Education and National Development

A COMPARATIVE PERSPECTIVE

SECOND EDITION

Education and National Development

A COMPARATIVE PERSPECTIVE

SECOND EDITION

by

INGEMAR FÄGERLIND
Stockholm University, Sweden

and

LAWRENCE J. SAHA
Australian National University, Australia

PERGAMON PRESS

OXFORD · NEW YORK · BEIJING · FRANKFURT
SÃO PAULO · SYDNEY · TOKYO · TORONTO

U.K.	Pergamon Press plc, Headington Hill Hall, Oxford OX3 0BW, England
U.S.A.	Pergamon Press, Inc., Maxwell House, Fairview Park, Elmsford, New York 10523, U.S.A.
PEOPLE'S REPUBLIC OF CHINA	Pergamon Press, Room 4037, Qianmen Hotel, Beijing, People's Republic of China
FEDERAL REPUBLIC OF GERMANY	Pergamon Press GmbH, Hammerweg 6, D-6242 Kronberg, Federal Republic of Germany
BRAZIL	Pergamon Editora Ltda, Rua Eça de Queiros, 346, CEP 04011, Paraiso, São Paulo, Brazil
AUSTRALIA	Pergamon Press Australia Pty Ltd., P.O. Box 544, Potts Point, N.S.W. 2011, Australia
JAPAN	Pergamon Press, 5th Floor, Matsuoka Central Building, 1-7-1 Nishishinjuku, Shinjuku-ku, Tokyo 160, Japan
CANADA	Pergamon Press Canada Ltd., Suite No. 271, 253 College Street, Toronto, Ontario, Canada M5T 1R5

Copyright © 1989 Pergamon Press plc

First edition 1983

Second edition 1989

Library of Congress Cataloging-in-Publication Data

Fägerlind, Ingemar, 1935–
Education and national development: a comparative perspective/by Ingemar Fägerlind and Lawrence J. Saha. — 2nd ed.
p.   cm.
Bibliography: p.
Includes indexes.
1. Education — Economic aspects. 2. Economic development — Effect of education on. 3. Education and state. I. Saha, Lawrence J. II. Title.
LC65. F33 1989 370. 19–dc 19 88-39186

British Library Cataloguing in Publication Data

Fägerlind, Ingemar, 1935 — Education and national development: a comparative perspective. – 2nd ed.
1. Social development. Role of education
I. Title   II. Saha, Lawrence J.
370.19

ISBN 0-08-036463-2 Hardcover
ISBN 0-08-036462-4 Flexicover

Printed in Great Britain by BPCC Wheatons Ltd, Exeter

Preface to the Second Edition

THE preparation for this second edition has given us an opportunity to review and reflect upon the events and changes of thought which have taken place during the early and middle 1980s. Most persons in the education and development field, whether academic, practitioner or both, rarely have the chance to step back to take a broad view of the field. Yet, as we are all immersed in our day-to-day activities, it is often the broad view that we require to understand not only our own special interests, but how these interests fit together with those of others.

The events of the past half decade or so have been important in forcing us to acknowledge some important facts about education, development, and the ability for education to bring about changes of a particular kind. What are some of these events? First of all, the recession during the late 1970s and early 1980s, sometimes gradual, sometimes swift, has shaken the confidence of education and development planners. Economically the world has become a small globe, highly interlinked, highly interactive, highly vulnerable and volatile.

Gone are the days of never-ending economic growth. We now face a world where the degrees of freedom in which to manoever have shrunk. In this environment, the condition of the rich and poor countries has become more visible, and the plight of the very poor can no longer be ignored. The zero-sum game of aid and development, of economic growth and recession, means that no longer can any country regard itself independently of others. Every plan and every strategy related to economic and social development may succeed or fail not because of factors within a country's borders but because of factors outside them. One country's success may be another's downfall. Within this context, the funds for education must compete with other demands on the limited resources of national governments, demands for social security and welfare, health, defense, scientific research, and so on.

v

As we reviewed what we had written over six years ago, we were surprised at how much still held true, and in some cases has become more important. The path of development of most societies seems to be upward, but cyclical nonetheless, with minor rises and falls in economic and social fortunes. Our overall organizing framework, the three dimensions of the *economic, political* and *social/cultural* appears as relevant now as then. We have become more aware that purely economic-based programs may flounder or fail if the social/ cultural and political dimensions are ignored. Furthermore, we are even more convinced that the political context has become all embracing, as all educational and development plans are inherently political, and all participants, whether academics, planners, politicians or recipient citizens, are caught up in the political process whether they like it or not.

In this revision, we have made major and minor changes as we thought were required, while keeping the original work more or less intact. In Chapters 1 and 2 we hope we have made more clear the theoretical underpinnings which we feel are essential to understand the assumptions of our plans and expectations about education and development. Chapter 3 has come in for some updating, due to the economic recession and the decline in educational funding. Chapters 4 and 5, on modernization and political mobilization, we think hold up well, and are as applicable today as when we wrote them.

Chapter 6 on development strategies, with its focus on Sweden, remains largely the same except for changes relating to recent events. Chapter 7 is a new chapter with a focus on women, education and development. We have included it with the conviction that many of the issues relating to development are also issues relating to women, and the topic deserves special treatment.

Chapter 8 on evaluation has been radically altered with the inclusion of several new examples. Chapters 9 and 10 have been extensively updated and the section on the State expanded. It is clear to us that no analysis of education and development relationships, or the formation of strategies, plans or programs is complete without a close examination of the role of the State, and the inescapable fact that all education and development origins, processes, and outcomes are inherently political.

There are topics in the education and development field which we have not given extensive treatment, although we believe they will emerge as significant in the next decade. Most discussions about educational plans and strategies focus on formal education, except perhaps for literacy and literacy campaigns. Adult education, lifelong education, or recurrent education have so far been in the background of current research and debate. Yet when pressed, many will acknowledge the importance or potential importance of education which takes place outside the formal structure, and which is aimed at adults. The education of adults remains to be integrated into research projects and planning strategies.

Another issue which we believe will dominate education and planning debates into the next decade concerns equity versus effectiveness, and expansion versus quality. In times of economic constraint commitments to equity often give way to concerns over effectiveness, whether measured in terms of getting the most for the money out of educational systems, or being satisfied with educating the talented few and leaving the rest to their own devices. These debates often give the impression that equity and effectiveness are mutually exclusive and competing goals. However we believe more attention should be directed to strategies which do not sacrifice equity concerns in order to maintain quality and effectiveness. Viable development strategies should strive for both.

A third concern focuses upon the many countries and people of the world who find themselves caught with one foot in the traditional and the other in the modern. Many societies are in a state of rapid change, and many of the problems of the developing countries have been attributed to problems of transition. The underlying assumption is that the tradition and the modern are in competition, and in choosing one, the other is lost. Yet some of the most successful countries in the developing world are those who have combined the best of both. We believe a greater recognition of the benefits of the traditional in the transition to the modern will ease the development process for all concerned. The structures and forms of education in developing societies need to build upon the traditional rather than replacing it. We see this as an emerging area for exciting and rich diversity in the expansion and the reforms of education around the world.

In short, we remain convinced that the field of education and development represents the crossroad which brings together academics, politicians, planners, practitioners, and the people in the pursuit of the world's biggest and perhaps most exciting challenge. We are pleased to be a part of that pursuit.

There are many institutions and individuals who deserve our appreciation in being able to produce this edition. First of all, we are indebted to the program experts and staff of the International Institute for Educational Planning (IIEP) in Paris where we were both Visiting Fellows in 1988, and where we found a stimulating environment for rethinking what we had written before. Acting Director Ta Ngoc Chau and Lars Mahlck facilitated our visit and looked after our needs. Similar appreciation is due to Martin Carnoy, Francisco O. Ramirez and the staff of the Stanford International Education Committee (SIDEC), Stanford University, where Saha vas Visiting Scholar in the latter part of 1988. Special thanks also to the **Centre Culturel Suédois** in Paris, where in the early spring Fägerlind was provided with accommodation in a stimulating environment. At the Institute of International Education in Stockholm the staff and students were critical but supportive in helping us "get it right", and persuaded us to explain the complexity of some issues more fully. At the Institute, Torsten Husén has given his constant encouragement and deserves special appreciation. Finally, we are indebted to Barbara Barrett at Pergamon Press for giving us another chance to have our say in this exciting subject area. Her advice has always been welcome and worthwhile.

Stockholm and Canberra   INGEMAR FÄGERLIND
30 January 1989   LAWRENCE J. SAHA

Contents

List of Figures and Tables

PART 1
Conceptions of Societal Development

1

The Origins of
Modern Development Thought

SINCE the end of World War II there have been few subjects which have received as much attention from social scientists, policy-makers and politicians as that of national development (OECD, 1978). The need to rebuild Europe, along with the simultaneous emergence of the new nations of Africa and the growth of old nations in Latin America and South East Asia, has brought into recent focus the importance of factors necessary for social and economic development. The theoretical debates and policy decisions concerning development have varied considerably, and have sometimes stressed technological advancement, but at other times have focused on social well-being. However, throughout these years a key variable in these discussions and practices has been the role that education plays in the development process.

It is our intention to explore in some depth the link between education and development. In doing this we summarize and critically evaluate the theories and cumulative research findings of this important and timely topic. In spite of some proportionate levelling off, nations and international organizations continue to spend vast amounts of money on educational programs (Coombs, 1985). In the mid–1980s some developing countries such as Bolivia, Philippines, and Equador were spending over one–forth of their national budgets on education (Unesco, 1987). In contrast, industrialized countries have tended to spend proportionately less. For example, during the same period, Sweden, the USA, Great Britain allocated roughly 10 percent of their national budgets to education. Investment in education has traditionally been justified by optimistic assumptions, the first being that an educated population contributes to the socio-economic development of the society as a whole, and the second, that education contributes to the well-being of individuals within the society (Schultz, 1980). In addition, it has become clear that rapidly changing technologies and the changing face of the world economic and political systems require a new flexibility and adaptability by societies and individuals. Education is increasingly

3

being seen as an essential component for an adaptable and flexible population.

Frequently some of these assumptions which justify educational expansion are called into question, and the age of optimism has given way to an age of caution. As one writer, speaking about educational expansion has said: "Educational expansion, as we now know, does not necessarily make either people or countries more prosperous; instead it may, and does, leave the former without jobs and the latter with increasingly burdensome claims on public funds" (Weiler, 1978:180).

In this chapter we examine the concept of development with the conviction that no discussion of education strategies can be effective without first clarifying the desired development strategy. Most of what follows concerns a discussion of theories of progress and development from early classical thinkers to contemporary writers. We conclude the chapter by identifying the salient dimensions of various development strategies, and leave the examination of the link between education and development to Chapter 2.

What is Development?

There have been few concepts in social and economic thought which have been as ambiguous as that of development. The term has been used in a variety of contexts, often clouded with political and ideological overtones. There are many words with similar meaning to that of development, for example, social change, growth, evolution progress, advancement and modernization. With the exception of the term social change, all the others imply change in a specific direction which is regarded by the users as positive or highly valued.

There have been attempts to resolve this ambiguity in the concept of development. Fletcher (1976) argues, for example, that there is a value-free meaning contained in the notion of development over and above the ideological and political uses of the concept. In discussing this meaning he states:

> Secondly, however, 'development' can mean the actualisation of an implicit potentiality, the simplest example being the patterned growth and maturation of a seed, or an initial germ-cell, to the full adult form of the individual plant, or animal, or human person. Without stipulating, at this point, anything too weighty or too precise, this can also certainly seem to apply to man and his *social* situations (p. 43).

This implicit logic of development about which Fletcher speaks is particularly useful in understanding and planning for change in human societies. It is based on the assumption that both societies and individuals have innate biological, psychological and sociological capacities which can be evaluated in terms of their level of actualization. For example, individuals can be physically healthy or sick, happy or sad and participative or not participative in their social environment. Likewise, societies can be judged as efficient or inefficient in making possible the actualization of their human potential. Following Fletcher (1976) we argue that any change which promotes or actualizes these dimensions of society represents development in an appropriate meaning of the term. We further contend that education in the formal sense is an essential component for the development process as we have defined it above.

Before proceeding to study and analyze this relationship between education and development, we first historically trace the conception of development as used by philosophers and social scientists.

Historical Analysis of Development Philosophies

Ideas and concepts do not occur in a vacuum but are products of the social, cultural and historical events surrounding them. Such has been the case in the thinking about development. Our present age has no monopoly on theories of social change and development. Throughout history people have always been confronted with the reality of change around them, and the philosophers and social commentators have from earliest times attempted to explain how and why these things happened.

On the other hand certain aspects of change have not always been apparent. It is relatively easy to perceive short-term changes that occur daily around us; it is more difficult to perceive broader changes over a long period of time.

For example, historians often think of the fall of the Roman Empire as though it occurred at one point in time in history. For some, this event took place when Rome was invaded by Alaric of the Visigoths in A.D. 410, by Attila the Hun in A.D. 452, by the sacking of Rome by the Vandals in A.D. 455, or by the deposition of the last Roman Emperor in A.D. 476. But how did the people of Rome regard these events? Were they aware that later writers and historians would describe them in such dramatic terms as the decline and fall of an empire? One early historian did not think so.

> The three centuries between the great age of Marcus Arelius and the overwhelming of Rome by barbarians in the fifth century A.D. is often called the epoch of Rome's 'decline and fall'. But

Romans who lived in those centuries did not know it was falling. To them, the business of empire appeared to go on as usual: petty tyrants paraded as emperors; rich men dressed up in senatorial togas; Roman soldiers went forth to battle barbarians, even if they did it more for money than for the glory of Rome. *It is only in the perspective of time that Rome's fall is evident* (Hadas, 1971:141, italics ours).

Social change, and in particular social development, is a phenomenon which might only be perceived over a long period of time from a macro perspective. This is certainly the point which Nisbet clearly makes in his work *Social Change and History* (1969).

No one has ever seen a civilization die, and it is unimaginable, short of cosmic disaster or thermo nuclear holocaust, that anyone ever will. Nor has anyone ever seen a civilization – or culture or institution – in literal process of decay and degeneration, though there is a rich profusion of these words and their synonyms in Western thought from Hesiod to Spengler. Nor, finally, has anyone ever seen – actually, empirically seen, as we see these things in the world of plants and animals – growth and development in civilizations and societies and cultures, with all that is clearly implied by these words: change proceeding gradually, cumulatively, and irreversibly, through a kind of unfolding of internal potentiality, the whole moving toward some end that is presumably contained in the process from the start. We see none of these in culture: death, degeneration, development, birth (p. 3).

One of the difficulties, then, not only in defining social change but also in empirically studying it, is that we do not always have the advantage of a macro perspective. Thus much of the ambiguity in the concepts related to social change, and the difficulties in identifying the variables which contribute to it, is due to the fact that often what we identify as change may only be short-term variations in a larger trend. Or conversely, we may conclude that over a given period of time no change has occurred, when in fact if seen from a long-term perspective, considerable change has taken place. The problem of temporal boundaries and a sufficiently macro perspective in the study of social change and development was equally as bothersome for the classical social theorists as for those contemporaries who are interested in change and development today.

Classic Cyclical Theories

The classical philosophers have a highly sophisticated view of progress and development. The Greeks in particular, not only knew, accepted and liked change, but they also were the first in history to make a science out of the study of change. They had a word, *physis*, which expressed the notion of development very well. *Physis* literally means growth in the sense of unfolding. They applied this term metaphorically to all living things – a tree, animal, man or society.

As an example one could take Aristotle's theory of the development of the State. According to Aristotle the origin of the State is found in the family, which he defines as a self-sustaining form of social organization but without the benefit of more elaborate institutions. A colony of families comes together to form a village and this represents the second stage of development. Finally the bringing together of several villages forms a new entity which Aristotle calls the State. There are three important elements of this theory. First the development of the State represents a growth or unfolding – *physis* – which is inherent in the nature of the family. Secondly the State is imminent in the family which is the cause of the development. And thirdly the development of the State did not occur by accident but was the result of a natural process. To this extent Aristotle's theory of the development of the State is similar to Fletcher's notion of the value-free logic of development about which we discussed earlier.

An essential element in this process for the classical thinkers was the fact that it took place in cyclical patterns involving the growth and decay of civilizations. Although the Greeks and Romans would not argue that history repeats itself, they did contend that the development cycles were always occurring. The Roman historian Polybius said of the Roman victory over Carthage:

> As every body or state or action has its natural periods of first growth, then of prime, then finally of decay, and as everything in them is at its best when they are in their prime, it was for this reason that the difference between the two states manifested itself at this time (cited in Nisbet, 1969:35).

The recurring cycles of development stages emerged from the closeness to nature experienced by the classical thinkers. The never-ending dramatic sequence of seasons in the Mediterranean climate with its periods of growth, prime and decay were reflected in their views of the ages of civilization. Like the perennial plant which produces flowers which bloom and die, only to bloom again at a later stage as the plant grows larger, so too the Greeks and the Romans saw civilizations rise and fall in the process of the historical development of mankind.

By the 5th century Christianity had become the State religion in

Rome. The fusion of Hebrew, Greek and Christian thought introduced a fundamental change in thinking about progress and development. The person most responsible for articulating the early Christian view was St. Augustine in his important book *The City of God.* The ideas contained in this work were to dominate European Christian thought at least until the 12th century.

Augustine and other Christian writers kept the growth metaphor, that is the notion of *physis*, in their theories of change and development. They did not, however, accept the never-ending cyclical element which was so important to Greek and Roman thought. In the Christian view the cycle of growth and decay was seen as a single, unique cycle, never to be repeated. Thus it was thought that there is one cycle in mankind which started with the creation of Adam, reached its full flowering with the coming of Christ, and would end with the death and destruction of the material world. It should be noted, however, that the Christian thinkers felt that this event would occur quite soon and their interpretation of history always tended to take this into account. While they were pessimistic about the future of the material world, they were optimistic about the eternal world which would follow, that is, the City of God. The notion of *physis* as a natural process was replaced by the "will of God" as the main force of change in the material world.

This expectation of the end of the world was to dominate Christian thinking for almost 1200 years. Medieval man was pessimistic about the future of the material world, and believed that progress existed only in planning for the coming of the City of God. Even during the flowering of the Renaissance, men felt that mankind was nearing an end and that the apex of civilization had long passed. This view prevailed in spite of advances in science and technology. It was only in the 17th and 18th centuries that the dominance of the Augustinian view began to wane and give way to new theories of development. However, remnants of the Christian view continue to survive in modern thought primarily in the various messianic movements which proclaim the coming demise of human civilization and the world itself.

The Enlightenment Optimism

The events of the Renaissance set the stage for the expansion of geographical and intellectual horizons giving rise to the belief in the possibility of an unlimited progress of mankind. The discovery of new worlds, the advancement of biological and natural sciences, the developments of new forms of art and architecture, and the preliminary stages of an international economy through trade and banking, all gave rise to new ideas and beliefs which seriously challenged the traditional Christian ways of thinking. The Protestant Reformation at the end of the Renaissance was a consequence rather than a cause of this breakdown.

The first major systematic departure from the prevailing Augustinian view of progress came in 1688, when the French intellectual Bernard Le Bovier de Fontenelle argued what became the modern view of development: that civilization made progress in the past, is now making progress, and will continue to make progress into the unlimited future. The idea of unending and unlimited progress is the cornerstone of the intellectual modernism of the Enlightenment which radically departed from the cyclical view of history of the classical Christian thinkers. According to Fontenelle:

> A good cultivated mind contains, so to speak, all minds of preceding centuries; it is but a single identical mind which has been developing and improving itself all the time...; but I am obliged to confess that the man in question will have no old age; he will always be equally capable of those things for which his youth is suited, and he will be ever more and more capable of those things which are suited to his prime; that is to say, to abandon the allegory, men will never degenerate, and there will be no end to the growth and development of human wisdom (cited in Nisbet, 1969:104).

During the Enlightenment period of the 17th and 18th centuries there emerged a number of beliefs which directly affected ideas about development. In particular it was thought that pure knowledge and science supersede theological knowledge, that natural processes are cumulative, logical and unlimited in terms of growth, and that the task of statecraft is to remove obstruction to the natural progress of nature and mankind.

In this period the ideas of the French mathematician and philosopher Descartes were extremely influential in that he established convincingly the supremacy of rational knowledge and the importance of doubting everything which cannot be proven. The German philosopher Leibniz further argued that progress was "not accident but a beneficent necessity", and that the process does not take place through discontinuities and leaps, but in a continuous, gradual, and cumulative manner.

One cannot speak about theories of change and development without mentioning the work of Immanuel Kant. Writing in late 18th-century Germany, Kant's conviction in the unlimited progress of mankind is reflected in his assumptions about the natural continuing advance of civilization, particularly in its moral existence. Furthermore, while Kant accepted that this unlimited progress might be interrupted, he believed that it would never be entirely broken off or stopped.

Somewhat later in France another typical Enlightenment view can be found in Condorcet's work *Progress of the Human Mind*. While hiding for his life from the Jacobins his faith in human progress was not daunted. Condorcet spoke of the indefinite perfectibility of mankind, and felt that this continuing progress would vary in speed, but would never be reversed. Finally, also reflecting the optimism of the Enlightenment, Rousseau praised the "noble savage" devoid of any contamination by civilization. At the same time he believed that only by entering civil society could an individual really become human and gain the power of self-control which he saw as the only true liberty. In other words, for Rousseau progress consisted in the ability of an individual to remain uncorrupted by civilization, and yet remain a part of it and carry out the responsibilities of a citizen. It is precisely in the resolution of this apparent contradiction that Rousseau placed so much emphasis on education (Rousseau, 1974 (1762)).

Convictions about the inevitability of progress are not restricted to the Western world. Chinese civilization developed an intellectual tradition which recognized the continual changing forces of society. The principles of *yang* and *yin* were seen to represent opposites which worked together in harmony to rule the world. Encompassing these two principles is the notion of *tao*: "All yin and all yang are tao." In traditional Chinese thought, *yang* was seen as the male or positive principle in nature: the sun, light, brilliant. On the other hand, *yin* represented the female or negative principle in nature: shady, dark, cloudy, cold. Finally, *tao* meant way, path or road which in its deeper meaning implied social and cosmic order, totality and responsibility. The possession of *tao* with *yang* and *yin* in harmony were seen as leading to the time of Great Happiness or original Golden Age. The main thinker in this tradition was Confucius (Becker and Barnes, 1961).

Additional non-Western views about social change and development can be found in the Near East and in particular in the Islamic tradition. While Western Europe struggled through the Dark Ages to the Renaissance there were important social thinkers in Islamic society who attempted to explain change as manifested in the Moslem world. The culmination of Islamic thought can be found in the ideas of Ibn Khaldun, who has by some been regarded as the world's first sociologist. Drawing upon Aristotelian philosophy

Khaldun saw change and development in terms of dialectic and cyclical processes. He was perhaps the first social thinker who put forth conflict as a major factor in explaining change (Becker and Barnes, 1961).

Khaldun never developed a complete theory to explain societal change, although his interests in historiography and the rise of Islam continually kept his attention on laws of society and social change. Khaldun definitely believed in ordered social change and rejected randomness, which he attributed to "hidden causes". He saw continuity in the rise and fall of states and empires and argued that "the past and future resemble each other as two drops of water" (Becker and Barnes, 1961:270). Yet he also saw all social change taking place within the conditional limits of climate and geography, particularly within the context of his experience of the North African desert in which he lived.

Khaldun's dialectic and cyclical theory is best illustrated in his description of the transition from nomadic tribal life to sedentary city life, which he saw as a basic historical process. For Khaldun, the nomads, by virtue of their rigorous and difficult life in the desert, were seen as having strong tribal discipline and intense *esprit de corps*. On the other hand, the sedentary city-dwellers, because of the relative ease and softness of city life, were seen as lacking bravery, fighting ability, discipline and ferocity. Thus Khaldun argued that any pastoral nomad group can conquer a sedentary city community of equal manpower. However, the nomadic victors soon become accustomed to sedentary city life, with its characteristics, and eventually become prey to new nomadic invaders. In this way, according to Khaldun, empires established by nomads rise to power only to fall, thus constituting a constant cycle of change (Khaldun, 1980 (1394)).

Evolutionary Theories of the 19th and 20th Centuries

At the turn of the 19th century the optimism of the Enlightenment gave way to more systematic and complex theories of change and development. These theories can be best described under the general rubric of evolutionary or organic theories. As such, evolutionary theories were based upon six assumptions about change. For the 19th-century writers change was seen as natural, directional, imminent, continuous, necessary and proceeding through uniform causes.

A forerunner to the evolutionary theorists, and one whose influence cannot be doubted, was the German philosopher, Georg Wilhelm Friedrich Hegel. Hegel's notion of development was similar in some respects to classical Greek and Roman thought, and was the same as that contained in the classical notion of *physis*.

The principle of development involves also the existence of a latent germ of being – a capacity or potentiality striving to realize itself. This formal conception finds actual existence in spirit; which has the history of the world for its theater, its possession, and the sphere of its realization (cited in Nisbet, 1969:159).

For our purposes Hegel made two contributions to the emerging evolutionary theory. His notion of the dialectic was to influence later thinkers like Marx and his followers and represents a contrast with those who saw development as occurring through stages of "levels of organizations", rising from the lower to the higher through historically conditioned transformations. In his description of history he was idealistic (history is the result of God's will), deterministic (what happens has to happen) and saw history as culminating in the progress of the Prussian state (Karier, 1967).

It was a contemporary of Hegel, the French philosopher and father of sociology, Auguste Comte, who was among the first to systematize evolutionary theory in his notion of a positivistic social science. Unlike Hegel, Comte did not place God at the center of his evolutionary theory, but saw progress and development as stemming from the scientific achievements of men. Comte described progress in terms of the Law of Three Stages through which he thought mankind was evolving. The first stage, which he called *Theological*, represented the level of society dominated by "priests", ruled by the military, and built upon the family as the major social unit. The second he called the *Metaphysical* which he saw as based upon the philosophical reasoning of men. The third and final stage toward which he saw mankind evolving was the *Scientific* or *Positive* one, which must be reached by the study of the laws of nature and the use of scientific experiments.

Later in the 19th century, evolutionary theory emerged in a somewhat different form through the work of the British philosopher and sociologist, Herbert Spencer. Building upon the notion of the "survival of the fittest", an idea which he, like Darwin, derived from Malthus, Spencer based his own theory of the evolution of society on its organizational structure. Spencer's definition of evolution has become classic:

Evolution is an integration of matter and concomitant dissipation of motion; during which matter passes from an indefinite, incoherent homogeneity to a definite, coherent heterogeneity; and during which the retained motion undergoes a parallel transformation (cited in Timasheff, 1964:32).

For Comte evolution consisted mainly of moral progress and the advancement of ideas; for Spencer evolution consisted of a greater specialization and differentiation of the structure of society.

Comte believed that evolution should be guided by human intervention. Scientific knowledge of society results in moral advancement and can be planned. Among the terms he frequently used were "social engineering" and "social hygienics". Spencer, on the other hand, was labelled a "Social Darwinist". He believed that like the evolution of the plant and animal kingdom, the "survival of the fittest" principle should be allowed to operate in society. For Spencer, the poor were poor because they were less fit; the rich on the other hand deserved to be rich. In effect the political implications of Spencer's thinking were in line with the *laissez-faire* political policies of his time, and which, indeed, are still with us today in some philosophical and political thought.

Evolutionary theory continued to be prevalent, sometimes in very subtle ways, in the late 19th and early 20th centuries especially in the works of the French sociologist Emile Durkheim and other social scientists. Permeating much of this evolutionary thought was the theme that society, as a living organism, develops from a simple primitive stage to a complex modern one. The practical application of this general theory for understanding societal development was that the poor non-industrial societies were seen as representing a primitive stage of evolution, while the industrialized countries were associated with the more complex and civilized stage. The higher more complex societies were seen as the end-points toward which the primitive (less-developed) societies would eventually reach. However, all societies, even the advanced ones, were seen as evolving in the direction of greater progress.

During this period evolutionary theory was used to justify the behavior of colonizing societies toward their colonies, in particular with respect to allowing them to remain in their preindustrial stage, while using their labor and material resources to support further industrialization in the mother country. The activities of colonial governments and the work of religious missions were based on the assumption that the peoples of the less-developed societies were primitive, "backward" and "uncivilized", and thus needed to be assisted in their development along the same unilinear evolutionary path as traversed by their own societies.

In the early 20th century evolutionary theory as a viable explanation for development began to be challenged. Critics argued, for example, that particular aspects of social behavior and the level of development of any society could not be effectively explained solely in terms of its origins. In other words, there was no basis for postulating the continuity of the historical evolution of a society. A second criticism of evolutionary theory was that it could not always explain social anomalies, for example, the survival of highly traditional religious rituals in modern industrial environments. For the most part evolutionists explained irregular patterns that did not fit the theory as anachronistic remnants of the past, whereas others preferred to explain them in terms of their functional interrelationships and utility in the society. A third criticism of evolutionism was directed at its assumption of unilinearity, which was increasingly seen as untenable. This became particularly evident with the emergence of the socialist states. Many critics felt that evolutionary theory had not specified the causal mechanisms and processes of change. In other words, the theory could describe the different evolutionary stages of societies but could not explain how a society passes from one stage to the next. Finally the assumption regarding the inevitable progress of mankind became untenable with the events of World War I and World War II. These events indicated that societies can decline as well as make progress.

Structural-Functionalism

Criticism of evolutionary theory by and large came from a new theoretical orientation emerging from both anthropological and sociological thought. From modest beginnings in the 1930s, the orientation known as structural-functionalism dominated sociology and other social sciences by the 1950s. The main proponents of structural-functionalism were Talcott Parsons and Robert K. Merton, who were responsible for its systematic formulation. The theory did not directly deal with social change or development, but since it is related to several of the major development theories (for example human capital theory and modernization theory) it merits our attention here.

The basic principles of structural-functionalism are quite simple and can for our purpose be stated briefly. In the first place society is seen as a system composed of interrelated parts (religion, education, political structures, the family, etc.). These parts are said to constantly seek equilibrium or harmony between themselves. The interrelationship of these parts is thought to occur by consensus, and pathological or non-normative events or arrangements are said to produce tension. In such a condition the parts strive to adjust in order to achieve equilibrium (homeostasis) again. For the structural-functionalists society is said to change, but there is no mention of evolution over a long period of time. Furthermore, conflict in society is seen as dysfunctional to social integration and equilibrium.

In spite of its general domination of social science theory and research from the 1940s to the 1970s, structural-functionalism has been criticized on several grounds. It has been accused of focusing solely on the static aspects of society to the neglect of change, process, conflict and dissent. In addition it is argued that the theory contains an ideological bias in favor of the *status quo*. Harmony and integration are seen as functional, highly valued, and to be preserved, whereas conflict, change or tension are seen to be dysfunctional and to be avoided. Therefore structural-functionalism has been criticized as conservative and against change, development or social reform . Nevertheless, there seems to be a renewed interest in functionalist theory, and the emergence of what is called neo-functionalism is attracting attention within the social sciences (Alexander, 1985).

Structural-functionalism and evolutionary theory were eventually fused in the later writings of Talcott Parsons into what is known as neo-evolutionism. The most important result of this fusion is that the new theory gave analytical force to the evolutionary perspective and provided structural-functionalism with the means for dealing with change. In other words, societies were said to evolve along an evolutionary path through the processes of integration, differentiation and reintegration, taking into account both internal and external factors. The importance of neo-evolutionary theory is that it was primarily responsible for the emergence of modernization theory, one of the most important of the contemporary development theories (Parsons, 1966).

Modernization Theory

Modernization theory, as we know it today, emerged in the 1950s and contrasted sharply with the evolutionary theory of the 1920s and 1930s. To some extent modernization theory was an intellectual response to the two world wars and represents an attempt to take an optimistic view about the future of mankind. Early forms of modernization theory had little to say about the further advancement of the already modern, industrialized societies; it was assumed that they had "arrived" and that their past was of interest only to show the future path of those societies still on the road to modernity. In fact some authors, for example Huntington (1976), argued that early modernization theory justified complacency (the *status quo*) at home and change abroad. The theory had no image of the potentialities of modernity's future, but only faith in the past.

According to Huntington (1976), the process of modernization can be characterized as revolutionary (a dramatic shift from tradition to modern), complex (multiple causes), systematic, global (affecting all societies), phased (advance through stages), homogenizing (convergence), irreversible and progressive. Modernization theory is also interdisciplinary. The theory has been used by sociologists, psychologists, political scientists, economists and social and cultural anthropologists. It has been particularly important for sociologists and social psychologists.

One of the first major studies that examined modernity is found in David McClelland's book *The Achieving Society* (1961). According to McClelland the rise and fall of civilizations is due to the individual values held by the majority of the population in the society. He argued that there is a personality characteristic which he called the achievement motive (n Ach), acquired through socialization which makes a society open to economic and technological advancement.

The notion of the need for achievement as a psychological trait (reminiscent of Weber's Protestant Ethic) was developed by the American sociologist, Alex Inkeles, who formulated a set of attitude questions known as the modernity scale. During the 1960s and 1970s the modernity scale was widely used to measure the extent to which members of a given society hold what are considered to be modern values. Inkeles and his followers argue that to modernize is to develop, and that a society cannot hope to develop until the majority of its population holds modern values. These theorists, along with all structural functionalists, also argue that the creation of modern values can be the result of human planning and that particular social institutions are of extreme importance for their emergence, for example, the socialization which takes place in families, schools and factories.

Modernization theory has stimulated a large amount of research and has been an implicit assumption underlying much development funding by governments, national and international foundations and organizations. Many studies have shown that education and factory employment are directly related to the acquisition of modern values. These studies have been conducted in a variety of countries, such that the relationship has been generalized to include most developing countries (Inkeles and Smith, 1974). However, research does not so far support the causal linkage between modern values and modern behavior. Modernization theory is based on the notion that there is a direct causal link between five sets of variables, namely, modernizing institutions, modern values, modern behavior, modern society and economic development. These links are illustrated in Fig. 1.1.

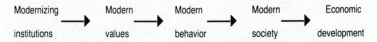

FIG. 1.1 The process of modernization (based
on Inkeles and Smith, 1974).

Whereas the link between the first two sets of variables have been well established in research, the links between the others are more problematic. For example, recent research has shown that developing countries with higher exposure to Western media do not manifest higher levels of modern values or indeed, economic development (Delacroix and Ragin, 1978). Likewise, farmers who score high on the scale of modern values do not show higher levels of agricultural productivity (Sutcliffe, 1978). Finally, it is clear that modernization has resulted in the convergence of some characteristics in world educational systems, for example, schooling as a public responsibility, as compulsory, and as structured both in terms student progression and teacher certification. Nevertheless, because of specific economic, political, cultural and historical contexts, considerable divergence in educational systems persists, namely repetition rates, teacher strategies and parental perceptions of schooling (Inkeles and Sirowy, 1983).

In general there are at least four criticisms of modernization theory. The first of these concerns the causal linkage between variables as indicated in the figure. The second concerns the underlying assumption of modernization, that modern attitudes and values are incompatible with traditional ones. In contrast, Gusfield (1967) argues that these values are not incompatible and cites the case of Japan where traditional forms of labor commitments seem to have contributed to economic growth while the same commitments were seen to be an impediment in the West. Thirdly, modernization theory assumes that modern values and behavior by individuals necessarily lead to socioeconomic development at the societal level. However, Portes (1973) and others contend that this causal linkage does not necessarily hold because a society is not simply the sum total of the individuals within it. For example, the emigration of professionals from less-developed countries is a form of modern behavior, but could not be said with any certainty to contribute to structural and economic development in those countries (Portes, 1973). Finally modernization theory in its assumptions about the end-point of the modernizing process is ideologically biased and ethnocentric. In terms of the criteria used to measure modernization, for a society to become modern, it must also become Western (Hoogvelt, 1976).

Human Capital Theory

While modernization theory dominated the thinking and research of sociologists, the economists also formulated their own theory of development based upon structural functional notions. Modernization theory for the sociologists was mainly a social psychological theory focusing upon individual values and attitudes. The economists, however, focused upon the productive capacity of human manpower in the development process and in so doing treated the improvement of the human workforce as a form of capital investment. Thus the human capital theory postulates that the most efficient path to the national development of any society lies in the improvement of its population, that is, its human capital.

One of the first systematic articulations of human capital theory occurred in 1960 when Theodore Schultz made his presidential address to the American Economic Association on the theme "Investment in Human Capital" (Schultz, 1961). In this widely cited address Schultz stated that education was not to be viewed simply as a form of consumption but rather as a productive investment. He argued that education does not only improve the individual choices available to men, but that an educated population provides the type of labor force necessary for industrial development and economic growth.

As with modernization theory, human capital theory provided a basic justification for large public expenditure on education both in developed and developing nations. The theory was consistent with the ideologies of democracy and liberal progressivism found in most Western societies. Likewise, both theories attributed the sources of underdevelopment or economic stagnation to factors within countries themselves rather than to factors outside the countries. Its appeal was based upon the presumed economic return of investment in education both at the macro and micro levels. For politicians and decision-makers, efforts to promote investment in human capital were seen to result in rapid economic growth for society. For individuals, such investment was seen to provide returns in the form of individual economic success and achievement (Karabel and Halsey, 1977; Blaug, 1970, 1976).

Human capital theory has been criticized on several grounds. At the individual level it has become highly controversial whether or to what extent education or other forms of human investments are directly related to improvements in occupation or income (Jencks *et al.*, 1972). In fact, it is now accepted that raising the level of education in a society can, under certain circumstances, increase the inequalities in income distribution. This is especially true with regard to the way education is financed and the way it is distributed in terms of facilities (Blaug, 1985).

Other factors which have been found to be important for occupational and income success are family background and innate ability (Fägerlind, 1975; Jencks *et al.*, 1979). Likewise individual attainment is also affected by structural factors, such as the economic, political and social systems and the way that they favor or discriminate against some strata in society. At the macro level the underlying assumptions of human capital research have also been suspect. Human capital theorists generally assume that after all the known inputs into economic growth have been explained, much of the unexplained residual variance represents the contribution of the improvement of human capital, of which education is seen as most important. Vaizey (1972), for example, cites figures from Schultz showing that the contribution of the improvement of human capital to economic growth in the USA between 1919 and 1957 ranged from between 36 and 70 percent of the unexplained growth.

However, as economists such as Blaug and Vaizey have been quick to point out, the residual in human capital analysis is generally assumed to represent the results of the improvement of labor quality, but in reality is more a "measure of ignorance". Human capital theory has intuitive appeal, but methodological difficulties, in particular regarding the measurement of the contribution of education to labor quality, has placed obstacles to its full acceptance. It is now only one of a number of approaches to the study of the economic value of schooling, and other theories such as the screening hypothesis and labor market segmentation approach enjoy current attention (Blaug, 1985). However the implications of these approaches for development are not always made explicit.

Marxist Theories of Development

Most theories of change and development assume that these processes occur in gradual and peaceful ways. As previously mentioned, the evolutionary and structural functionalist theories have tended to overlook the element of conflict in social systems, or conversely have regarded it as pathological or abnormal to the system. Indeed one of the most frequent criticisms of these theories is that they virtually ignore conflict as a major dimension in social change. Yet, a close scrutiny of history, from past to present, often highlights the importance of conflict in social events. Examples of these kinds of conflicts include the innate contradictions of a social system, revolution, exploitation, colonialism, dependency, struggle for survival, and class and racial conflicts.

Nisbet (1969) argues that the principle of conflict has been implicit in all theories of change and development. He contends that conflict and change are two sides of the same coin and to emphasize one does not mean that the other is not recognized. Even St. Augustine spoke of the struggle between good and evil; Spencer also acknowledged conflict in the notion of the struggle for survival. However, in European thought Hegel was perhaps the first and most important of the social thinkers who gave conflict a central focus in his theory of change. His principles of the dialectic whereby all change is seen as the result of a process of thesis, antithesis and synthesis, was the foundation for Marx's theory of society which has had profound impact on several schools of development theory today.

According to Marx, society is polarized into two classes which are in conflict, the exploiting and the exploited. Like other evolutionary theorists, Marx saw society as progressing through stages from an original primitive communist stage, through slavery, feudal, capitalist, socialist and finally to a visionary communist society. But unlike the evolutionary theorists, Marx saw these changes from stage to stage as the result of dramatic and qualitative leaps due to the conflicts within society and changes in modes of production.

Although the principles of Marx's theory of the structure of society are well known, it will be useful to summarize them here in the context of our later discussion of education and development. For Marx the major agent of social change is the economic structure of society. Class societies (which include the capitalist) are those where private ownership of the means of production exists, whereas classless societies (which include the socialist and communist) are those where the means of production are publicly or collectively owned. In the former type of society there are two major classes, those who own the means of economic production and those who do not, which Marx called the bourgeoisie and the proletariat respectively. The capitalist system is dependent upon the extraction of profit by the owner from the labor of the proletarian class (surplus value). In order to accomplish this the bourgeois class (those who control the means of production) must legitimate their claim to the surplus value either by social norm or by force. For Marx the remaining social institutions (the superstructure) exist to reinforce and reproduce the social norms relating to the economic structure, that is the control of the means of production and the legitimation of this control. Through the legitimating force of these institutions, the working class, as Marx saw it, was ignorant of its exploited condition (false consciousness). As this class becomes aware of its condition, the conflict of interests between the classes emerges, giving rise to revolution and thus major structural social change. It is this inevitable transition that Marx saw as part of a necessary process of development and progress (Smelser, 1973; Melotti, 1977).

In socialist societies, change is said to occur in a somewhat different manner. Marx saw socialism as an intermediate stage between capitalism and communism. While eradicating the capitalist structure, remnants of capitalism were seen as still surviving in the socialist stage. Thus for Marx it was essential that there be strong centralized rule by a proletarian elite, the so-called dictatorship of the proletariat, in order to prevent society from regressing again into capitalism. The purpose of the socialist system, in Marx's view, is to strengthen and mobilize the masses in their struggle to completely overcome the capitalist system of production and exploitation. Thus two essential components for a Marxist program of development are mass literacy and ideological consciousness-raising through which the proletariat is made aware of its exploited situation (Melotti, 1977).

There is nothing incompatible between Marxism and a development strategy based upon industrialization. In the case of the Soviet Union, Lenin is generally regarded as applying Marxism to a policy of industrialization under socialism. In so doing he emphasized the importance of centralization of control in the State, nationalization of the means of production, and democratic participation in economic planning (Lane, 1974).

Marxist thinking about social change, and implicitly about development, has had considerable impact on development theory. Recent interpretations of Marx's original position and further applications of his thought have given rise to a number of different forms which have been called neo-Marxist theories of development. For the most part these recent versions of Marxism focus upon selected, problematic aspects of Marx's original theory. For example, Marx spoke about colonialism and the stunting effect it sometimes has on development, for example, Ireland, but he never extended his idea to include the notion of underdevelopment. Likewise one of the most important concepts in Marxist analysis is that of mode of production, which is the combination of two aspects of production: production as a material process and as a social one. For example, feudal and capitalist societies represent two modes of production in which one social class exploits and dominates another. Recently there has been considerable debate about the nature of various modes of production, and in particular the transition between modes of production and the possibility of two modes coexisting in the same society (the theory of a dual economy). The absence of a crystallized class structure in many less developed societies has made the application of Marxist concepts problematic for development theory and strategies. Mao Zedong recognized this difficulty and incorporated different types of the agricultural population into the Marxist class structure (Mao Zedong, 1967). On the basis of this extension of orthodox Marxism, Mao's revolutionary program for socialist development in China has been influential in many third world countries today.

The orthodox Marxist-Leninist perspective on development formed the basis for the emergence and application of a currently dominant general theory of development, known as dependency theory. Although dependency theory exists in many versions, it is possible to understand its basic characteristics and subsequent implications for a unique approach to the problems of development.

Dependency Theory

In contrast to evolutionary and modernization theories, dependency theory focuses upon the relationships both between and within societies in regards to social, cultural, political and economic structures. The underlying assumption of this theory is that development and underdevelopment as relational concepts within and between societies are inversely related. The underdevelopment of a region or society is seen as a process which is linked to the development of another region or an outside society. The term dependency is used to emphasize that the causal relationship between the development of central or metropole societies and the underdevelopment of peripheral or satellite societies is an historical and at least indirectly an intentional process.

The intellectual origins of dependency theory can be traced to Marx. It was Marx's concern with the exploitation by the bourgeois of the proletariat which led the American economist Paul Baran, in his work *The Political Economy of Growth* (1957), to see underdevelopment in the poor countries as caused by capitalism in the Western world. A further contribution to the intellectual origins of dependency came from Lenin's concept of imperialism, which dependency theorists used to describe the process whereby capitalism dominates and exploits the poor countries.

In some respects dependency theory can be seen as the obverse of the theory of imperialism; whereas the theory of imperialism concentrates on the domination and exploitation of the poor countries by the rich, dependency theory focuses on the extent to which poor countries are dependent on the rich. Without question the most important popularizer and systematizer of dependency has been Andre Gunder Frank, who began to study and write about development problems in Latin America in the late 1950s and 1960s.

According to dependency theorists the world can be divided into the core and the peripheral countries (Galtung, 1971). These countries are seen as part of a global system dominated by a capitalist economic network. The process of dependency whereby the rich core countries dominate and exploit the poor peripheral ones is best described in the following words of one writer:

> The mode of articulation of the underdeveloped economies with the world economic system may result in a transfer of resources from the periphery to the centre and/or this articulation may give rise to various 'blocking mechanisms' which hold back or 'distort' the economies of the periphery, thereby preventing an allocation of resources which will produce economic growth (Roxborough, 1976:118).

According to dependency theory the transfer of resources can occur in many ways, including plunder, colonial or neo-colonial relationships, or the operations of multinational corporations. Dependency theory provides an alternative to theories of capitalist development. It rejects the linear and progressive view of development and places importance on factors external to society. Furthermore, dependency theory focuses on the process whereby the condition of the less developed regions and countries in the world are seen to be caused by the activities of the rich countries. The process whereby the metropolis dominates the countryside within a country is identical to that which occurs between countries.

In considering the dependency relationships between countries it is not necessary that the rich country physically dominates the poor. It is enough that the leaders or the elite of the poor countries hold attitudes, values and interests consistent with those in the rich countries. Andre Gunder Frank gave these elites the name "lumpenbourgeoisie" and regarded them as major instruments of the dependency relationship (Frank, 1972).

It may be useful to compare dependency theory with modernization theory in order to highlight its unique approach to understanding development and underdevelopment. Firstly, whereas modernization theory treats the nation-state as an autonomous unit, dependency theory focuses on the relationship between nation-states. Secondly, modernization theorists accept that elites may play a positive role in the development process, whereas dependency theorists regard elites as an obstacle to real development. Thirdly, modernization theorists see education as providing skills necessary for development, while dependency theorists regard education as reinforcing the dependency condition of less developed societies. Finally, dependency theorists do not deny that education promotes modernization, but question whether modernization promotes autonomous national development (Walters, 1981).

There have been a number of variations of dependency theory which have focused to a greater or lesser degree on specific aspects of the theory itself. Indeed, some authors have tended to prefer the terms "paradigm" (Foster-Carter, 1976), "school" (Lall, 1975), or at the least, a collection of theories (Palma, 1978) to designate what we call, in a broad sense, dependency theory. However, there can be little doubt that dependency theory has been extremely important on thinking about development, and some have argued that the notion of dependency has replaced modernization as the dominant conceptual model in the development literature (Webster, 1984).

At the same time there have been numerous criticisms. One is that dependency theory, at least in its early formulation, focused too heavily on the factors external to societies and neglected the internal structures of underdevelopment. A second criticism concerns a combination of historical accuracy and conceptual ambiguity. In its early formulation by Frank (1967) it is argued that dependency occurs through participation in a world capitalist system. Yet it is further argued that the process of underdevelopment in Latin America began with colonization by the Spanish and the Portuguese during the 16th century. However, it is difficult to concede that the agricultural economy of Latin America, both then and now, can be described as a capitalist mode of production. In other words, there is a confusion in the theory concerning the two concepts of the "capitalist mode of production" and "participation in a world capitalist economic system" (Booth, 1975).

There are other criticisms worth noting. For example, recent studies suggest that foreign investment, trade and aid to a given country does, in the short run at least, contribute to economic growth in that country (Bornschier *et al.*, 1978). In this context it makes more sense to speak of *dependent development* rather than the development of underdevelopment (Cardoso, 1972). Related to this is the fact that the dependency theorists have failed to take into account that some dependent nations have succeeded to become rich while others have remained poor (Warren, 1980). Lastly the dependency theorists have not explained the participation of non-capitalist countries such as the Soviet Union in the development of the poor countries, and the extent to which it promotes its own form of dependency and underdevelopment in them.

Perhaps the most serious difficulty with dependency theory has been its failure to provide a viable strategy for development without creating some degree of dependency in the poor country. To sever trade relations, to refuse international aid or to nationalize multinational companies are simplistic policies, which are not likely to eliminate dependency or promote economic growth.

The goals of complete self-sufficiency and autonomy by a nation are unrealistic in the present-day world condition. Therefore the important question is what kind of dependency and what kind of development should be pursued in any given context. The dependency theorists have given few guidelines in this regard.

Finally the dependency theorists have not explained how the national elite of a poor country, who are seen as collaborators with the elites of rich countries in the dependency process, can be made to ignore their own interests and positions in favor of those of society as a whole. Yet in spite of these difficulties it must be said that the dependency perspective has provided us with a critical starting-point and understanding of important aspects in the process of development among the poor countries in the world.

Liberation Theory

Closely related to the Marxist and dependency theories of development are the so-called liberation theories. The authors of these theories do not completely reject the Marxist and dependency perspectives, but offer an alternative focus as to the source of underdevelopment and the means to overcome it. Furthermore, the liberation theories are not intended to be complete systematic theories of development but represent attempts to prescribe specific means to promote certain aspects of it.

The liberation schools of thought are built upon the conviction that nothing good or profitable can be secured for the poor members of an underdeveloped society without a drastic and radical change in the structure of that society, as well as a broader radical change of the current socioeconomic, political and cultural world order. The liberation theorists basically take a humanistic approach to questions of development. The underlying assumption is that members of the underdeveloped societies are oppressed by the powerholders of their own societies, who control the relevant economic resources such as land, industry and wealth. Some liberation theorists argue that the main remedy for overcoming this oppression lies in the education of the oppressed to be aware of their condition. This practice is called "conscientização" by the Brazilian educationist Paulo Freire. He explains the practice as follows:

> As the cultural revolution deepens 'conscientização' in the creative praxis of new society, men will begin to perceive why mythical remnants of the old society survive in the new.... I (Freire) interpret the revolutionary process as dialogical cultural action which is prolonged in 'cultural revolution' once power is taken. In both stages a serious and profound effort at 'conscientização' – by means of which men, through a true praxis, leave behind the status of 'objects' to assume the status of historical 'Subjects' – is necessary (Freire, 1972:158).

Freire is one of the main proponents of liberation theory whose focus tends to be on the role of education in the liberation and development process. Indeed, for Freire, liberation *is* development, and for those espousing the liberation approach, development is more a question of justice rather that wealth (Curle, 1973).

Liberation theory has been adopted at various times by policy-makers in some countries where education has been seen as the main tool for development, for example Guinea Bissau, Angola, Mozambique and Nicaragua. At the same time, however, the writings of Freire, for quite a few years, were banned in his own country, Brazil, and some other Latin American countries.

In many less developed countries the governments have tended to regard education, and particularly literacy, as neither economically beneficial nor politically desirable. Education, by producing a literate peasantry or workforce, has been seen by some as a potential threat to the *status quo,* and especially to the economic and political systems. Freire agrees, and as he states: "It would be extremely naive to expect the dominant classes to develop a type of education that would enable subordinate classes to perceive social injustices critically" (Freire, 1985). For Freire, literacy is a potentially political act which is important for liberation and therefore for development.

So far, there is little evidence available upon which to base an evaluation of development strategies derived from liberation theory, particularly those related to education. The perspective in general has been criticized by some as being utopian in its optimistic view of education as an agent of social change (Paulston, 1977). A further difficulty in the educational method is that it can be used to serve any political position. In other words, liberation can also mean oppression to a new master, and does not necessarily resolve the problems of development previously discussed in this chapter.

Four Models of Development Theories

Thus far in this chapter we have reviewed the ideas of philosophers and social scientists about the process of social and economic change and development. All of these theories continue to exert influence on current day-to-day thinking and planning among laymen, scientists and politicians about past changes and future directions of the world. These are living theories, and although not always made explicit, aspects of all of them in some way pervade much of modern thought.

We have identified four different major schools concerning change and development into which most past and present theories can be subsumed. Idealized illustrations of these schools are found in Fig. 1.2 which may help in visualizing their salient characteristics, their similarities and differences.

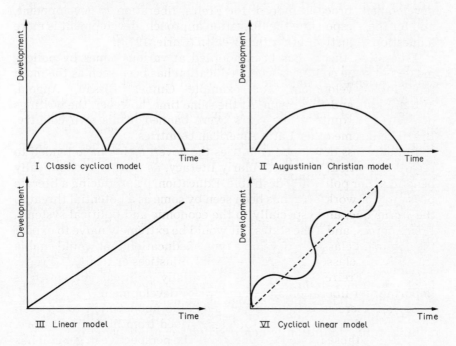

FIG. 1.2. Idealized illustrations of four theories of change and development.

The first pattern we call the Classic Cyclical Model, which includes the Greek and Roman views about the never-ending cycles of growth and decay of all material things, including nations and civilizations. There were variations, for example Plato's view that there were general cosmic cycles, lasting for thousands of years, within which were smaller concentric-like cycles. Ibn Khaldun's view of the repetitiveness of history puts him into this school, although with an added emphasis on never-ending conflict.

The importance of the "great catastrophe", which classical thinkers saw as ending the cycles, found its way into the schema of Judeo-Christian thought, which represents our second school of thought. The Christian notion of one major cycle, in particular Augustine's view of the City of God, continues to be found among those who today see the world as heading toward a major catastrophe, whether by nuclear destruction or the notion of the "second coming" which is part of much of present-day Christian belief.

The optimistic views of the Enlightenment and evolutionary theories generally are represented by our third school of thought which we call the Linear Model. Here we include all theories which see development as a never-ending progressive movement based on a faith in mankind and the conviction that societies evolve through similar stages. Structural-functionalism, human capitalist theory and modernization theory are, we would argue, part of this school of thought.

The combination of the optimism of the linear model and the conflict orientation implicit in the cyclical model is found in our fourth school of thought, which we call the Linear Cyclical Model. The dialectics of Hegel and Marx, which are found in much of conflict theory generally, are included in this category. We would also place liberation theory here. Dependency theory, however, has not been sufficiently systematized or articulated for us to assign it to this school of thought without equivocation. However, it seems to share many of the characteristics of other theories in this category.

A common feature of models three and four, which influence much of present-day thought, is that the notion of development assumes that societies can change consistently in a direction which is generally regarded as desirable or highly valued. In this respect, the Swedish economist Gunnar Myrdal states the matter plainly: "...by development I mean *the movement upward of the entire social system*, and I believe that is the only logically tenable definition" (Myrdal, n.d.:1). While Myrdal does not speak explicitly of conflict, there is nothing in his definition which precludes conflict being part of the development process.

Myrdal's understanding of development, because it is directed to the social system level, includes both economic and non-economic factors, for example, health, education and other social needs. Development, then, at its most general level is multi-dimensional in both conceptualization and reality. Most theories of development tend to focus on only one dimension of the process. To this extent the numerous theories appear confusing. However, if one takes the position suggested by Myrdal, it may be possible to see consistency in the many strains of thought found in the theories we have considered.

At this point it is also useful to draw the distinction between development and social change. Whereas social change includes the possibility of the "downward" movement of a social system as well as an "upward" one, the notion of development is generally restricted to the latter meaning.

In the final section of this chapter, we turn our attention briefly to what we identify as the basic dimensions used in the literature in the study of development.

Dimensions of Development Models

Throughout the history of social thought, the notion of development has been understood as change in a desirable direction and encompassing many different dimensions. In order to organize our discussion of these dimensions, we borrow the three criteria used by Furtado (1977) to analyze the concept further. They are:

1. an increase in the efficiency of the production system of a society;
2. the satisfaction of the population's basic needs;
3. the attainment of the objectives sought by various groups in a society, which are linked to the use of scarce resources (Furtado, 1977:636).

Without question the most common measure of increased growth or the efficiency of production in a society has been the Gross National Product (GNP) or its related measures like Gross Domestic Product (GDP). However, as Galtung (1976) has pointed out, this measure, "developed by experts and for experts", was useful and important as long as development was defined solely in terms of economic growth. The general assumption underlying these related measures of economic growth has been that the level of development, in terms of stages of growth, can be quantitatively measured in a way that represents the life conditions of the general population of a given society. Many studies have used indicators of this type such as GNP,

GDP, level of industrialization and level of technology, and have tried to explain why some societies are more developed than others.

The use of economic indicators as representing a single dimension of development has come under considerable criticism. In the first place, apart from the inaccuracies of such indicators, it is generally recognized that they only tell part of the story. High level of economic growth is quite compatible with a deterioration of life conditions. As Furtado (1977) states: "We cannot rule out the possibility that the deterioration of the living conditions of the population at large is due to the introduction of more "efficient" techniques" (p. 636). Likewise, as Furtado also comments, it is possible to have a rise in living standards without any change in economic growth or increase in efficiency of production. This occurs, for example, when there is a discovery or greater utilization of natural resources such as oil, minerals and so forth. The difficulty with a rise in living standards as an indicator of development is that it may be short-term, as it involves an irreversible process of the depletion of non-renewable resources, and hence contributes to what Furtado calls "universal entropy".

There has been general recognition that the living conditions of a population may be a better indicator of level of development than the economic indicators. These life conditions are sometimes divided into basic human needs of a material nature and basic human needs related to satisfaction. With regard to the needs themselves, food, water, energy and shelter, on the one hand, and education, security, recreation and communication, on the other, are included in the material and phycho-social categories.

The notion of basic human needs first came into being at the Declaration of Cocoyoc in 1974 which resulted from a symposium sponsored by the United Nations Environmental Program and the United Nations Conference on Trade and Development. While the notion of basic needs is not incompatible with economic growth, to measure development in terms of these needs is to place stress on the *distributive* aspects of society. Thus, indicators of the satisfaction of human needs, for example, education or health, show the extent to which societies are distributing their resources and thus raising the level of human quality of life. In constructing new indicators which reflect this process, Galtung (1976) argues that we might even reintroduce the idea of growth "not as the accumulation of machineries, of production, or of marketable goods, but in the sense of dynamism of progress, along the many dimensions of *true* development" (p. 265).

The third dimension, as stated by Furtado (1977), concerns domination and power. In addition to focusing upon economic growth and the equal distribution of the society's resources in meeting human needs, attention must also be directed to levels of decision-making whereby these resources are distributed. The idea here is that societies are more developed to the extent that there is greater *participation* in the decision-making process, and no one group completely dominates another group. In this dimension as well as the other two, the choice of indicator is crucial. Thus attention is directed to indicators of political development, such as political participation, access to political positions, and the development of national integration and cohesion.

There are many writers who have acknowledged the multidimensionality of development. There are very few who have attempted to deal with the interrelationships between these dimensions. One of the basic assumptions of our work is that education cuts across what we identify as three important dimensions, the economic, the cultural-ideological and the political. To this extent education is a common element for all three in the process of development. In Chapters 3, 4 and 5 we propose to critically examine in depth the crucial role that education plays in this multidimensional development process. In the following chapter, however, we focus our attention specifically on the controversial link between education and development.

2

Education and Development:
the Emerging Confidence in
Formal Schooling as an Agent
of Change

IF theories about the nature and direction of societal change have been numerous and diverse, so too have explanations of change. Classical thinkers and their early Christian counterparts saw the causes of societal development as largely outside the control of mankind. If the fate of civilization was seen to be in the hands of the gods, which in some form or other dominated men's minds until after the Middle Ages, it was also seen to rest in the continual conflict between Good and Evil, between God and Satan. However, man was not seen to be completely passive in the complexity of forces which affected his long-term destiny, for even Augustine recognized that part of the struggle for this destiny took place within man himself, between virtue and vice, between love and hate, and in the strife of man against man. Yet even at this level of explanation, the struggle nevertheless was seen to take place because it was "willed by God" (Nisbet, 1969:85–90). As we noted in the previous chapter, it was only after the Middle Ages that men began to believe that the destiny of mankind and the progress and development of civilization rested not in the hands of the gods but in the hands of men. And with this belief came the view that through rationality and knowledge, human civilization could develop and make progress forever. No longer must life on earth be wretched, subject to disease, war and other catastrophes, because with the improvement of rational thought man's control over his environment would increase and the quality of life improve. It was this shift in comprehension about the cause of social change which gave rise to an optimism about change itself. With the Enlightenment, social change, because it meant the possibility of progress and development, became regarded as desirable rather than feared (La Piere, 1965).

32

Improvement of the human mind, then, with its potential powers of rational thought and ability to discover knowledge about nature and its laws, became regarded as the key to human progress. Rather than regard the learning of skills and knowledge as a virtuous pastime or merely to carry out important political and civil operations (as in the case of Egyptian, Greek and Roman scribes), men of the Enlightenment saw cognitive development and the pursuit of knowledge as essential not only for the survival, but also the advancement of society itself. Education in the modern sense, as a formal and deliberate process by which the cultural and normative heritage of a society is transmitted from generation to generation, and through which that heritage is improved through scientific discovery, had its roots in the Enlightenment. The precursors of the modern school and university, with their presumed functions relating to progress, became established during this period.

However, the Enlightenment did not have a monopoly on schooling. Formal and deliberate education through institutionalized schooling existed long before, and was known in ancient societies. How or why these ancient schools emerged, or in what ways they were seen as agents of social change is not altogether clear. In retrospect, however, contrary to the prevalent beliefs of classical thinkers, formal education may indeed have contributed to changes in society, and possibly to societal progress and development.

The Emergence of Formal Schooling and its Transformation

There have been relatively few authors who have attempted to document, or even explain, the emergence of formal schooling in human society. Most available evidence suggests that the deliberate and institutionalized training of scribes in the art of writing existed in 3000 B.C. in Mesopotamia and Egypt, almost as soon as writing itself began. Clearly the development of writing represented a major breakthrough in the development of civilization, and the acquisition and use of this important and strategic skill was soon institutionalized so as not to be left up to chance learning, to informal training, or indeed to be learned by the wrong persons. From the beginning, it appears that schools and their skilled products were seen as serving the State and the society as a whole.

This is precisely the argument put forth by the anthropologist Yehudi Cohen (1970) who contends that schools in antiquity emerged as political instruments to serve political purposes. In developing his position, Cohen defines school very much in its modern form, that is "...an institution devoted to instruction, with specialized personnel, permanent physical structures, special apparatus (of which texts are an important part), formal and stereotyped means of instruction, a curriculum, and rationally defined manifest objectives" (p. 56). He contends that these separate institutions came with the emergence of what he calls "civilizational states", or the political union of smaller economic and socio-cultural sectors of civilization networks. He cites as examples, the societies of ancient Egypt, Babylonia, Greece and Rome.

According to Cohen, one of the requirements for the survival of civilizational states (the unification of small, local, political and/or tribal entities which formed what we call today nations) is the breaking down of local loyalties and replacing them with loyalties to the State. This is particularly important for the elites whose task it is to maintain the boundaries of the State. Thus, for Cohen, in the early period of the development of civilizational states it was necessary that at least some of the population, that is, the elite, be schooled.

Cohen's theory becomes more compelling when he deals with the question of the introduction of formal schooling from civilizational to non-civilizational states, and of more recent concern, the emergence of mass schooling and its political implications. With respect to the first, Cohen argues that schools in civilizational states developed indigenously ("autochthonously") whereas in non-civilizational states they have always been introduced from without, generally as an instrument for the conquering of or expanding into the new society. The relevance of this point of view for contemporary debates about the appropriateness of Western-type schools for Third World development should be self-evident and is a topic to which we will turn later in this chapter.

Until relatively recent times, formal schooling has always been restricted to a small proportion of the population. This was no less true for the schools for scribes in Mesopotamia as for pre-19th-century England. As such, the political nature of schooling is, at least potentially, overt and visible. However, the emergence of mass schooling in Western industrial societies, and the multiple functions of formal education, including that of self-development, can be seen within the same political context as the education of the elites in former times. With more complex economic and political structures, boundary-maintenance, political loyalty and conforming behavior become even more important for state survival, and indeed for societal advancement. Thus for Cohen, factors leading to the emergence of schooling in antiquity have continued to the present. State machinery has become more complex but the educational needs of the State remain the same.

Although there are exceptions, every state system knows that a 'good' student becomes an obedient subject. Repeated examinations in arithmetic and biology are integral aspects of what is called 'political socialization' (Cohen, 1970:134).

In spite of the fact that at different times and places the form of education appears far removed from the political system, it is difficult to disregard Cohen's explanation for the emergence of schools. Even among the Mesopotamians and Egyptians, the skills of the scribes soon became available to the military, and later to professional bureaucrats, in whom the responsibility for the boundary-maintenance of the State rested. Even in Greece and Rome where much learning was admired for its own sake, the advantages to the State of an educated citizenry were recognized. Plato, in particular, was concerned with education, for only through proper training could the State be assured of a loyal citizenry and talented leaders. According to one writer, Plato's argument can be summarized as follows:

> If the state is to be preserved it must take care of the young, control their education in a state system independent of the whims of parents and the power of wealth, and place their training in the hands of teachers more competent and more responsible than the poor schoolmaster and pedagogue (Castle, 1961:81).

Without passing judgement on the historical validity of Cohen's interpretation, we do feel that implicit in his argument is a theory of education and development. It would appear that what Cohen is saying is that the school not only made and continues to make it possible for the old and new civilizational states to survive, but also to grow and develop. Conversely, not to have at least some educated citizens in these societies meant not to survive or develop. Yet in the classical period, the survival of the State, and also its progress, was still seen to be a matter for the gods. But then the distance between the gods and men was not perceived as very great.

A somewhat different approach to explaining the emergence of schooling has been developed by another anthropologist, George Kneller (1965). He has focused on the continuities and discontinuities between primitive and modern education. Rather than the needs of the State, Kneller argues that the emergence of schooling, and the organizational forms that schools have taken in history, have been related to the complexity of social organization and social institutions.

Kneller suggests that with increasing societal complexity, the transmission of specialized skills and knowledge from generation to generation could not be left to traditional educational methods. Therefore, not only did there emerge special institutions for this training in society, but also special agents to whom was entrusted the responsibility of carrying out this function, namely teachers.

Kneller provides little empirical evidence to support his theory, but nevertheless uses it to explain the contrasts between educational institutions in primitive and modern societies. The "Bush Schools" of Africa and the initiation rites of tribal Australian Aborigines represent primitive forms of schooling which were suited for simple but not complex social structures. Nevertheless Kneller, in agreement with other social scientists (for example, Mead, 1966; and Havighurst, 1968), contends that some qualities of simple educational forms retain value even in the highly complex industrial societies of today. The link between the structure of schooling and the level of societal development does not necessarily imply strict causality in one direction or the other. It does, however, suggest that any conflict or discontinuity between the two will possibly be detrimental to the development process.

> One reason that we study the educational methods of primitive cultures to is acquire a more balanced and critical view of our own educational system. Clearly, we cannot transplant primitive practices into our own vastly more complex culture and expect them to work, for we would be removing them from the only context in which they make sense. On the other hand, the success that primitive peoples have had in managing certain aspects of their educational life should encourage us to tackle our own problems with greater perspective and optimism (Kneller, 1965:78–79).

There seems to be considerable room for debate about the nature of the interrelationships between schooling and society, from the very origins of schooling to the most recent reforms in many Western industrialized societies. In his discussion of the evolution of the French educational system from the Middle Ages, the sociologist Durkheim (1977), writing in the early 20th century, argued like Cohen and Kneller that changes in society always precede changes in the educational system. Durkheim emphasized that "Educational transformations are always the result and the symptom of the social transformations in terms of which they are to be explained" (p. 166). Indeed before the emergence of Renaissance schooling and its interest in the classical writings of Greece and Rome, it was necessary for people to change their intellectual and moral outlook. The classics were *known* to those in the Dark and Middle Ages, but they were not *needed*.

Schooling and the Industrial Revolutions in England and Japan

Durkheim recognized that changes in the economic sphere have much to do with changes in education. The link between schooling and the economy, and in particular economic development, has become even more debated with reference to the Industrial Revolution in England. The expansion of literacy in the 16th and 17th centuries was partly due to changing views about learning in general, especially the emphasis on reading which was encouraged by the Protestant Reformation, and partly due to the invention of the printing press and the increased publication and circulation of books. In the mid-17th century, it has been estimated that there was 30 to 40 percent literacy in England, although the actual figure varied and was higher in cities than in the countryside, and almost completely concentrated in the upper classes (Shipman, 1971).

In the several centuries prior to the Industrial Revolution, when the variety and numbers of schools were expanding, schooling was sometimes criticized as detrimental to worker productivity, and by implication, to national interests. In 1723 one opposition voice to the expanding number of schools wrote:

> Going to School in comparison to Working is Idleness, and the longer boys continue in this easy sort of life, the more unfit they will be when grown up for downright Labour, both as to Strength and Inclination (cited in Shipman, 1971:104).

In the early "take-off" stage of industrialization in England, which is generally agreed to have lasted from about 1780 to 1850, schools were never seen as being related to economic advancement. The skills and knowledge required for jobs in the first factories were not complex, and indeed were probably less demanding in this context than those required for successful farming. Furthermore, these skills were generally learned on the factory floor and were never seen as having any connection with schooling. This view even prevailed with respect to most middle-class occupations, as the requirements for pursuing careers in military, teaching and administration contexts were learned on the job. The universities during this period, although catering for the education of future religious and legal professionals, did little to match their curricula to vocational needs (Shipman, 1971). Even historians generally agree that at least in the beginning, the Industrial Revolution was not due to British scientific and technological superiority. The cotton industry, which was the initial impetus for more widespread industrialization, was largely created as a byproduct of overseas trade, particularly with the colonies. It certainly was not due to the quality of an already-existing labor force, for in the words of the English historian E. J. Hobsbawm (1977), "English education was a joke in poor taste" at the time that early industrial development occurred (p. 45).[1]

As the pace of British industrialization quickened, the pressures to improve and expand the educational system increased. However, these pressures seem to have been only marginally vocational in nature. The social consequences of industrial development, for example greater geographical mobility and widespread criminality in the new urban centers, required new measures of social control. For many, schooling replaced the family as a means of inculcating discipline and a respect for one's place in society. Thus even in the mid-19th century, schools for the poor were seen more in philanthropic and disciplinary terms, and less, if any, in vocational. However, by the beginning of the 20th century, with the passing of Balfour's Act in 1902, and subsequently to Butler's Act of 1944, schooling became a compulsory process through the two stages of primary and secondary education. This was in sharp contrast to the voluntary nature of schooling which prevailed throughout most of the industrial development period, until 1870 (Shipman, 1971; Williams, 1961).

The transformation and expansion of the school system in England during the Industrial Revolution did not occur without considerable debate. There were many who saw schooling, especially of the poor and the emerging working class, as unnecessary, time consuming, and potentially sowing seeds of discontent and social instability by raising the consciousness and aspirations of workers. Alternatively, there were others, in the beginning a minority, who saw in schooling a source of discipline, and indirectly a means of improving the quality of the workforce by inculcating the norms of organized work. However, as schooling expanded it was also seen as a basic human right, but at the same time was designed to match the increasingly complex stratification structure of British industrial society. Its function was in practice, therefore, conservative rather than progressive in terms of maintaining the social structure.

The expansion of formal schooling was more a result rather than the cause of industrialization in Britain. Available evidence suggests that a similar relationship prevailed in the transformation of schooling in the United States in the late 19th and early 20th centuries. "The changes in the occupational structure have raised the educational aspirations of large parts of the American population, and the educational system has been responsive to these higher aspirations" (Trow, 1961:147). It would be simplistic, however, to assume that education was only a passive agent throughout the technological and social changes of the 18th and 19th centuries. Clearly the relationship was more complex, and as the complexity of industrial skills increased, the importance of schooling in producing an appropriately skilled workforce also increased. What is of most significance for our investigation, however, is that schools were not regarded as agents of change and development throughout this period. Rather, they played a role somewhat similar to schools in earlier societies, where the purpose and consequences of schooling were seen in individual and elitist rather than in societal terms.

This does not mean, however, that formal education has not and cannot play a more direct and causal role in economic development. Post-World War II development in Japan is generally regarded as the classic example of education being deliberately utilized as a contributing factor to rapid industrialization and economic and social development. Much has been written about the modernization of Japan, and in particular the use which was made of education during this period. The details of this process have been well documented and discussed elsewhere and will not occupy us here.[2] However, a number of significant points are relevant for our concern, as the Japanese experience, although similar in many ways to the British, departs in ways which are informative. After political and social stability had been established during the Tokugawa period, which began in the early 17th century, education in Japan was used as a main unifying force to combat the fragmentation of the previous feudal period. Even though Japan was a closed nation for over two centuries while Britain and Europe were slowly undergoing industrialization, important events took place which made for an easy and rapid transition into an industrial state. Before 1850, it has been estimated that 40 percent of the male population was literate, and in 1872 a universal and unified education system was introduced. When Japan decided to industrialize in the late 19th century, it had a model to follow, for the technology of the West was known and desired. Furthermore, in order to industrialize, Japan did not have to progress through the long and sometimes agonizing process experienced by Britain, starting with the simple to the more complex levels of technology. Thus the level of skilled manpower required to modernize was high from the beginning. Schooling was, from the outset, regarded in Japan as essential for economic growth (Stone, 1970; Shipman, 1971). To this extent, the Japanese example is unique when compared to industrialization in the West, and represents perhaps the first overt commitment to the belief and practice that education can make a direct contribution to economic growth and advancement. This conviction was to become more widespread throughout the West such that by the end of World War II, education was seen as the most important, and indeed an essential engine for both the "take-off" into industrialization by less-developed countries, as well as for the transition of the already developed countries to post-industrial stages.

It is difficult to pinpoint exactly when this shift in thinking about education and social and economic development began. However, it is certain that by the late 1950s and early 1960s there was general agreement among politicians, educational and social planners, and scholars that education was a key change agent for moving societies along the development continuum.[3] There were a number of reasons, both theoretical and practical, which presumed to explain this direct relationship. One of these was based on the very simple belief that literacy was essential for modernization and industrialization to occur, specifically for the less developed countries. Thus during the period following World War II we entered what has rightfully been called the "age of innocence", which manifested itself in a world-wide explosion in educational enrolments and expenditure, both in the developed and less-developed countries.[4] With respect to the latter, the attainment of a literate population by means of universal primary education became a major goal for many development programs.

The Importance of Literacy

There is general agreement among scholars that one of the fundamental breakthroughs in the emergence of civilization was the invention of writing as a means of communication. With the written word it became possible for historical events to be accurately recorded, and for knowledge to be more widely and quickly disseminated within and between generations. In writing about the importance of literacy, Goody and Watt (1977) point out that not only was trade, commerce and the economic sector of society radically altered, but also the nature of human interaction was transformed. With the birth of writing, it was no longer necessary to depend on memory as a record of events, even though the practice of oral history was well developed. The use of written accounts and the ability to communicate by the written word greatly reduced the margin for error, making it possible for individuals to validate knowledge for themselves rather than depend on the credibility and accuracy of the accounts of others. For example, there are compelling arguments which suggest that in spite of the widespread use of memory and oral history, it is unlikely that the classical epic literary and historical works, such as by Homer and Hesiod, could have been produced without the use of writing and therefore of a partly literate population (Kenyon, 1951).

Closely associated with literacy, and interdependent with it, was the development of numeracy. Basic writing and basic arithmetic appear to have been a major requirement for the emergence of civilizations. There is a qualitative difference between pre-literate and literate societies in terms of the mobilization of human resources through more effective and efficient communication, more complex forms of social organization, and the ability to create and utilize higher levels of technology. In short, the literate person has greater powers of communication, critical consciousness and control over his or her environment. The mobilization of human potential for social and collective action in ancient Egypt, Babylonia and Greece, even with partially literate populations, dramatically surpassed that of pre-literate tribes or nomadic groups.

In the ancient classical societies literacy and numeracy were restricted to a small portion of the population. For example, in Egypt and Babylonia schooling was specially designed to train scribes whose task it was to officially record commercial and other matters for the State. The position of the scribe was considered to be an important one. The same can be said for the *literati* in China, who had to pass rigorous examinations before they could carry out duties for the State. In these early societies the role of the small group that could read and write were essential for even the moderate advancement which these societies were able to make at that time.

Historical evidence suggests that formal education and thus literacy expanded considerably in ancient Greece and Rome. By the 5th century B.C. most Greek citizens sent their sons to schools at least up to the age of 14, and this privilege was extended to daughters sometime during the 4th century B.C. Because of the strong belief in democratic processes, particularly in Athens, schooling and literacy were seen as essential for all Greek citizens. However, there is little empirical evidence that schools and literacy either caused or were the result of Athenian democracy, since schools and the ability to read and write are also found in the tyranny that preceded its establishment (Harvey, 1966).

There is little indication that literacy, and indeed education in general, was seen only in utilitarian terms. Above all, learning was considered a requirement for the "whole man", and humanistic rather than instrumental values seem to have prevailed (Marrou, 1956).

Although exact figures are impossible to obtain, it is almost certain that there was at least "minimal literacy" among most male citizens, with perhaps less literacy competence among females, slaves and in the countryside (Harvey, 1966:621–629; Bowen, 1972:75–78).[5]

In early Rome, education took place within the home and grew out of a predominantly rural civilization. In contrast to Athens, Roman education was "a utilitarian response to the urgent demands of rural life" (Castle, 1961:106). It is difficult to determine to what extent this early form of schooling included training in literacy skills. Castle (1961), for example, suggests that the main focus may have been on other matters deemed important for traditional Roman life.

> To the Roman father education was not a matter of instruction from books or of cultivating aesthetic appreciation in his children, but rather a means of inculcating an indelible reverence for a few definite moral qualities, and of imparting such practical skills as were essential to good farming and brave fighting. Elementary instruction in letters and simple calculation was given by the father, but this was a small part of his children's upbringing (Castle, 1961:113).

However, if we can generalize from some surviving writings of prominent Romans, the ability to read and write were considered essential components for the education of children. In fact, the evidence seems to suggest that literacy may have been more widespread in the Roman world than in the Greek. It seems that many slaves were literate and even served as readers or secretaries in Roman households (Marrou, 1956:266). Although the evidence suggests that literacy was more widespread among Roman males, many Roman women apparently excelled in learning to read and write, and their accomplishments were recorded in Roman documents (Best, 1969).

Formal schooling began to expand in Rome in the 3rd and 2nd centuries B.C., and followed the Greek model. However, the literary tradition of the Greeks did not assume as prominent a position in Roman schooling, with the result that Roman education has been seen as inferior in quality. Indeed, Castle remarks that "as the pre-Christian era drew to its close the mass of Rome's citizens emerged as no more than a poor, ignorant, overworked, unhealthy, and undisciplined mob" (p. 123).

There seems to be general consensus among historians that literacy began to decline with the deterioration of the Roman Empire. Yet, during the following centuries literary activities continued to flourish in some European locales, for example, in monasteries and cathedral schools established for the training of the clergy. In addition, the perceived importance of literacy continued to exist in the Arab world which, during the so-called Dark Ages, was responsible for preserving Greek Philosophy and eventually reintroducing it into Western thought.

As early as the 13th century we have documentation of the gradual increase in the literacy of laymen in particular in North-western Europe. Many merchants were literate. By 1850 it has been estimated that over half of the workers in English and French cities had some literary competence (Bowman and Anderson, 1973). Current research in Sweden has documented the fact that almost all adults could read long before schooling became compulsory in that country (Johansson, 1977). Likewise, in the 19th century literacy and school attendance became widespread in the United States (Meyer *et al.*, 1977).

Our main concern in examining these patterns of literacy is to raise the question of the link between literacy, schooling and development. Scholars are not in agreement about the causal relationship between literacy and economic growth. In the case of literacy and education in antiquity, Marrou has even suggested that its potential as an agent for change and development may have been wasted.

But the point is that the historical conditions of the period – political, economic, social and technical conditions – did not really know what to do with the admirable human capital with which it had thus been so well provided. I must repeat that classical education supplied the *materia prima* for a higher human type than had hitherto been known, a type capable of anything – if only it could have discovered something, or someone, to devote itself to (Marrou, 1956:226).

In effect, Marrou argues that the form of classical education became inappropriate for the needs of Greek and Roman society and failed to contribute to societal development, and perhaps was even detrimental to it in the long run.

Bowman and Anderson (1973) argue that a literacy rate of about 40 percent is necessary but not sufficient for a sustained level of economic growth. However, they further contend that industrialization and more rapid economic expansion cannot occur until 70 to 80 percent of any population is literate (p. 250). Psacharopoulos and Woodhall (1985) seem to confirm this view for individuals, as they argue that the young do benefit economically from additional schooling. To this extent, it seems that a least for a certain level of economic and industrial development, a fairly high level of literacy is required. The strong link between literacy and level of development is clearly apparent in the figures in Table 2.1., keeping in mind that the span in years between the three dates are not equal. Although literacy has increased for low and middle-income countries, they still lag far behind the industrialized countries. While it is impossible to argue that raising levels of literacy would directly result in increased economic development, the correlation between the two is clearly apparent. Yet there is growing evidence that the relationship between the two is also complex and requires further conceptual clarity.

TABLE 2.1. *Adult Literacy Rate*
(percent) for Countries of Different
Levels of Development

	1960	1975	1985
Low-income countries	29	38	32
Middle-income countries	54	71	72
Industrialized countries	—	99	98

Source: World Bank, "Education", *World Development Report, 1980,* Washington, 1980b, Table 23, pp. 154–155. Unesco Office of Statistics, The Current Literacy Situation in the World. Paris, 1985.

There are ways to improve the economic productivity of society without literacy. This is particularly true of the agricultural sector where output can be increased through basic innovations and technology, for example fertilizers and irrigation. Indeed, as Fuller *et al.* (1987) point out, the evidence suggests that the relationship between literacy and economic growth is stronger in urban centers for manufacturing and trade than in rural areas. With respect to the latter, there are even examples where peasants have resisted literacy training and schooling, seeing it as a form of indoctrination to another social order. Nevertheless there have been higher levels of literacy in rural areas where higher levels of agricultural technology and productivity have prevailed.[6]

In like manner, lower levels of industrial technology probably do not require a large literate population. As already pointed out, this seems to have been the order of events with respect to industrialization in the West. This fact is particularly relevant for developing countries where development strategies progress from simple levels of industrialization to the more complex. The problem arises when it is generally assumed that the only suitable development strategy for the Third World is to imitate the industrialized countries at their present level of development. Only then does it seem that rapid mass literacy campaigns would be essential for economic growth.

Throughout this discussion we have tended to treat literacy only in terms of its role as a basic requirement for learning skills for high levels of industrialization. But some have questioned this as the most important consideration where mass literacy is concerned. Literacy is also a basic human right which expands personal choice, control over one's environment, and allows for collective action not otherwise possible. Much of the concern today in less-developed and developed countries about illiteracy stems, at least in part, from this consideration. However, even in industrialized countries, various forms of illiteracy continue to exist. In 1975, for example, it was estimated than in the United Kingdom over two million adults were considered semi- or completely illiterate (Limage, 1986:59) and although £ 1 million was allocated to combat this illiteracy, the results are still in question (Wells, 1987). According to UNESCO, in 1980 the illiteracy rate in Northern and Western Europe was estimated to be about 0.5 percent, which is generally regarded as an underestimate (Brand, 1987:203). In this context, current concern in the industrialized countries has tended to focus on the "right to read" as a justification for the eradication of these last vestiges of illiteracy. However, only several decades ago literacy, and indeed all of education, was seen in terms of human resources. Irrespective of country and level of development, a literate and educated population was regarded as more productive and desirable, and to tolerate pockets of illiteracy and undereducation was to tolerate wastage of human talent potentially available for society's benefit.

Literacy campaigns have attracted much attention during the 1970s and 1980s, especially in post-revolutionary societies of the Third World. Some government programs had the eradication of illiteracy as a primary goal. In 1961 Cuba reduced illiteracy from 24 percent to four percent. Nicaragua, in 1979–80, reduced illiteracy from 50 percent to 13 percent, while southern Vietnam, from 1976 to 1978, reported reductions of 25 percent to 14 percent (Lind and Johnston, 1986:67). Starting with a much higher illiteracy rate, Ethiopia's campaign from 1979 to 1982 resulted in a decrease from 93 percent to 55 percent (Carron and Bordua, 1985:119). These dramatic examples of rapid decreases in illiteracy, or conversely the increases in literacy, are reflected in Figure 2.1 which shows changing patterns of literacy in various parts of the world between 1850 and 2000 (projected). The success of several literacy campaigns suggests that some parts of the less-developed world are attaining in 20 years what the industrialized world took over 100 years to accomplish.

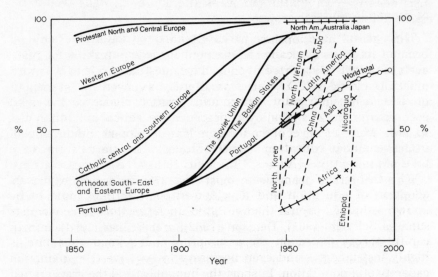

FIG. 2.1. World literacy in a historical perspective. Population about 10–15 years of age and older. Percentage figures. (Adapted from Johansson, 1977: Figure 20).
_____ Literacy in Europe 1850–1960 estimated from censuses.
_/_/_/_/_/_/_ Literacy in the world 1945–1970 and prognosis 1970–1980 according to UNESCO
–o–o–o–o–o–o–o– Total world estimations up to 2000 according to UNESCO
_ _ _ _ _ _ _ _ Mass literacy campaigns in some countries (according to papers at the International Symposium for Literacy, Persepolis, Iran, September 1975).

Literacy campaigns also serve ideological goals. In some of the newly independent socialist countries literacy has been seen as an essential instrument for informing the people of aspects of government social and economic policy, and a means to mobilize the masses to political solidarity and to giving their energy to the attainment of national goals. However, some literacy campaigns have been short-lived, as their cost increased and political usefulness decreased. The rise and fall of the Mozambique literacy campaign, from 1978 to 1982, provides an example of a program which slowed down before it achieved its objectives (Lind, 1988; see also Chapter 8).

The maintenance of literacy in a society, once it has been attained, is not always easy. For example, the level of literacy in individuals must reach a certain threshold of minimal competency (estimated to be the equivalent of about six years of schooling) so that literacy gains will not be lost. Thus, in addition to literacy programs, a society must have available a literate environment, including reading materials and newspapers, which will sustain the momentum of the campaign (Wagner, 1987).

Formal Education and the Mobilization of Human Resources

The causal relationship between education and development became accepted by academics and policy-makers in the late 1950s and early 1960s. Supported by the publications and funding programs of OECD and UNESCO,[7] education came to be viewed almost without question as an important, and indeed "crucial" agent for the rapid economic growth of nations. The degree of theoretical conviction was so high, while the level of empirical evidence so scant, that the belief in the benefits of education has been called "one of the most romantic tales of the century" (Adams, 1977:300).

The theoretical framework most responsible for the wholesale adoption of education and development policies has come to be known as human capital theory. Based upon the work of economists such as Schultz (1961), Denison (1962), and Becker (1964), human capital theory rested on the assumption that formal education is highly instrumental and even necessary to improve the production capacity of a population. In short the human capital theorists argued that an educated population is a productive population.

How, and on what evidence, did the human capital theorists develop their arguments? As indicated briefly in Chapter 1, the human capital theorists contend that for any economic growth and development to occur two requirements are necessary. The first of these is the improvement and greater efficiency of technology, because higher technology results in greater production. The second component, however, concerns the utilization of human resources in the employment of technology. The skills and the motivation for productive behavior are imparted by means of formal education. Therefore the human capital theorists believe that an investment in education is an investment in the productivity of the population. To be sure, other factors are also seen as essential for full utilization of human resources, for example food, housing and health. Put simply, a well-fed, healthy and well-housed population is seen as more productive, both physically and psychologically.

In spite of the theoretical and methodological difficulties in the work of human capital theorists, educational planning and development strategies were dominated by it until the 1980s.[8] Numerous studies have shown the consistent patterns between levels of education and economic levels of development among countries. Harbison (1973), in a now classic study, documented this pattern by showing that school enrolment ratios at all three levels are considerably lower for the less advanced countries than for the advanced. Although he pointed to many difficulties and critical issues in the use of education to bring about development, he nevertheless argued that education was a major component in the development of human resources.

Theodore Schultz, one of the originators of the concept of human capital, demonstrated his continuing commitment to the theory in his 1979 Nobel Lecture (1980). In this address, Schultz reiterated the main arguments in much the same way and with the same conviction that he did some 20 years previously. Speaking broadly about the general transition from agricultural to industrial societies, Schultz stated that "a fundamental proposition documented by much recent research is that an integral part of the modernization of the economies of high and low-income countries is *the decline of the economic importance of farmland and a rise in that of human capital – skills and knowledge*" (p. 642). Furthermore, Schultz argued that due to the improvement of farm technology the productivity of agricultural activity was far greater than it once was. Speaking about what he called "land augmentation", Schultz observed that the "corn acreage harvested in the United States in 1979 was 33 million acres less than in 1932. Yet the 7.76 billion bushels produced in 1979 was almost three times the amount produced in 1932" (p. 642). Throughout his address Schultz emphasized the importance of improving population quality in order to enhance the economic prospects and the welfare of poor people. Furthermore, he stated without ambiguity that "education accounts for much of the improvements in population quality" (p. 647).

A review of research based on the human capital approach in 44 countries has tended to confirm Schultz's arguments. In conducting his survey of rates of return to educational investment, Psacharopoulos (1981) found the following patterns: (1) the social and private returns are highest for primary education, (2) private returns exceed social returns, especially at the university level, (3) all rates of return to investment in education are above the 10 percent criterion of the opportunity cost of capital, and (4) the rates of return are higher in less-developed countries than in developed countries at comparable levels. In spite of this accumulation of supporting evidence, human capital theory always has been controversial.

In the early 1960s the investment value of education for the improvement of human productivity was virtually unquestioned; by the end of the same decade human capital theory as the basis for a viable development strategy had been brought into doubt. No longer was it universally accepted that an increase in educational expenditure and of participation rates was sufficient to improve economic productivity both in industrialized and non-industrialized countries. By the early 1970s belief in education as a panacea for development had entered an "age of scepticism" (Weiler, 1978).

Criticisms of the human capital approach have generally focused on the underlying assumptions of the theory itself. For example, the theory assumes that the labor market in which the educated worker must compete is a perfect one, such that the better educated, with more skills, get the better jobs and are more productive. Secondly, the human capital theory does not take into account other factors, such as job satisfaction and the reward structure, which might contribute to higher worker productivity irrespective of education. Thirdly, human capital theory does not consider the possibility that education only serves as a "screening device", whereby it is not used as an indication of skills, but of other features of individuals which promote higher productivity, such as appropriate attitudes, motivation and other personal characteristics (Blaug, 1985; Woodhall, 1985).

Human capital theory, much like modernization theory, contends that the key to economic growth lies in individual characteristics. It makes no reference to aspects of the social structure, and rather than advocating structural change to promote development it advocates individual change. As such it also completely neglects the nature of international ties between countries and assumes that differences between advanced and non-advanced countries and between rich and poor countries rest in characteristics within the countries themselves.

Radical critics of human capital theory, such as Bowles and Gintis (1976), do not deny the investment value of education in promoting human productivity. They do contend, however, that education should be examined more critically in its relationship to development. For in addition to the imputation of skills and values they point out that education serves, at least in capitalist societies, to maintain the *status quo* and in the long run may be detrimental to the continued economic growth of a society. In effect, the radical critics argue that it creates a docile and adaptive work force which serves the needs of the power structure of the economy. For the radical critics, an education system which does not alter the structure of an inequitable capitalist society, does not contribute to the change and development of that society.

The methodology of human capital theory also leaves much to be desired. For the most part, attempts to demonstrate the development outcomes of improvements in the quality of human capital rely upon linear equation models whereby gains in national productivity (usually measured as GNP) over a period of time are explained in terms of known factors, such as improvements in technology and other forms of capital investment. The residuals, or the gains in productivity, left unexplained after all known factors are taken into account, are attributed to improvements in the quality of "human stock". However, as indicated in Chapter 1, a basic fallacy in this reasoning is that the size of residuals in linear models can be the result of many factors, not the least of which concerns the specifications of the model itself (including the underlying assumptions), as well as the adequate measurement of the variables in the model. In short, the strength of human capital theory rests upon theoretical assumptions and methodological procedures which, to say the least, are tenuous with the best of data. Given the dubious quality and inadequacy of the data available for most early human capital research, it is not surprising that policies based on the theory have produced unexpected results, such as greater inequality in society rather than greater equality (Blaug, 1985).

Without doubt, however, human capital theory has had considerable influence over policies concerning education and development strategies, for example in international organizations such as the World Bank, OECD, and UNESCO. Indeed, much of the early optimism regarding the direct contribution of education to development was based in part on beliefs in human capital theory. In many respects human capital theory represents the contribution of economists to development strategies. When human capital theory began to be questioned, so too did the link between education and development.

The Modernizing Influence of Education: a Pre-condition for Economic Development

While the economists were busy developing measures to support the investment value of education for increased productivity, sociologists were adopting similar positions from a sociological framework. Starting from the 1950s through to the early 1970s the general view among many sociologists was that there is a direct relationship between education and socioeconomic development. Like the human capital theorists, sociologists also focused upon individual-level characteristics within a population to explain different levels of economic growth and development.[9] Also like human capital theorists, sociologists maintained that education brings about a change in the individual which promotes greater productivity and work efficiency. Whereas human capital theorists spoke in terms of improvements in the quality of a population through education in the productivity process, sociologists spoke of education's modernizing influence on values, beliefs and behavior. For sociologists the underlying assumption of what has come to be called modernization theory is that in order for a society to become modern (to develop economically and socially), it must be composed of a modern population, meaning modern values, beliefs and behavior.

Modernization theory had its origins in the work of David McClelland, a social psychologist who in the 1950s and 1960s attempted to explain why some societies have attained higher levels of social and technological organization than others.

McClelland (1961) argued that the factor most responsible for differences between societies in social and technological advancement was in the cultures and modal personalities of those societies, specifically in what he called the need for achievement (n Ach). Advanced societies contained high proportions of individuals with a high need for achievement, while the populations of less advanced societies contained lower proportions.

In sociology, an approach similar to McClelland's was being pursued, but with a focus on attitudes, values and beliefs rather than personality traits. Largely based on the work of Alex Inkeles and his modernity scale, it became generally recognized that social and economic development could not occur until an appropriate proportion of the population held modern attitudes, values and beliefs about work, quality of life, the ability and desirability to control one's environment, and other related values (see Chapter 1). The so-called modernity thesis is clearly summed up in the following passage from a six-country study of modernization by Inkeles and Smith (1974):

Mounting evidence suggests that it is impossible for a state to move into the twentieth century if its people continue to live in an earlier era. A modern *nation* needs participating citizens, men and women who take an active interest in public affairs and who exercise their rights and perform their duties as members of a community larger than that of the kinship network and the immediate geographical locality. Modern *institutions* need individuals who can keep to fixed schedules, observe abstract rules, make judgements on the basis of objective evidence, and follow authorities legitimated not by traditional or religious sanctions but by technical competence. The complex production tasks of the *industrial order*, which are the basis of modern social systems, also make their demands. Workers must be able to accept both an elaborate division of labor and the need to coordinate their activities with a large number of others in the work force (pp. 3–4).

The unique contribution of the sociological version of modernization theory to development theory in general rested on its contention that education, and particularly schooling, was perhaps the most important agent for transforming a traditional society into a modern one. During the 1960s and early 1970s considerable research effort tended to support the modernization thesis that schooling has a modernizing effect on the ways that people think, and consequently the ways they behave.

Like human capital theory, however, modernization theory has been subject to considerable criticism, much of which was given in Chapter 1. Clearly at the most fundamental level, many of these criticisms have been directed at the very premises which underlie modernity as a viable development target. However, even if one accepts modernization and all that it implies, there remain several weaknesses which are critical for the argument that education constitutes an important agent for the modernization process. First of all, because modernization theory focuses only on factors internal to a society in seeking the cause for development, education, as a societal institution, is generally assumed to be a part of the internal modernization prcess. However, modernization theory does not account for the external influences on education, and therefore the problematic aspects of education's contribution to development, nor to its possible negative impact on development (Anosike, 1977; Hanf *et al.*, 1975). Secondly, since modernization has generally been regarded as a unidimensional phenomenon, little regard has been given to the more complex nature of the process, in particular disjunctures and even conflicts which occur through the uneven and inconsistent impacts of the transformation. Education, because it generally is more strongly directed to some segments of a population, for example urban youth from higher status backgrounds, can contribute to rather than alleviate these disjunctures and conflicts. The underlying ethnocentric bias of modernization represents a further aggravation of the points already made. To the extent that education for modernization shares this bias, as an institution and process its effects may be unintended and its efficiency less than economical or tolerable.

Finally, the causal chain linking education with the formation of modern values, attitudes and behavior to social and economic development can, at this stage of our theoretical and empirical knowledge, be held only with extreme caution. As noted in the previous chapter, already some doubt has been cast upon the causal model which modernization theory assumes, and it may be that social-psychological modernization without comparable structural changes, both within and without societies, may create more problems than it solves for the development process. Possible "breakdowns" in the modernization process are many, and the vulnerable role of education in this process is now recognized and acknowledged.

Nevertheless these crucial weaknesses were virtually unknown or were disregarded during the period when modernization theory was thought to represent the most viable strategy for Third World development and the continued advancement of the industrialized countries. It should not be surprising, then, that both human capital theory and modernization theory played major roles in justifying the massive expenditures on education virtually throughout the world in the 1960s and early 1970s. The expansion of educational enrolments throughout the world between 1960 and 1975 was remarkable. Even among the developing countries this expansion was, by any standard, impressive. According to UNESCO, for Third World countries the enrolments of primary, secondary and tertiary levels increased from 122 million, 22 million, and 2.6 million to 247, 72 and 11.8 million respectively (UNESCO, 1983:11). Approximately during the same period there was a decrease in illiteracy from 44 percent of the adult population to 32 percent (cited in Habte, 1980:88). However, as impressive as these figures may be, the evidence that education contributed unambiguously to social and economic development has been challenged on many fronts. In the words of one writer, "the systems of education now to be found in the developing countries still resemble those that preceded them. *They have expanded more than they have changed*" (Ward, 1974:vi, emphasis ours). Ironically, by the mid-1970s as rapid educational expansion occurred, the link between education and development was questioned with increasing frequency.

Although there were examples of decreased educational costs during this period, as Coombs predicted by the mid-to-late 1970s educational systems everywhere began to feel the squeeze between rising costs and limited economic resources. By the mid-1970s the expenditure on education as a proportion of GNP flattened out and in some cases declined. In his follow-up report on the world crisis in education, Coombs (1985) noted that reductions in educational expenditures came sooner and were more severe than his original prediction. Furthermore, the economic squeeze affected both developed and less-developed countries.

Educational Costs and Development

One of the first factors to undermine the confidence in education as an agent for development was that of increasing costs. In one of the early critical examinations of world-wide educational expansion, Philip Coombs (1968) asked: "Is money – or the lack of it – at the root of the educational crisis?" In the late 1960s and early 1970s economists became concerned not only with costs in the expansion of educational systems but also with the increasing costs in maintaining them at all levels at any point in time. In other words, "...each year, ad infinitum, an educational system needs more finances simply to accomplish the same results as in the previous year" (Coombs, 1968:47). The reasons for this, of course, were rising costs for capital expenditures and increases in teacher salaries, both of which are subject to general inflation.

To be sure, there have been examples of declines in some aspects of educational costs. Coombs observed that in the late 1960s some developing countries experienced an apparent decline in cost per student primarily at the university level. However, he also noted that this decrease was mainly due to five factors: (1) the lag between inflation and rise in teacher salaries; (2) the use of unqualified teachers with low salaries; (3) an increase in pupil/teacher ratio; (4) a shift away from higher cost types of education, e.g. boarding schools; and (5) the use of the double-shift system (Coombs, 1968:49).

However, questions concerning educational costs must be weighed against those resulting from educational quality. Recent comparative data from studies of educational outputs clearly indicate the continuing disparity in student achievement between developed and less-developed countries. The most ambitious documentation of this disparity can be found in the twenty-one-country study undertaken by the International Association for the Evaluation of Educational Achievement (IEA) in the early 1970s. From the analyses of science and reading ability, based on standardized tests, it was consistently found that students in the developed countries scored considerably higher than their counterparts in less-developed countries (Comber and Keeves, 1973; Thorndike, 1973). Preliminary results from the second IEA science survey of 17 countries suggests that this pattern remains, except that students from the Southeast Asian societies of Hong Kong, The Republic of Korea and Singapore performed at a level equal to or better than some western industrialized countries (IEA, 1988). Furthermore, a more detailed study of one African country found that students in their final year of secondary school (about 18 years of age) had acquired a reading ability only to the level of 14-year-olds in England (Husén, 1977).

While there may be many factors to explain the persistence of these disparities, the question concerning educational costs cannot be resolved until both the causal relationship between expenditure and output is established, and the more fundamental question of desired and appropriate educational outcomes and targets for particular societies is determined.

The relative decrease in government expenditures on education since the 1970s has been uniform and dramatic. Between 1972 and 1985 the low-income countries, on average, reduced allocation of total expenditures to education from 13.2 percent to 7.6 percent. The middle-income countries reduced their allocation from 14.0 percent to 11.5 percent. The comparable figures for the industrialized countries were 5.4 percent to 3.8 percent (World Bank, 1987). These figures indicate that most countries of the world have not been able to sustain previous allocations of budget expenditures to education, or that education is no longer the high priority sector that it once was. Many governments now regard education as less their own responsibility and more the responsibility of consumers. The privatization of education is currently seen by some as a way of minimizing the public costs of education, particularly since inequities appear inevitable. Thus the investment value of education to governments has become doubtful, and the debates concerning quality of educational output and the apparent inappropriateness of much education in some countries have called into question the contribution of these educational costs to social and economic development. The costs of education therefore have been one factor which has made education appear to be, at least in some contexts, counter-productive to development efforts, In simple terms, this means that development requires expenditures in many sectors of society, and if a disproportionate share of limited resources is given to education, less will be available to the needs for investment on other vital sectors of the budget, such as health, welfare, and other infrastructures required to support development policies.

Education and the Labor Market Crisis

A basic assumption about education and its link with development strategies was its role in creating a skilled and viable workforce. We have already seen how both human capital and modernization theories contended that a more educated population is more productive and would have the attitudes and behavior required for a sustained modern industrialized economy, which was assumed to be the goal of most development strategies. Although there was considerable research evidence in the 1960s and early 1970s to support these assumptions (Psacharopoulos, 1973), by the middle 1970s the world economy, and the economies of individual countries, was such that this aspect of education and development was no longer tenable. What development planners had overlooked was the strength of economic ties binding nations together, and concurrently educational planners had failed to recognize the inflexibility of educational systems to quickly adapt to changing social and economic needs within countries.

During the 1970s and 1980s there were two major world economic recessions which contributed to labor market crises. There were many causal factors which brought about the world economic recession of the 1970s. One of these of course was the increasing costs of fuel and energy. Another, however, was the increasing competition for the sale of certain manufactured products which began to be produced both in developed and developing nations. While production costs soared and economic expansion levelled off, the rapid increase of participation in educational systems in most countries continued to produce larger numbers of skilled and qualified manpower. Between 1960 and 1970 unemployment gradually rose at a world-wide level, but after the first oil crisis in 1973 it rose quickly. In the industrialized countries unemployment reached 5.2 percent in 1975 and by 1983 it was up to 8.5 percent. In the less-developed countries unemployment had reached an average of 6 percent in 1980 and by 1985 had reached 7.5 percent in Latin America. Although rates vary widely between countries and over time, it is clear that unemployment will constitute a major problem for most countries into the 21st century (ILO, 1984:1987). Youth unemployment, especially among school leavers and graduates, is several times above the average rate in many countries.

In addition to the general problem of unemployment, there also arose considerable scepticism about the relevance of schooling for specific kinds of work, and more particularly about the tendency to use educational credentials as a screening device for job recruitment and selection (Berg, 1971; Dore, 1976; Blaug, 1985). Critiques of the relevance of schooling for employment have occurred both in the developed and developing countries. Credentialism, sometimes called the "diploma disease" (Dore, 1976), has been recognized as a world-wide phenomenon (Collins, 1979). And finally in some developing countries it has been argued that schooling has trained students for the wrong kinds of jobs and created a skilled workforce inappropriate to the demands of a Third World labor market. Thus, for example, the unusual situation was found in Nigeria where there were large numbers of unemployed school graduates with inappropriate skills, while an appropriately trained labor force had to be imported from abroad for certain sectors of the economy (Anosike, 1977).

Schooling raises levels of aspirations for post-school careers and jobs. Consistent with modernization theory there is evidence that schools have direct influence on levels of aspirations and expectations among students. These aspirations appear to be higher for disadvantaged groups and in developing countries (Saha, 1982). Furthermore, some have argued that these aspirations are inconsistent with opportunities in, and the needs of, the labor market (Husén, 1977; Little, 1978), while others contend that the unemployment crisis may be a capitalist structural phenomenon rather than an educationally related one (Blaug, 1980; Carnoy, 1980, 1988). Irrespective of its source, the disjuncture between level of educational attainment, levels of aspiration, and job opportunities have been regarded with concern by some who contend that disruptive social and psychological consequences, both for individuals and societies, might result (Wober, 1975). Therefore it could be argued that insofar as schooling raises ambitions to levels inconsistent with labor market opportunities, its contribution to this aspect of economic development is doubtful.

Clearly in certain circumstances schooling can produce a workforce with needed skills. However, schools are not the only way in which these skills can be acquired, and sometimes schools can be the least appropriate way of acquiring them. Furthermore, the employment crisis in many developed and less-developed countries probably would exist irrespective of whatever skills were taught in the classroom. Nevertheless we contend that much of the cynicism which has emerged about the role of education in economic development has been due to the perceived breakdown in the relationship between schools and the workplace. Further complexities of this relationship are discussed and empirically examined in Chapter 3.

Education and Development: Radical and Neo-Marxist Critiques

The most undermining challenge to the education and development hypothesis has come from radical and neo-Marxist camps. These writers are in agreement concerning their rejection of development theory derived from evolutionary, structural-functional and modernization perspectives. Likewise they represent departures from the linear and cyclical linear models of social change (see Chapter 1) in that the current situation in most Third World countries is not seen as an "original state", soon to follow and imitate the paths of already developed societies, but the result of many centuries of decline, due to a process of dependency and underdevelopment. "Underdevelopment is no longer to be regarded as a residual and passive condition, but is a phenomenon resulting from a particular historical process" (Bernstein, 1979:83).

Some of these writers have included education in their critique of current political and social development conditions. The radical views have become persuasive and influential, particularly in the less-developed countries. In many respects their critiques of education and development incorporate and are part of a larger movement in the sociology of education generally, where structural-functional and consensus approaches have been rejected in favor of conflict and sometimes micro-oriented perspectives (Karabel and Halsey, 1977). Here we will confine our attention primarily to the neo-Marxist critique, as it more directly addresses questions related to education's place in the development and underdevelopment process.

Important in the neo-Marxist critique is the almost exclusive focus on societies with capitalist economies and on the world economic system rather than on particular nation-states considered independently of others. With respect to the latter, it is regarded as impossible to assess the role of education in development without an international perspective. The crucial unit of analysis is the world system made up of networks of relations between countries in which some countries are dominant while others are subordinate. Education, like manufactured commodities, is seen both in terms of domestic and international consumption. The important question is not, How does education contribute to social and economic development?, but rather What kind of education is appropriate for what kind of development, and in whose interests?

Neo-Marxists do not deny that education can contribute to economic growth. However, they contend that this growth in advanced capitalist societies has served mainly the interests of those in power and has perpetuated the inequalities of the social system. Critics in Britain, France and the United States all agree that schools in capitalist societies reflect the values and interests of the upper and middle classes and operate to the disadvantage of the working class. Furthermore, somewhat consistent with views held in 19th-century England during the period of rapid school expansion, they contend that schools reinforce and reproduce the class structure of capitalist society by producing a docile and compliant workforce (Bowles and Gintis, 1976). Empirical research in France by Pierre

Bourdieu has shown that schools provide the dominant classes with "cultural and material capital" which enables them to participate more fully in the social system and its rewards (Bourdieu, 1973). According to critiques such as these, there is no question concerning the contribution of education to the production of skilled manpower and therefore to economic growth. However, it is regarded as problematic whether such an education contributes in the long run to social and political equality which in their view is essential for continued development in advanced capitalist societies, and for the reversal of patterns of underdevelopment in less-developed societies.

In the latter context, the concern of neo-Marxists is more complex. Most societies in Africa, Latin America and South East Asia have experienced colonial rule at some period of their past. Schooling in former colonies has been imported from the Western industrial societies and has served the same dominant social group as did the colonial system as a whole. Carnoy (1974) argued that schools in many developing countries are simply a form of neo-imperialism and neo-colonialism. They continue to serve the interests of the elite of previous colonial powers or what the dependency theorists call the "core countries" (the USA, UK, Western Europe), and perform this task through their selection mechanism and curriculum structure, producing what Frank following Marx calls the "Lumpenbourgeoisie" (Frank, 1972). "Lumpenbourgeoisie" are local elites who serve overseas interests rather than the interests of their own people. Clearly from this perspective traditional education is not seen to serve the development interests of the Third World countries, but rather contributes to the continuing process of underdevelopment. The rejection of the education and development hypothesis is not based on a general rejection of education, but rather on the particular form that education has taken as it has historically evolved in Western capitalist societies. The critique, then, is directed more fundamentally at the capitalist model of education, and the diffusion of this model to other societies subordinate to capitalist influence. The fact that resistance and conflict did occur in some colonial schools, for example in Vietnam between 1918 and 1938, does not effectively reduce the strength of the neo-Marxist argument (Kelly, 1987).

As we might expect, views concerning education and its role in development are less negative in socialist countries. Both in the Soviet Union and other Eastern European countries education has been regarded as an essential part of strategies for social and economic advancement. This is particularly true in the Soviet Union since the advent of *Glasnost* in 1986. The importance of education in the Soviet Union today is reflected in government programs to improve the quality of education, to modernize the curricula, to promote creative thinking, and to improve teacher education (Szekely, 1986, 1987).

In the People's Republic of China, education, from literacy programs to high levels of scientific and technological training, continues to be in the forefront of policy, planning and expenditure. However, there have been differences of opinion about the most appropriate organization, curriculum and levels which should receive top priority.

In China, there have been alternating educational strategies which on the one hand have placed emphasis on an academically based curriculum structure, while on the other have favored a more practical-oriented school program. Like many other socialist societies, China has displayed a very high commitment to educational expansion, and even though dramatic accomplishments were achieved between 1949 and 1979 (primary enrolment increased 3.4 times, secondary 36 times, and tertiary 4.5 times), contradictions in the system (for example the tension between rural–urban, individual–society and economic–political needs) have prevented the Chinese educational system from matching expectations. As Löfstedt has observed:

...we have seen that China has performed rather well in educational development since 1949, considering the resources available and the difficulties left over by the old society and aggravated by the liberation war. But we should also note that serious setbacks have occurred. Many problems exist and the educational system at present is far from able to meet needs of national development as defined by the present leadership (1980:178).

An important component of educational policy in socialist countries has been the strong concern about illiteracy, which is generally regarded as detrimental to development. In the Soviet Union following the revolution, as well as in socialist-oriented countries such as China, Cuba and Tanzania, literacy campaigns constituted a first major effort in educational strategy.

The literacy rate in Russia after the revolution increased from 32 percent in 1920 to around 98 percent in 1959. By the early 1980s, the adult literacy rates in China and Cuba were 70 and 98 percent respectively, very high when compared with progress in other societies. After liberation the new socialist developing societies of Guinea Bissau, Mozambique and Angola began their own literacy campaigns which had already started during the liberation wars, again based on the conviction that literacy is a key requisite both for economic advancement and the social and political restructuring of society[10]. Literacy and the incorporation of the theory-practice dialectic (manifested in work-study programs) have constituted the pillars of educational programs in socialist societies. It would appear that like the capitalist societies of the 1950s and 1960s, socialist development policies have embraced education as the key agent for the control of social, economic and political social change, and until recently its potential contribution has gone largely unquestioned.

However, recent evidence from several socialist societies suggests that many of the questionable aspects of education in capitalist systems can be found in the former as well. The reproduction of the social structure and the pervasiveness of unequal access and attainment can be found in socialist-oriented societies as widely diverse as the Soviet Union (Dobson, 1977) and Tanzania (Court, 1976).

Likewise unemployment and the disjuncture between school and work is now being recognized as a major problem in some socialist societies, for example in the Democratic Republic of Germany and Poland, just as in many Western countries. The creeping doubt about the potential role of education in development seems to be coming from many diverse political and economic systems, and does not seem confined to capitalist societies which have adopted human capital theory or modernization theory as the basis for development strategies. The ability for education to act as a means for controlling social change seems to touch factors much more fundamental to the forces of social structures and systems, and thus may not be amenable to simple generalization and manipulation.

Conclusion

This chapter has covered considerable ground, both historically and theoretically. We began with the proposition that education represents a major agent for the control of social change, and have seen how this belief very early was responsible for the increase in educational facilities and expenditures. In more recent times, we have identified the two major theoretical and policy-relevant orientations which we feel were largely responsible for the complete confidence by researchers and policy-makers in education as a means for social and economic development. In both cases, human capital theory and modernization theory, the outcomes of practices based on these theories were not as expected. We have discussed the failures of both theoretical orientations and have examined the conditions leading to their drop in popularity. In short, human capital theory and modernization theory failed largely because of questionable assumptions and international events such as the downturn in the world economy in the middle 1970s and the early 1980s and the persisting evidence of inequalities in societies, in spite of rapid and massive educational expansion in most countries.

Neo-Marxist theories have given us an explanation for this failure. Their focus on international networks and the more subtle aspects of educational processes have enabled them to explain why massive investment in education could in fact be detrimental to development. In their view, the failure of education to completely resolve problems of development in both industrialized and non-industrialized societies is due not so much to education *per se*, but to its place in capitalist economies. Education, as a tool of the capitalist state, operates to maintain the *status quo*, enabling those in power to reinforce their privileged position and deprives those not in power, either by socialization into a passive role or by depriving them of the necessary cultural capital, from launching a challenge to the capitalist hierarchy. At the same time, however, socialist societies motivated by Marxist perspectives have looked to education to control their own development plans. Ironically the evidence slowly emerging from these societies suggests that they have experienced many of the same problems which they had previously attributed to the capitalist system itself. For whatever reason, whether because of the inescapable influences of a world capitalist economy, the vestiges of an old order in new socialist states, or more fundamental links between education and society itself, the euphoric view that education can help change and build economies, social structures and political systems has been seriously called into question. For us, the discussion must be resumed but perhaps by posing different questions. For example, what is the basic relationship between education and society, and to what extent can its effects be manipulated in the transformation of social, economic and political systems?

Our view, which will be elaborated in subsequent chapters, is that the relationship between education and development is highly complex. However, it is important to determine what kind of development is desired, what kind of education is more suitable for this development, and whose interests in the development process should prevail. In the next three chapters we examine what we feel are three crucial dimensions of any education and development question: economic, social and political. Our intention is to critically examine each of these dimensions, both theoretically and empirically, in order to achieve a better understanding of the ways that education does and does not contribute to social change, and why in recent decades attempts to utilize it have resulted in disappointment and disillusionment. In doing so we come closer to understanding the relationship between education and society at its most fundamental level. With this in mind, we now turn to the first of the three dimensions, the economic, and examine the impact of education on economic growth and the labor market structure.

Notes

1. It was the poor reputation of established educational institutions during the 17th, 18th and early 19th centuries which accounted for the prevalence of domestic education among the middle and upper classes. A study of 18th-century men whose names appeared in the *Dictionary of National Biography* found that 28.5 percent were domestically educated: a quarter of the peers' sons and a third of the gentry's sons were educated at home (Musgrave, 1970:121).
2. Perhaps the most basic study of this process is that by Dore (1965). Other sources which are useful are Jansen (1965), Makino (1966), Passin (1965), Shipman (1971) and Stone (1970).
3. One indication of this conviction can be found in the proliferation of books and collections of articles which attempted to demonstrate the direct link between education and development. Examples of these writings can be found in Anderson and Bowman (1965) and Adams (1977).
4. The dramatic increase in education is evident from statistics on the expansion of educational participation and expenditure
5. As an example of working-class literacy, Bowen (1972:75) refers to a passage in a popular play where a sausage merchant in the market-place "states that he is uneducated and knows only his letters, the implication being that even the most ignorant can at least read and write". See also the examples given in Harvey (1966).
6. Even though literacy rates tend to be lower in rural areas, there is evidence that considerable regional diversity has and continues to exist. In France areas of high agricultural productivity became literate faster than the poorer areas, and indeed could continue only where there was a market economy. Likewise in the United States education expansion occurred in those areas where mechanization and the use of wage labor were well established (Limage, 1980:144).
7. Early statements in the belief in education as a main producer of development can be found in Herbert Parnes (ed.), *Planning Education for Economic and Social Development* (1962) and two UNESCO and OECD publications, *Qualitative Aspects of Educational Planning* (UNESCO, 1967) and *Social Objectives in Educational Planning* (OECD, 1968).
8. The assumptions of human capital theory and its research are crucial. A good example can be found in the work of Denison (1962), who used linear equation models to remove the variance in economic growth due to known and measurable factors (for example, capital investment), and attributed the residual variance to unknown factors such as the improvement of human capital through education and similar variables.
9. Generally speaking modernization theory can be formulated at different levels of analysis, that is, at the level of social structure, culture or personality. The first is best exemplified by theories of increasing social differentiation and complexity, as in the work of Emile Durkheim and Herbert Spencer.

The second has its classic origin in Weber's thesis concerning the protestant Ethic and the emergence of capitalism. More recently the work of social psychologists such as Inkeles and Smith, fall into this category. Finally modernization at the personality level is best typified by the work of McClelland on the achievement motive.

Clearly, as Figure 1.1 in Chapter 1 illustrates, these levels are not independent of each other. The modernization school as we discuss it here postulates that change must occur at all three levels before society can become truly modern. What concerns us here is the role which education plays in the modernization process, and the order of importance of change at each level.

10.   As far as we are aware, major literacy campaigns have been conducted in the following countries: Angola (1976–   ), Birma (1969–72), China (1950–66, 1976–   ), Cuba (1961), Ethiopia (1979–   ), Guinea, Mozambique (1978–82), Nicaragua (1979–80), Peru (1974), Portugal (1976), Somalia (1973–75), Southern Vietnam (1975–78), and Tanzania (1971–83).

PART 2
Dimensions of Development

3

Education, Economic Growth
and Employment

Economic Growth as Development

THERE have been few models of development which have enjoyed the prestige and influence of the economic growth model. Both theoretically and empirically the notion of economic growth has long been at the heart of development thinking and has dominated policy and research at national and international levels. There have been many points of view as to how economic growth is best measured. However, whether seen in terms of increases in per capita income, a shift in the labor force from the agricultural to the industrial and service sectors, a rise in energy consumption or the expanded use of high technology such as automobiles, telephones or television, there can be little doubt that the recent histories of most Western societies, at least until the 1980s, have been characterized by steady economic growth and increased productivity.[1].

Economic growth models are of relatively recent origin, although most have links with 18th-century theories of progress, as, for example, the theory articulated by Adam Smith in *An Inquiry into the Nature and Cause of the Wealth of Nations* (1970 (1776)). In general, economic growth models have been concerned with describing and planning the advancement and well-being of nations as wholes. Although some models may consider the attitudes and beliefs of individuals within societies, it is societal advancement which is of primary concern in most explanations of economic growth. Furthermore, while acknowledging the importance of the agriculture sector in economic systems, most economic models focus on the process of industrialization, and include its origin and growth and the way that it promotes or impedes economic growth.

Early theorists such as Smith and Malthus believed that specialization, division of labor, exchange and population growth were the key elements of rapid economic growth. The first three were thought to affect the efficiency of labor output while the last was seen as directly related to the volume of output. However, neither felt that the process of growth could continue indefinitely because of limitations of resources, particularly the increased competition for land. Thus most early economic growth theorists, with perhaps the exception of Marx, did not believe in the unilinear, steady and uninterrupted improvement of economic productivity. But neither did these theorists anticipate changes in those factors which were seen as potentially inhibiting the growth process, for example the decline in population growth, rapid technological advancement and a steady rise in real wages.[2]

Most contemporary economists argue that while there may be short-term interruptions and even declines in the growth process, in the long run there have been striking regularities and consistencies in the basic upward trends of most advanced countries of the world. They agree that technological change, specifically in the form of labor or capital saving, inventions and innovations, and the accumulation of capital (machines, tools, raw materials, factories, etc.) largely account for these trends.[3] The improvement of the quality of manpower (human capital) is of course a component of capital accumulation.

As has been discussed in Chapter 1, there have been many theories of the stages of economic growth. For example, Marx saw history in terms of a one-way evolution from primitive cultures, through feudalism, capitalism and finally to socialism and communism. Stages of growth theories are but special cases of more general theories of economic growth, all of which serve as useful devices for the study of the progressive growth of one society, or the comparative analysis of many economic systems. As such, they are ideal types or constructs of actual historical developments (Chodak, 1973). The most widely known and most influential of contemporary stages of economic growth theories is that put forward by Walt W. Rostow (1960). His theory has exercised impact not only on economic strategy and policy in developed countries, but in the less developed as well.

Rostow contends that there are five linear stages of economic growth through which all societies must pass in order to reach full economic maturity: the traditional stage, the stage of preconditions for economic take-off, the take-off, the drive to maturity and the stage of high mass consumption. The take-off represents the tipping point or the "watershed" whereby the resistances and obstacles to growth are overcome, and growth itself then becomes the normal condition of a society. For this to occur, traditional societies require changes in political, social and economic structures, as well as changes in values. Whether due to outside intervention or innovations from within, traditional societies become dynamic and enter a transition stage whereby the preconditions for take-off are reached. Among these preconditions, Rostow lists not only the access and exploitation of available science and technology, but also the acquisition of values which predispose a population to the possibility and desirability of change itself. Education is seen as an important factor in this value-acquisition process.

The implications for development policies of Rostow's stages of growth theory, particularly as related to the improvement and expansion of education, are self-evident. The weaknesses of the theory have been often noted and have focused mainly on its questionable historical accuracy, its teleology and its failure to describe the dynamics of the change process itself (Frank, 1969; Myrdal, 1972).[4] Rostow, however, has stood firm by his original model in subsequent editions of his work (1971a), and more recently has produced considerable empirical support for the theory in *The World Economy* (1978), in which twenty countries are analyzed in depth and their passages through the various stages are identified.

Rostow admits that his stages of growth theory is not entirely economic, but in reality is a larger part of modernization theory. Indeed, once the first stage of take-off is accounted for, there is an element of "automaticity" in continued growth. However, continuity is not "mechanically assured". In order that sustained economic growth take place within a society, Rostow (1971b) contends that a "profound set of changes" must occur "which touch every dimension of society". These changes require the "development of an institutional, social, and psychological setting such that the society reacts positively to the potential spreading effects of modern industrial activity" (p. 58). The engine which drives the economy through the various stages of growth, particularly through the take-off stage, is an increase in net savings and investment which represent additions to capital resources. Rostow and others argue that a saving of 15 to 20 percent of the GNP enables a country to grow economically much more rapidly than a country with a lower rate. But in order for this type of economic behavior to occur, appropriate attitudes and structures must first exist. But these attitudes and structures are characteristic of non-traditional, modern societies. Thus Rostow's stages of economic growth theory is inherently Western-oriented, based on the assumption that industrialization and modernization are necessary conditions for economic growth to occur, and that there are no alternatives to this linear path except stagnation.

An example of Rostow's analysis is found in Table 3.1 which shows the dates of take-off (Stage 3), the drive to technological maturity

TABLE 3.1. *Take-off and Subsequent Stages: Some Dates for Twenty Countries*

	Take-off period	Drive to technological maturity	High mass consumption
Great Britain	1783–1830	1830–1913	1920–
United States	1843–1870	1870–1910	1910–
France	1830–1870	1870–1913	1920–
Germany	1840–1870	1870–1913	1925–
Sweden	1868–1890	1890–1925	1925–
Japan	1885–1905	1905–1941	1955–
Russia–USSR	1890–1905	1905–1956	1956–
Italy	1895–1913	1920–1940	1950–
Canada	1896–1914	1915–1950	1919–
Australia	1901–1920	1920–1945	1925–
Argentina	1933–1950	1950–	–
Turkey	1933–1961	1961–	–
Brazil	1933–1950	1950–	–
Mexico	1940–1960	1960–	–
Iran	1955–1965	1965–	–
India	1952–1963	1963–	–
China	1952–1967	1968–	–
Taiwan	1953–1960	1960–	–
South Korea	1961–1968	1968–	–
Thailand	1960–	–	–

Source: Compiled from Rostow (1978), chs. 28–47.

(Stage 4) and high mass consumption (Stage 5) for twenty countries, including both the developed and less developed. On the basis of his most recent investigation, Rostow concludes that some of the late starters in the take-off stage (for example Sweden, Japan, Russia, Canada and Italy) have had the capacity to catch up with early starters, and that many of the countries which have most recently entered the take-off stage are rapidly absorbing technology and knowledge and will also quickly close the development gap. He contends that economic, social and political indicators give support to his model of economic growth.

The argument is a narrow one and is based on assumptions which can be problematic. Its simplicity makes it intuitively appealing, and strategies for development based on the model are straightforward and focus on clear objectives. The refinements of the growth model, such as the Harrod–Domar Model, which focuses on savings and investment as the key agents of economic growth, even further justify development strategies which call for large transfers of capital through aid programs, and for changes in attitudes and behaviors, both collectively and individually.[5] Ultimately the theory assumes that savings and investments increase through adherence to values of deferred gratification (save now for later returns) and in some cases by the reduced consumption of produced goods.

All models of economic growth rest upon additional assumptions which are equally problematic for development planning. For example, they assume that a number of key variables will remain constant, when in fact they can be unpredictable. Thus population growth, capital accumulation, the motives to maximize profit and the improvement in general conditions of life are but several of such variables upon which the working of the model depends (Meier and Baldwin, 1957). Thus the economic model turns out to be, in part, a psychological and sociological one.

The difficulty with economic growth models such as these is that they cannot be easily extrapolated to societies which are not based on a capitalist free-enterprise system, and which have not already experienced a certain level of industrialization and modernization. The strategies appear more suitable for countries which have already reached a level of economic advancement and strive to expand development and yet remain politically and socially stable. Difficulties arise, however, when one attempts to extrapolate the economic growth model in its Western form to countries with different socio-cultural values and structures, and whose natural resources preclude normal strategies for industrialization.

Economic growth in this conventional sense, therefore, represents only one kind of development, and the indicators generally used as measures point only to the economic dimensions along which development might be said to occur. A brief examination of the contrasts between Western urban capitalist industrial societies and other societal types may help to clarify the complexities of equating economic growth with development as such. Furthermore, the problematic location of education in supporting economic growth and other development policies in various national contexts becomes more apparent when seen in a wider perspective.

Economic Growth in Capitalist and Socialist Societies

The essential difference between capitalist and socialist societies with respect to economic growth and development is the extent to which national policies and individual behavior are centrally planned and controlled by the State. Capitalist modes of production assume freedom from State intervention and open competition in the market-place. The profit motive, the surplus value in the process of production, and the accumulation of capital for reinvestment are seen as the dynamic forces for economic growth, and economic growth for all practical purposes has been seen as synonymous with development. At the collective level the laws of development are seen to best operate in a *laissez-faire* environment so that the supply and demands of the market-place are allowed to reach their own equilibrium. At the individual level there is presumed freedom to aspire to and achieve high levels of status and income, and the motives to do so are assumed. In actual practice, pure *laissez-faire* capitalism has virtually ceased to exist, particularly following World War II, and has given way to what is known as mixed economies. Thus even in highly capitalist countries such as the United States, government intervention does occur and takes the form of welfare programs, public services, and taxes and laws controlling business practices. The extent of this intervention varies considerably across capitalist societies, as is apparent in comparisons between countries like the United States and Sweden.

The relationship between education and economic growth, according to general theories of capitalist economies, is a close and necessary one. In mixed economies education is promoted by the government and protected to some extent from the vagaries of the market system. Schooling in particular is seen as an important agent for instilling appropriate motives and aspirations for economic behavior within the capitalist system.

Economic-growth theories are consistent with human capital and modernization theories and with the mechanism of the capitalist mode of production in Western societies. To the extent that the benefits from economic growth in this type of system are thought to "trickle down" to all members of society, development in a broad sense can be said to occur.

Socialist economies, however, provide a different context for the interpretation of economic growth and development. The role of the State in controlling the planning process precludes open competition in the market-place. State or collective control over the means and modes of production as well as the allocation system of personnel implies not only greater control over economic growth iself, but also of participation by individuals in it. Factories, mines and land are almost entirely owned by the State, while private enterprise is virtually unknown. Individuals may have some choice in occupation but the mobilization of human resources is always a part of general development planning. The consumption of goods is likewise regulated by the State and subservient to production objectives. Savings and investments, so essential for economic growth, are not left to the motivations and aspirations of individuals, but enforced through State control over wages and consumption.

There have been significant variations in the application of socialist ideology and practice, as is best exemplified by the Soviet Union and the People's Republic of China. While both societies profess to follow the Marxist–Leninist line in building a socialist society, China is far less developed and industrialized, and in a theoretical sense, has been in the 1970s more fundamentalist and politically to the left of the Soviet Union. There has been less flexibility and choice for individuals in China and a greater attempt to link theory with work.

This latter emphasis has been particularly evident in schooling. While education in the Soviet Union and China are more carefully controlled and monitored by the State than in capitalist societies, China has been more committed to school-work programs. In both societies education has been strongly guided by professional and vocational needs. At the same time there has been a strong emphasis on moral education and a commitment to the communist party ideology. The differences between the Soviet Union and China, in policies related to education and economic growth, continue to exist, in spite of the fact that by the early 1980s, China had introduced a number of changes which modified and even reversed many of its educational practices of the 1970s. The rapid expansion of higher education, the utilization of overseas universities for graduate education, and a move toward privatization at the tertiary level suggests that in the late 1980s China had incorporated, at least in part, the Western economic growth model for its education system.

It is assumed in socialist societies that the benefits of economic growth will not trickle down to the general population unless the distribution of profits is also planned. Nevertheless, in the socialist framework, like the capitalist, economic growth is also seen as a major dimension of development, but as highly constrained and goal-oriented. However, the role of education is clearly affected by the socialist economic model and thus takes on unique organizational structures and patterns, which we will discuss in a later chapter.

Economic Growth in Developed and Less-developed Societies

A second distinction which must be taken into account when examining growth models and their link with development is that between developed and developing societies. In one respect economic growth of whatever kind represents a form of development in both developed and less-developed societies. However, the nature of this growth, for example the economic structure and the material and human resources on which it is based, determines the type of education which more adequately responds to the needs of any particular type of societal development.

Economic growth in developed societies is shaped by several distinct characteristics. The distribution of the labor force is very much skewed towards the manufacturing and service sectors or what have traditionally been called secondary and tertiary industries. For example, in 1980 the United States and the Soviet Union had 31 and 39 percent of their labor force in the industrial sector, and 66 and 36 percent respectively in the service sector. Similar average figures for all middle-income countries such as Egypt and Chile were 16 and 29 percent in the same sectors. Conversely the proportion of the work-force in the argicultural sector is the reverse, with both the United States and the Soviet Union having much smaller proportions than middle- and low-income countries.

Secondly, developed societies are characterized by relatively higher per capita incomes, higher levels of public use and consumption of energy and other sophisticated technology, for example, automobiles, telephones and television. In such societies the current rate of economic growth may not be higher than that found in some developing countries, and as such may not be a distinguishing feature. Many less-developed countries are currently growing at a more rapid rate than the developed, while the total productivity of the latter, of course, is much higher. Table 3.2 points to some of these more general differences.

The higher level of productivity of the developed countries implies high accumulation of capital, as the surplus after consumption needs have been met allows for saving and reinvestment into the system.

TABLE 3.2. *Summary of Prospects for Economic Growth*

Country group	Population 1980 (millions)	GNP per person 1980 (dollars)	Average annual percentage growth of GNP (high case)		
			1970–80	1980–85	1985–90
All developing countries	2290	791	2.9	2.6	3.3
Capital-surplus oil exporters	69	4614	5.0	2.8	2.8
Industrialized countries	671	9684	2.4	2.8	3.5
Centrally planned economies	1386	1720	3.8	3.3	3.3

Source: Adapted from World Bank (1980b), Table 2.8:11.

The distribution systems and opportunity structures of developed societies include both capitalist and socialist. Although it was pointed out earlier that there is greater flexibility in the capitalist system, it is clear that some restraints do exist. The theory of labor market segmentation, for example, holds that there are system-level forces which operate to limit the opportunities available to some groups in the labor force. As a result of this segmentation, groups have different experiences of work settings which result in patterns of behavior which condition job structures and even the development of technology (Carnoy, 1977). At least three segments have been identified in modern work structures. The first consists of well-paid jobs requiring high levels of education. The second has been called the "unionized" segment, and is characterized by internal hierarchies, job security and relatively high wages, but not necessarily job satisfaction. The third segment has been called the "competitive" segment and consists of jobs with low wages, poor job security, poor working conditions and little opportunity for advancement (Carnoy and Levin, 1985). One implication of labor market segmentation for developed capitalist economies is that the market system may not operate as freely in the occupational structure as is generally believed, with the result that the motives and attitudes of the workforce may not fully maximize the growth potential of the economy. However, the extent to which labor market segmentation fluctuates with more general economic and social conditions is less known. In addition, difficulties concerning the definition and measurement of labor market segments has, at least for the time being, precluded generalizations about the process of segmentation in capitalist societies (Cain, 1976).

Although it is difficult to project the nature of future economic growth in modern developed societies, it is clear that such growth represents a form of development in the general sense. This is not to say that economic growth has necessarily been evolutionary or linear in nature, but the history of Western societies gives strong evidence of this, at least in terms of past patterns as illustrated by Rostow and other growth theorists. However, even within the stages of growth models, the possibility of fluctuations, stops and starts, and other vacillations in economic growth are not seen as contradictory to the general evolutionary pattern.

The link between education and development in developed societies clearly manifests characteristics appropriate to their level of economic development. Whether we speak of developed capitalist or developed socialist countries, the amount of schooling, the nature of the curriculum, and the structure of the education system is clearly oriented toward the needs of economies based on high-level technologies and a flexible and mobile labor force. What this means is that the actual skills imparted in such schools (apart from advanced literacy and numeracy) may be less important than the creation of attitudes and cognitive abilities which enable individuals to adjust to frequently changing job situations. Although there may be differences between capitalist and socialist societies in emphasis on technological training (for example physics and chemistry), this may be due more to different types of technology rather than the different functions of education. Finally, as we already noted, the selection system varies between the two types of societies, the socialist being more planned and controlled, while the capitalist, at least on the surface, being more open.

When we turn our attention to developing societies we must keep in mind the wide range of economies that this term usually includes. We find countries ranging in GNP per capita from below $ 390 (including India, Mozambique, Tanzania, China, Haiti, and twenty-seven other countries) to between $ 2130 and $ 7420 (for example, Singapore, Hong Kong, Argentina, Venezuela and six other countries) (World Bank, 1987: 232–233). Likewise there are equally wide variations in levels of industrialization, with some countries being much more oriented toward high industrialization programs (Republic of Korea, Singapore, Hong Kong and Brazil) and others being more oriented towards agricultural development and mining (Tanzania, Kenya, Botswana, Peru and Zambia). Nevertheless there are certain commonalities which make it possible to group these countries in the category of developing societies. The per capita income of the less-developed countries is generally lower than that of the developed countries, and their rates of growth are much more variable. They tend to have a small modern employment sector with a much larger informal employment sector, which can sometimes include between 25 percent and 60 percent of the urban labor force (World Bank, 1980a: 48). Often these countries are based upon what economists have called a dual economy, in that the modern and traditional sectors co-exist side by side. The needs of rural development policies, both in technology and education, are frequently given much attention. The distributive system is such that the gap between the rich and the poor is more pronounced and visible than in the developed societies.[6]

The different economic structure and life condition of the less-developed countries requires the educational system to build upon human resources and societal needs which are somewhat unique. The simple transferral of school models from the developed societies to the less developed becomes, on close examination, logically indefensible and empirically and historically largely unsuccessful. The assumption of the linear evolution of societies, as in the stages of growth theories, ultimately suggests that educational systems must correspond to (both causing and being caused) not only the level of economic advancement but also the particular type of economic growth which is being sought, as for example between those countries committed to industrialization and those choosing to pursue argicultural development or the extraction, and perhaps the processing, of natural resources.

Thus in societies such as the above, the Western model of schooling may not only be inappropriate, but even dysfunctional for economic growth and development. For example, there is nothing sacred about the number of years of schooling required for maximum productivity in agricultural or mining societies, nor is it necessary that the levels of education – primary, secondary, tertiary – be expanded to the same extent as they are in the industrialized developed societies. Greater diversification of the curricula, taking into account variation in regional economic and human resources, may in the long run make the most contribution to economic growth. Considerable effort is being expended in many developing countries to modify and change traditional Western systems of education to those which are more suitable to their particular needs and to avoid what one writer has called "educational irrelevance" (Habte, 1980). However, as will become evident in a later chapter, it is not entirely clear what range of educational options are available for the less-developed economies, nor how deviation from the Western model of schooling may affect a society's position in the international social and economic system.

Economic Growth in Industrial and Non-industrial Societies

A third dimension in the analysis of economic growth, development and education is that which differentiates between industrial and non-industrial societies. The industrialized societies of the world include both capitalist and socialist countries, such as the United States and the Soviet Union, and most developed and some less-developed countries. In the latter case it is more conventional to speak of the new-industrializing countries (NICs), among which are Brazil, the Republic of Korea and Taiwan.[7] It is more difficult to find examples of totally non-industrial societies which follow a pure capitalist or socialist model and which are recognized by the international community as "developed".

Like the notion of economic growth, industrialization in the Western sense has often been considered synonymous with development. In this context the term means more than the expansion of the industrial sector of an economy, for example the shift in labor force from agricultural to manufacturing or other industrial pursuits. It implies also the accumulation of industrial capital, the use of technologically sophisticated machinery and equipment throughout the economy, the use of mass-production techniques, mastery of scientific and technological knowledge, means for promoting the accumulation of capital, material prosperity (including a wide distribution of goods and services) and a high level of urbanization (Kasdan, 1973).

Given this notion of industrialization, conventional indicators of it are readily available. Economic growth as industrialization in this context can be measured in terms of increases in production, increases in the rate of growth of GNP, and increases in the utilization of sophisticated technology, usually capital intensive rather than labor intensive. Industrialized societies have their labor force concentrated in manufacturing or service sectors of the economy and the distribution system is reflected in the wage structure. However, a principal driving force in the industrialization process is the quality of the workforce itself, and for this reason education is seen as an important component of industrial growth and expansion.

Education for an industrial or industrializing society is generally oriented toward the production of skills and attitudes necessary for efficient and productive output. Flexibility and adaptability of manpower skills have become more important as changes in industrial technology become more rapid. As the level of industrialization becomes more sophisticated, a well-developed tertiary educational sector becomes essential and is thought to justify the investment necessary to support it. Thus educational expenditures, because they improve the quality of the workforce and its output, are seen as directly comparable to investment in physical capital.

When we come to non-industrial societies it becomes somewhat more difficult to speak in general terms about economic growth, development and their relationship with education. Since the notion of non-industrial includes not only those societies whose economies depend on agriculture, but also those based upon mining, fishing or other primary industries, the identification of unique indicators of growth and development is more problematic. To be sure, an increase in production of any kind, or an increase in rate of growth in GNP would, as for the industrial societies, indicate progress in the desired direction. Furthermore, as in the industrialized economies, the skills and attitudes of the farmers, miners or whatever type of workforce, appears to make a direct contribution to increased productivity. Elkan (1976), for example, suggests that the higher production of rice per hectare in Australia and Japan in 1964 (6100 and 5200 kilograms) compared to India (1600 kilograms) is at least partly explicable "in terms of what is described as human capital produced by education" (p. 21). However, in non-industrial societies, it is less likely that the level of technology and its utilization would be as high or complete as in the industrial societies; rather the technology will be at a level appropriate to the types and structures of the economies.

In non-industrial societies, a relatively high percentage of the labor force is employed in the non-industrial sector, and to a lesser extent in the informal sector of the economy. In the case of agricultural societies, the distribution of land and the ability of those on the land to maintain relatively high levels of productivity and obtain returns for their products are an important part of the production and distribution system.

Education in non-industrial societies will not take the same form as for the industrial. While there is a need for the training of skills appropriate to non-industrial work activity, it also appears that high levels of educational attainment are not as important for agricultural and other non-industrial economies as for the industrial. School and work programs have recently become more common in non-industrial societies, and many contexts appear more relevant. Finally, in agricultural societies, schools for rural development not only stress skills related to agricultural technology, but also are instrumental in inculcating the values, attitudes and behavior related to rural life. Economic growth for non-industrial societies requires an increase of productivity in the primary sector, and it is essential that the education system promotes the skills and individual motivation appropriate for that sector.

This brief overview of the three selected societal dimensions: capitalist–socialist, developed–less developed and industrial–non-industrial, illustrates not only the variations in models of economic growth, but also the clear implications that these variations have for the education system itself. In each case, however, the link between the economy and education is complex and entails both costs and gains to the society and to the individual. Thus in designing an education system to promote a particular kind of economic growth, the expenditure on education has to be weighed not only against returns in the form of increased productivity, but also in tangible benefits for individuals themselves. Otherwise the demands for education will decline or remain low, and the potential for greater mobilization of human resources will be lost.

Education: Costs and Gains to Society and to the Individual

On the basis of the previous discussion, it clearly cannot be assumed that the link between education and economic growth is a direct and linear one, or that it operates in the same manner for every kind of society. The decision to invest in education, whether by expanding facilities or by improving efficiency, requires considerable costs to any society, and these costs become more important to the extent that they take away funds from other areas of potential economic or social investment, such as factories, machines, health, nutrition or housing (Edwards and Todaro, 1972; World Bank, 1980a). Likewise the decision by individuals to participate longer than necessary in school also requires short-term costs to both the individual and society in that entry into the labor market is postponed while additional schooling is subsidized. The personal costs to individuals from continued participation in the school system, for example in meeting school requirements (i.e. the discipline of the school regime) and deferred entry into the adult world, are rarely included in cost-benefit analyses. Yet at the macro-level all factors ultimately become important in the assessment of education's contribution to national economic growth and development.

As we pointed out in Chapter 2, the rate of expenditures by national governments on education since the 1960s and 1970s has levelled off, and in some countries even decreased. Even though education is funded from sources other than government budgets (for example, from state and local budgets where applicable, or from private sources, such as parents and churches), the allocation from governments is indicative of national commitment to education. The allocation from national budgets during these two earlier decades reflected a conviction that the returns to investment in education outweighed costs. However, since the 1970s, the low-income countries have cut their rate of allocation by almost half, the middle-income countries by almost 20 percent, and the industrialized countries by almost 30 percent (World Bank, 1987: 276–277).

In spite of cutbacks, the range in public expenditures on education is considerable. In 1985 the lowest public expenditure was 0.8 percent for Zaire to a high of 27.7 percent for Equador. However, in absolute figures the developing countries are spending far less on education than the developed countries because of their lower productivity. At the same time, their unit costs of education as a percentage of GNP per capita are much higher. This is particularly true for the secondary and tertiary levels. In West African countries, for example, the unit cost of higher education as a percent of GNP per capita in the period 1970–1973 was 1405 compared to 55 for the OECD countries (World Bank, 1980a:70).[8] The unit cost of secondary and higher education for Africa continued to be high into the 1980s. For example, in 1981 the unit cost of secondary education for all Africa was seven times higher than that of primary education, while the unit cost of higher education was fifty-seven times higher (Cocco and Nascimento, 1986: 265). With this rate of expenditure and at the present rate of educational growth it will be highly unlikely that the economies of the developing countries will be able to afford these costs, with the result that they may be unwilling to maintain this level of investment in education in the future or at least may have to rethink their priorities in terms of investment in primary, secondary or tertiary education.

Studies have shown that the returns to society from investment in education are generally positive. Even in rural areas, as pointed out earlier in this chapter, it has been shown that educated farmers have higher productivity than less educated ones. In a review of twenty studies on farmer 'education it was found that with 4 years of schooling farm productivity increased 7.4 percent (World Bank, 1980a:50). In another study of sixty-one countries the average social rate of return to primary education ranged from a high of 27 percent for Asia to a low of 13 percent for "intermediate" countries (for example, Cyprus, Iran, Israel and Spain). In all parts of the world the returns to investment in primary education were greater than secondary education, and the returns to secondary education greater than higher education (Psacharopoulos, 1985).

Apart from whether these costs can be sustained even with subsequent returns, other events have occurred which complicate the apparent contribution of education to economic growth. The increasing levels of unemployment in most countries, which in recent years has paralleled educational expansion, suggests a certain inappropriateness of a certain kind of schooling during periods of rapid educational and social change. The study of education by the International Labor Organization (ILO), in what was then called Ceylon, observed that the school functioned well for the needs of that society when participation in schools was low. However, when participation to the tenth-year level reached 35 to 40 percent of the cohort, many school graduates had no alternative but to become farmers and manual workers. In the words of the writers of the report: "Instead of becoming adapted as instruments of general education, the secondary schools retain their single-minded concern with qualifying pupils for white-collar jobs, achieving this today by pushing as many students as possible as far up the ladder as possible" (ILO, 1971:134).

Further sources of school inefficiency were identified in the ILO study. It was shown that because of dropouts and the repetition of grades in 1966, it took 100 pupil-years at the primary level to produce one tenth-year or C-level graduate. In an ideal world where no one dropped out or repeated, it would take 10 pupil-years to produce such a graduate. In addition to the ILO observation, a UNESCO study of school children in fifty-four developing countries in Africa, Latin America and South East Asia estimated that of 100 pupils starting grade one in 1970, only 60 eventually reached the third grade, and in some of the low-income countries only 37 reached the fifth grade (Habte, 1980:89).

In view of the increasing costs of education and of the competition for limited funds, the question of gains outweighing the costs becomes highly problematic. The inefficiency of schools, the wastage of human resources through unemployment, the frustrations of large segments of the population because of unemployment or underemployment, and the demands of other sectors such as health, food and other human needs, suggests that if schooling is to make an optimum contribution to economic growth, considerable improvement in efficiency and a rethinking of the structure must be made. Some have argued that education should be supported more by those who receive it, either through tuition fees or loans. Others, however, have suggested that more attention should be directed towards improving school efficiency by reducing repetition and attrition as much as possible, and by a greater utilization of school facilities and resources. Nevertheless, in any type of society, developed or less developed, capitalist or socialist, the link between education and economic growth is more tenuous than has previously been assumed.

Many of the observations made above also apply to the individual returns from education, in particular since a degree or diploma has almost always and everywhere been considered a ticket to a white-collar occupation. Indeed, the analysis of sixty-one countries cited earlier showed that individual returns to education exceeded social returns, and that the individual returns to primary education are the greatest, followed by returns to higher education (Psacharopoulos, 1985). The belief that more education leads to better jobs has been a principal motivating factor for young people to stay in schools longer. Furthermore, the relationship between education and occupational attainment has been one of the most well-researched and documented phenomena in the social sciences, both in developed and less developed societies. However, there are those who take a more skeptical view. As early as 1961, Anderson (1961) argued that education contributed only to part of a person's prospect for mobility. In an analysis of data from three industrialized societies (Britain, the United States and Sweden), Anderson found that mobility independent of schooling occurs frequently, and that ability (not necessarily genetic) and relevant motivation plays a "powerful" role for a person's occupation prospects. He concluded that "even with more equal distribution of educational opportunities, the independent operation of 'intelligence' will probably damp the impact of schooling upon individual careers" (p. 176). More recently, Boudon (1974) took virtually the same position but for a different reason, and stated that:

> Except under very special conditions which are unlikely to be met, a highly meritocratic society will not necessarily give to those who have reached a high level of education more chances of promotion or fewer chances of demotion than those whose level of education is lower. This apparent paradox derives from two circumstances. First, since those who obtain a high level of education more frequently have a higher background, they have to climb still higher in the hierarchy of social status in order not to experience demotion. Second, one consequence of the discrepancy between educational and social structure is that even under a high degree of meritocracy, people with the same level of education will reach different social status. Thus, even if a society has a strong tendency toward granting the best social positions to those who are better educated, education may have no apparent influence on mobility (pp. 13–15).

When we turn to education in less-developed societies, we find that at least until recently, there was a direct relationship between years of schooling and occupational attainment. With educational expansion, however, this relationship is no longer a certain one, for the number of educated individuals has outstripped the abilities of the economies to absorb them. Large numbers of educated unemployed are one of the major problems facing the less-developed countries today. In a study of seven countries, four of which were less developed, Little (1978) concluded that the proportion of males and females who aspired to non-manual jobs far exceeded the proportion of the economically active population actually engaged in those jobs. Thus unless the economic structures themselves were to expand, there would be little likelihood that these aspirations could be fulfilled.

Likewise, using data from eighteen countries, Saha (1988) found a strong inverse relationship between level of social and economic development and the educational and occupational aspirations of 14-year-old students, even with controls for home background, school quality and academic performance. Consistent with Little's and Saha's findings, it has been estimated that from the year 1970 to about the year 2000 the rate of unemployment will increase 2.7 percent a year (World Bank, 1980a:42).

The increasing numbers of educated unemployed youth in less-developed countries calls into question the contribution that education can make to economic growth at the societal level and to individual job prospects at the individual level. There have been numerous efforts to argue that education, particularly in its transported Western form, has ill-served the manpower needs of many less-developed countries. Anosike (1977), for example, has argued that in Nigeria there has been the "paradox" of a high and worsening rate of unemployment along with a shortage of workers with particular skills. Yet Nigeria has made great strides in educational expansion, but of the wrong kind:

> ...given contemporary Nigeria's low stage of development, it is clear that she does not legitimately need the kind of high level manpower and educational expansion that she has frequently cried about as a precondition for her development project implementations (p. 41).

On the other hand, there is little evidence to support the notion that education "creates" unemployment. Rado (1972) has pointed out that at least in Kenya and Ghana most school-leavers are quite flexible about the jobs they obtain and are realistic about the job opportunities available to them. Some have suggested that education raises expectations such that many young people have false hopes about jobs, particularly in the cities. Although in rural areas they migrate to the cities thus swelling the pressures on the already restricted job market, the problem may not be with the schools. Rural – urban migration may exist as much from push-factors, due to limited land in the countryside, and pull-factors, such as the discrepancy between rural and urban wages. The migration of the more educated becomes a "rational" solution rather than an irrational one: the less educated remain in the countryside because their chances of finding jobs in the city would be even more remote.

Ironically the limitations and even the restrictions of the job market and the rising rate of unemployment increases the demand for education and raises the aspirations for higher educational and occupational attainment. The rising number of those with educational credentials has tended to escalate the requirements for jobs, and has increased the use of credentials by employers as a screening device, or what some have called "the diploma disease" (Dore, 1976). Likewise this expansion effect has also resulted in greater demand for higher education which is at the same time more expensive. This "educational displacement phenomenon" means for the individual that some "who for some reason are unable to continue their education will fall by the wayside as school leavers while the others continue to overqualify themselves through more years of education" (Edwards and Todaro, 1972:111). Using education as a means to employment under these circumstances is somewhat like a lottery. For the society the implications are that educational facilities must be continually expanded to cope with the demands, with higher education serving in effect as an "absorber of last resort" for large numbers of potentially educated unemployed. For both the society and the individual the costs of education appear to be outstripping the apparent benefits.

Matching Education with the Job Market:
Recruitment, Curriculum and Performance

If the relationships between education and employment are as tenuous as we have first suggested, then surely the most crucial question facing planners in all societies concerns the content of schooling: what do schools teach, and what should they teach in order to promote economic development?

The debate concerning the content of the curriculum in education has been an old one. Generally there have been two points of view; the first being the traditional which sees schooling mainly in terms of instilling the norms and values of society in creating the ideal adult. It was thought that the best way to bring about this result was to teach subjects such as religion, history and the classical languages, in order to acquire an understanding and an appreciation of the golden ages of classical Greece and Rome. This view of education can be found in past and contemporary school curricula in the form of the classical academic program.

The opposite perspective stresses the utilitarian aspect of education, the origins of which can be traced back to the writings of Rousseau, and in this century, to Dewey (1966 (1916)). In this view the emphasis is on the learning of subjects useful for practical life, for example mathematics, physics and chemistry, or even more practical and vocationally-oriented subjects like typing, woodwork and industrial arts. Irrespective of how these subjects are taught, either through self-discovery of teacher-centered approaches, the goal of this type of education is the same, namely to promote both the economic development of the society and the practical well-being of the individual.

Both philosophies of curriculum content argue that in the long term, their's is the best for the benefit of the country and for the individual. However, those who adopt one or the other of these two views of education have not found it easy to understand each other. In a society where one view is dominant, for example the traditional, it has been extremely difficult to introduce a curriculum based on the other view. Because of this wide disparity in educational philosophies, the matching of school to jobs in both the developed and less-developed societies has been extremely difficult. The differences in educational philosophies are not only found between countries, for example between Britain and the Soviet Union, but also between generations or segments of the population in the same country. It can also be found to exist between educational policy-makers, teachers and parents. In this case many parents in some advanced societies expect schools to teach their children the norms and values of approved behavior, while educational planners are frequently more concerned with teaching children the skills and knowledge necessary for the economic development of the society.

One of the major difficulties in matching schools to jobs is the dual aspect of curriculum content. The most obvious contribution which schools make in the preparation of young people for entry into the job market is through the official curriculum. As we noted above, the official curriculum can be either of a general nature or highly specific in vocational content. With respect to the appropriateness of these types of curricula we have already pointed out that a general curriculum might be better suited for a rapidly changing and more sophisticated economy, where a higher level of education is attained by a relatively large proportion of the population. On the other hand, a more vocationally-oriented curriculum may be more appropriate for a society which has specific occupational needs, and in which the levels of educational attainment of the general population are not so high. Schooling in the United States, Britain, or Sweden may be taken as examples of the first, while schooling in Nigeria, Botswana or Tanzania might be taken as examples of the second. We would furthermore argue that the important distinction is between industrialized and non-industrialized countries rather than between capitalist or socialist countries. The problem of matching curriculum content and workforce needs in industrialized societies are the same under both capitalism and socialism. The difference between the two, as we have already noted, lies in the extent to which the State intervenes to regulate individual access to both education and occupation.

There has likewise been considerable discussion about the relevance of vocational education in developing societies. This is particularly true in societies where the model of development is an agricultural one rather than an industrial one. As early as 1961 the British economist Thomas Balogh argued that since most African countries were based on agricultural economies, the essential needs in education would be large-scale technical and agricultural programs within the schools. "The school must provide the nucleus of modern agriculture within the villages" (cited in Foster, 1965:142).

However, the development of vocational curricula for schools in less-developed countries has not been without criticism. For example, Foster (1965) has written a fundamental critique of vocational schools and the fallacies involved in regarding them as the solution for matching education with occupational needs. Foster contends that schools cannot alone solve the manpower problems in the less-developed countries, and in fact may be very "clumsy" instruments for this purpose. He argues that the immense wastage in schools, the high levels of aspirations created by schooling, and the almost "irrational" nature of African demand for academic as opposed to vocational education, constitute the heart of the problem. Foster contends that this is precisely because academic education has been seen in the eyes of most Africans as vocational education in that it leads to clerical and white-collar jobs. As long as the economic structure gives greater rewards to the white-collar sector, vocational or practical schooling will be unsuccessful in achieving its goals.

The predictions which Foster made in 1965 seem to have been borne out by subsequent experiences. In its 1980 report the World Bank, after evaluating many experimental and research results, observed that the attempts to introduce rural curricula at the primary-school level in low-income countries have been difficult and have tended to create a dual system of education: one for the urban industrial sector and another for the rural. The former has tended to give considerable advantage to the students being schooled in the urban sector in terms of life style and career choices, while the latter has tended to give limited access to both. In other words, a dual system of education to cater to the different sectors of society tends to increase and institutionalize the inequalities in the society. While everyone agrees that technical skills at all levels are needed in agriculturally based economies, as long as the modern sector is disproportionally rewarded, attempts to introduce vocational schools will encounter considerable difficulty (World Bank, 1980a). Subsequent studies of vocational education continue to confirm these cautionary comments. Benevot (1983) found, in his analysis of up to 124 countries, that enrolments in vocational education between 1950 and 1975 had declined on a global scale and could only be explained in terms of an ideology which emphasized egalitarianism and deemphasized formal differengiation of children while still in school. On a more practical level, Psacharopoulos (1985) reports that the rate of return for general academic education is higher, 16 percent, than for vocational education, 12 percent. Finally, the World Bank continues to regard vocational education with caution, arguing that it is unequal, too costly, and not sufficiently flexible to meet the needs of modern industrial technologies (World Bank, 1985).

Clearly the matching of school with manpower needs may require changes in the social and economic structure whereby the income and lifestyle gap between the industrial and agricultural sectors is reduced. As long as the systematic inequality between those employed in different sectors exists, the aspirations and motivations of individuals will be to the favored sector and will result in phenomena such as rural-urban migration, low response to those schools leading to jobs in the less advantaged sectors, and possibly frustrations, and criminal hostility due to perceptions of blocked opportunities.[9]

Does this mean that it is impossible to match education with the needs of the labor market? In a study sponsored by the International Institute for Educational Planning (IIEP) the relationship between education and recruitment to and promotion within occupations was studied within four countries (Panama, Indonesia, Kenya and France). The conclusions of these case studies throw additional light on our previous observations regarding the matching of education and jobs. In the first place, the authors, Hallak and Caillods (1980), found that employers in firms use several different criteria for initial hiring or promotion decisions. These include cognitive criteria, for example educational level, vocational training experience, knowledge of foreign languages, and results on tests. A second type of criterion is based on ascriptive characteristics, such as age, sex, marital status, and police record. And, finally, a third criterion concerns affective characteristics, for example personal attitudes and behavior. In all four countries educational attainment was a very important factor in access to any job category. In Panama and Indonesia it was the first criterion among the list of requirements, whereas in Kenya and France a certain level of education was stated as the minimum criterion for access. However, in all countries education was not the *decisive* criterion for entry into every job category, and it was less important for internal promotion than for initial hiring. Other cognitive criteria, including experience and vocational training, were also regarded as important factors but less so than educational attainment. Ascriptive criteria were generally less important, except in some cases where there were quotas by sex or region, as in the case of Kenya and the recruitment of teachers.

After considerable investigation of these four countries the authors were unable to present clear-cut directives for matching the educational system with the needs of the workforce, at least at a general level. Their conclusion therefore failed to resolve the dilemma facing both the industrialized and the non-industrialized countries.

> ...the crux of the debate concerns the criteria for developing a modern workforce and comes down to the question of whether it is enough simply to increase the correspondence between training and work – which could lead to the dilemmas mentioned earlier – or whether, on the contrary, one should maximize the choices and the individual's occupational mobility by putting the emphasis on a very wide general training which would enable him to move freely from one activity to another. The theory of credentialism does at least emphasize the fact that the deliberate or uncontrolled expansion of the educational system is not the incontrovertible answer to the problem of training a modern workforce. It all depends on the social, political and economic context involved (Hallak and Caillods, 1980:25).

There is, however, more to the linking of schools and occupations than the skills and knowledge that are deliberately taught. Schools also teach ways of thinking and doing things which are not part of the official curriculum. The so-called "hidden curriculum" has received considerable attention in recent years, and it has been suggested that what is taught informally and indirectly may be more important than what is taught formally and directly. In his work *On What is Learned in School,* Dreeben (1968) argues that the learning of attitudes and behavior, such as punctuality, competitiveness and bureaucratic organization, are three dimensions of normative systems which, in effect, the child must learn if he or she is to survive in the larger society. This point of view, while not presented within a radical framework, is similar to that developed further by Bowles and Gintis (1972, 1976). Their critique of the school in capitalist societies was initiated by their concern over the IQ ideology which they saw as a legitimating factor in the selective mechanisms of schools. To the extent that at the primary- and secondary-school level, measures of IQ effectively differentiate between working-class and middle- and upper-class students, it operates as an agent for the reproduction of the social structure and legitimates these social relations in the consciousness of workers. In other words, the working-class students learn to accept their place in society through the successful application of the IQ ideology.

There are, then, two important dimensions to the relationship between education and the manpower needs of a country: the formal curriculum which produces an appropriately trained and skilled workforce, and the informal curriculum which instils values and attitudes consistent with the economic and social structure. Both dimensions have been important in current assessments and critiques of education in developed and less-developed societies. With respect to the latter, additional arguments have been put forward by those who contend that Western-type schools have been used as instruments for maintaining dependency relations between countries and for attaining neo-imperialist objectives. Thus the technical skills taught in the schools, as well as the values and attitudes of the students regarding their possible (and appropriate) careers in a highly dependent economy, only serve to perpetuate that dependency.

However, there are grounds for suggesting that these problematic aspects of the relationship between education and occupations may be somewhat exaggerated and oversimplified. First of all it is inconceivable that schools in any modern or modernizing society could dispense with at least minimum standards of orderly behavior. Such demands for order seem legitimate not only in capitalist but also in socialist societies and in both industrial and agricultural societies. All schools in every society are engaged in the process of socialization of some kind: it is unlikely that education could ever take place in an attitudinal or cultural vacuum. The problem then is not whether the skills, attitudes or values inculcated through schooling are consistent with a particular society's economic structure or ideology, but whether a particular kind of education is appropriate for a particular kind of social and economic structure.

However, the relationship is even more complex. The entire argument concerning effects of overt and the hidden curricula is based on the assumption that schools teach what they say they teach and what others say they teach, and that students learn what they are supposed to learn. Recent research suggests that it is difficult to demonstrate this relationship, and that schools cannot be seen to operate independently of other important factors, for example the family, the media, and the occupational structure itself (Hurn, 1978).

Thus there are limitations which constrain the power of schooling, and through which unexpected consequences flow. Not every student accepts the class structure of the capitalist system, nor does every student in less-developed societies accept a colonial or dependent mentality. Yet overall there is justification for asserting that the overt and hidden curricula are effective, because social order would otherwise be more problematic than it is in reality for most societies.

What Kinds of Education? – Some Concluding Remarks

Our examination of the link between education and economic growth has left us with a highly complex picture. At the most general level it is possible to argue that education can support or contribute to economic growth when considered in its broadest sense: an educated population is more productive than an uneducated one, irrespective of type of society. However, beyond this general statement specific assertions are more difficult to support.

It appears that universal primary education of at least 4 to 6 years can be regarded as the minimum requirement to sustain any kind of economic growth. For the poor societies this means that universal literacy and numeracy through primary schooling should be given high priority in educational policy decisions. In industrialized societies this concern is less salient, as most countries virtually have full educational participation. For the poor countries, however, this target may not be easily obtainable. The proportion of children from 6 to 11 years of age enrolled in primary schools in 1984 ranged from a low of 25 percent in Bhutan and Somalia to 100 percent in countries like China and Sri Lanka (World Bank, 1987: 292). The figures for all less-developed and developed countries in 1990 are expected to be 75 and 93 percent respectively. The world total for net enrolment ratios by this date, and for this age group, is expected to be 78.6 percent (UNESCO, 1983 : 35, 48). Clearly much effort remains even to be made before primary education can be said to be universal.

This does not imply, however, that mass primary education is best carried out following the urban, Western industrial model in all parts of the world. The study of twenty-one countries by IEA showed that neither the age of starting primary school nor the number of instructional hours per year made an appreciable difference in science and reading achievement (Passow *et al.*, 1976). Furthermore, from an historical perspective, primary education itself gradually evolved and was implemented in a number of countries by patterning the school year around the relevant agricultural seasons and also by holding classes on alternate days or during alternate periods. For example, in a study of 19th-century schooling in south-east Sweden, it was found that many pupils only attended school about 50 days per year, and yet effectively learned to read, write and count (Gerger and Hoppe, 1980). Likewise in Norway a study of different school-day cycles found that children attending school every other day achieved just as well as those who attended every day (Husén, 1972). Countries with high levels of illiteracy might try to experiment with alternate educational structures in order that schooling be more compatible with local cultural and economic patterns.

It does not appear that mass secondary or tertiary education is necessary to sustain all kinds of economic growth. Industrialization in the West and in the Soviet Union occurred without universal secondary education. Furthermore, it has been argued that the unrestrained expansion of American secondary education not only affected the credentials required for entry into the workforce, but also changed the nature of secondary schooling by making it part of "mass education", and thus but a stepping stone to the acquisition of skills and requirements which afterwards could be found only at the tertiary level. The effect on the tertiary level was to exert pressures to provide not only purely academic credentials but vocational ones as well (Trow, 1961). The experience of countries like Ceylon (Sri Lanka), about which reference was made earlier, suggests that similar phenomena take place in other societies, including the less developed (Dore, 1976). There can be little doubt that as a general preparation for life, some secondary or tertiary education may be desirable, and that certain skills for high-level technologies are necessary to a limited extent in advanced societies and thus justify explicit vocational content in secondary and tertiary training. However, in some contexts the pressures for universal secondary schooling and the rapid expansion of tertiary institutions, especially when they are regarded as vocationally linked, may produce contradictions which prove to be dysfunctional to the society as a whole. The acquisition of narrow vocational skills during periods of rapid social change may be less preferable to more general educational programs, and as Foster (1965) rightly observes, all education is inherently vocational even if it prepares for a well-adjusted life. In view of the high costs of tertiary education, at least in some developing countries, it would seem that a reallocation of funds to the primary level may be necessary to obtain maximum efficiency from educational expenditures for development. This may be an easier policy to accept at an academic level than a political one.

Future Trends and Future Needs

In this chapter we have attempted to present a persuasive argument showing that the relationship between education, economic growth and development is like a two-edged sword. There is little doubt that in some contexts education can be an extremely important motor for economic growth. The human capital theorists were not entirely wrong in their assumptions concerning the mobilization of human resources as a *sine qua non* for certain kinds of economic growth. On the other hand, neither were they entirely correct in that they failed to emphasize that education does have limits in what it can do for an economy. The problem of education is not only that it is both determined and a determinant of the society in which it is located, but that other factors likewise contribute to the mobilization of human resources.

Looking ahead to future needs with respect to education is difficult. One thing, however, is certain: it is impossible to assume that the direction of social change and development in societies, as in the past, will continue unlimited into the future. The rapidly diminishing sources of energy and their increased costs is putting pressure on many advanced societies; it is making many poor societies even more poor; ironically, it is making some poor societies into rich ones.

For the advanced industrial societies, be they capitalist or socialist, it may be time to take careful stock of educational expenditures in order to ensure maximum efficiency. The transition to mass secondary education radically changed the role that secondary education fulfilled in those societies. Likewise, if trends continue, the gradual transition to mass tertiary education will likely bring about a radical change in the role that tertiary institutions will play. Such a transformation, even if yet at an early stage, requires careful evaluation, assessment, and planning.

For the poor societies which remain relatively poor, it will be a case of spending limited resources in those areas of education most suitable to their needs. A focus on primary and some secondary education with a careful selection of vocationally-oriented subjects appears to be a viable strategy, even though such a strategy may be difficult to follow in the first instance. In addition, all poor countries need to consider the utility of non-formal education, particularly for adults, at the same time that primary and secondary schooling are improved and expanded. Basic literacy, numeracy and fundamental vocational skills for adults can be effectively taught in this manner, and an appreciation of these school-based skills by adult parents is an important impetus for improving the efficiency of schools in general.

For the newly rich developing countries, particularly those with oil funds such as Saudi-Arabia, Indonesia and Nigeria, the educational problem is only partly solved. Monney can buy buildings and textbooks but not human resources. What is apparent is that economic growth alone cannot bring about the full range of changes required for development to occur in the broad sense. Education contributes to economic growth by producing skills and knowledge which promote it and make it possible; on the other hand, economic growth potentially contributes further to educational expansion and efficiency through increases in national productivity, accumulation of capital and savings for reinvestment into the system, and in the improvement of human resources. However, as we have stressed throughout this chapter, this improvement of human resources is not limited to the inculcation of skills and knowledge, but includes having values, attitudes and motives consistent with the goals and methods of development plans. Here education is again inextricably linked with development, since it is the major vehicle for bringing about the social and psychological changes necessary for the improvement of productive labor and openness to change. It is to this process that we turn in the following chapter, namely education's abilities and limitations to promote social-psychological changes in a population consistent with the needs and objectives of development strategies.

Notes

1. Hagen (cited in Chodak, 1973:214) for example, identifies eleven indices of economic development under five general headings:
    Welfare:
    1. GNP per person
    2. Doctors per 1000 persons
    Communications:
    3. Vehicles per 10,000 persons
    4. Telephones per 10,000 persons
    5. Radios per 1000 persons
    6. Newspaper circulation per 1000 persons
    Industrialization:
    7. Energy consumption per person (usually in kilowatt hours)
    8. Percent of labor force employed outside the agriculture and service sectors
    Urbanization:
    9. The percent of population inhabiting urban centers of more than 100,000 inhabitants
    Education:
    10. Percent of population literate
    11. Ratio of enrolment in primary schools to population of school age. These indices are generally used, in various combinations, to measure the level of economic development of a society at a given point in time, or to measure change over time. Agreement varies as to their reliability. However, some economists

argue that "an increase in national income... is the most relevant, as most convenient, single measure of development for both poor and rich countries" (Meier and Baldwin, 1957:8, cited in Chodak, 1973:214).

2. In general, the terms economic growth and economic development are used synonymously. However, some would argue that they are conceptually distinct, with growth referring primarily to a rise in income per capita while development pertains to an expansion of the overall economic structure, for example advances in technology and the discovery and exploitation of natural resources (Chodak, 1973). While we do not wish to make a sharp distinction between the terms, we argue that economic growth leads to economic development and for the most part is inextricably linked with it.

3. For a more thorough discussion of economic-growth theories, in particular the weaknesses of the classical "labor theory of value" and its replacement by contemporary theories emphasizing technical change and the accumulation of capital, see Samuelson (1976), Ch. 37, "The Theory of Growth".

4. With respect to the historical accuracy of Rostow's theory, Frank questions its assumption that all countries are classifiable in terms of stages of growth. For example, he asks where and when has the traditional stage ever existed? Furthermore, Frank accuses Rostow of denying the less-developed countries of having a history insofar as they have not yet reached certain stages. Rostow's replies to these and other criticisms are found in the appendix to the second edition of *The Stages of Economic Growth* (1971a).

5. For brief explanations of the Harrod-Domar and other growth models, see Samuelson (1976 : 748–51, or Todaro (1977 : 51–55.

6. For a more detailed discussion of the differences between developed and less-developed countries, and the particular characteristics of the latter, see Todaro (1977).

7. The OECD has classified the following as newly industrializing countries (NICs): Brazil, Greece, Hong Kong, South Korea, Mexico, Portugal, Singapore, Spain, Taiwan and Yugoslavia. See *The OECD Observer*, No. 113, November 1981:12–13.

8. The unit cost as a percent of GNP per capita is defined as "the geometric average of the corresponding unit costs as percent of GNP per capita for individual countries in the group" (World Bank, 1980a:70).

9. A good example of these behaviors is found in Marshall's (1976) account of his experiences as teacher in a private Ugandan school, some 200 miles east of Kampala. Although somewhat isolated from the urban area and life-style, there nevertheless was, each year, considerable pressure from the surrounding region for admission to the school. Marshall describes the attitudes and behavior of those who did not get accepted to the school as follows:

Although every available vacancy had been filled, crowds of youths thronged the school in the vain hope of getting a place. They queued up outside his office [the headmaster's] and trailed after him as he bicycled around the compound. The bolder spirits hammered on his front door and demanded to see him. Even when told in the most emphatic terms that there were no more vacancies, they still persisted.... There was something terribly pathetic about the way in which these forlorn rejects clung to their shattered hopes. A vision of a glittering world of motor cars, bungalows and status shimmered before their eyes; a school place was their one hope of escaping a life of drudgery... (pp. 59–60).

Evans (1975) reports a study conducted in Kenya on 699 male African students. He found that 18.7 percent of his sample expressed fears and worries about becoming a thief or engaging in some other crimiral activity. Over 20 percent expressed fears about law and order for Kenya as a whole. According to Evans, these fears were related to increasing unemployment.

4

Education, Modernization and Quality of Life

> We proposed, then, to classify as modern those personal qualities which are likely to be inculcated by participation in large-scale productive enterprises such as the factory, and, perhaps more critical, which may be required of the workers and the staff if the factory is to operate efficiently and effectively (Inkeles and Smith, 1974:19).

> Our first concern is to redefine the whole purpose of development. This should not be to develop things but to develop man. Human beings have basic needs: food, shelter, clothing, education. Any process of growth that does not lead to their fulfillment – or even worse disrupts them – is a travesty of the idea of development (The Declaration of Cocoyoc, cited in Ghai, 1978:6).

We begin this chapter with two quotes, both of which describe aspects of the process of modernization and ultimately of socioeconomic development. To this extent they represent a development perspective which departs considerably from that taken by economic-growth theorists described in the previous chapter. Yet economic growth and modernization also focus on similar goals or endpoints of the development process. The major difference between the two is that economic-growth theorists consider economic factors as central to economic development, while modernization theorists emphasize the importance of the sociological and psychological attributes of a population in order that economic growth can occur in a stable and consistent manner. Within both perspectives, however, education is seen to play a major role in the attainment of development objectives.

Although modernization theory is generally thought to represent a unified and integrated approach to the study of the processes whereby societies have and continue to become "modern", it nevertheless is

96

manifested in a variety of forms in different academic disciplines. Thus while social, organizational and political modernization are part of the same process, sociologists and political scientists prefer to define and document the process quite differently. In this chapter we focus on two aspects of the modernization process, the social-psychological and the sociological. With respect to the first we examine the importance of attitude and value change on social change generally, and regarding the second we focus on the impact of modernization on improvements in the quality of life, or in meeting what recently have come to be known as the basic human needs. In both contexts we critically evaluate the contribution which education makes to the modernization process.

The Modernization Process

While most social scientists agree that societies can be ranked according to the extent to which they are more or less modern, and that the process of "becoming modern" has dominated the changes experienced in societies during recent times, there still does not exist a single comprehensive theory of modernization. The term has been called a "blurry word", a concept which is "big and slippery" (Tilly, 1972). Some writers have conceptualized modernization as industrialization in the Western sense, and have defined it both in terms of factory organization structures and the utilization of inanimate power in the improvement of human productivity (Levy, 1966; Nash, 1973). Others, however, have preferred to define modernization as a form of human adaptation and the increasing use of man's rationality and knowledge in mastering his environment (Black, 1966).

At a more general level, it has been suggested that modernization is best conceptualized in terms of the "growth in moral, social and personal choices", in other words the liberation of a human population from the environmental, political and cultural constraints which place obstacles to its freedom to choose its destiny (Apter, 1965). Carrying this line of thought further, Moore (1979) contends that the process of modernization is fundamentally the process of becoming more rational. He argues that a modern society is one characterized not by particular technologies or institutions, but rather by a mode of thought and decision-making. Thus the ethnocentricity of other conceptualizations of modernization are avoided. Moore, for example, states:

> If modernization is defined as the process of rationalization of social behavior and social organization, one avoids the

vagueness of 'joining the modern world' and the ethnocentric connotations of 'becoming just like us'. More positively, rationalization suggests particular aspects or processes that partially cut across the more conventional attention to major functional aspects of society that are analytically and perhaps structurally differentiated... (p.29).

Societies of widely differing circumstances and economies become more modern to the extent that they become more rationalized. Ultimately a rational society is one which regards people as having the knowledge and ability to control their own destinies. Essential for rationalization to occur is the secularization of beliefs such that fate or destiny is not seen as being in the hands of the gods but rather of men.

In order to more accurately conceptualize the process of modernization, one must first differentiate between kinds of modernization, for example the "modernization of new nations" as is currently taking place in many post-colonial societies of the Third World (Weinberg, 1972), and "modernization of old nations" such as found in Sweden in the early 20th century (Hancock, 1972).

The tendency to regard modernization as a single linear process, shared by all societies, is common but clearly problematic. In this respect, a linear view of modernization is similar to the stages of growth theories discussed in the previous chapter, which postulate that all societies pass through the same stages in the process of economic development. Thus Weinberg (1972) suggests that the term modernization be limited in usage primarily to designate the social change careers of new nations following their political independence. Western-trained elites, heterogeneous populations, often the scarcity of basic resources, and economic dependence on the older developed nations exercise an influence on, and sometimes limit the modernization of new nations. These characteristics certainly shape their modernity process with a different mold compared to that experienced earlier by the older nations of the West. Weinberg designates the current changes taking place in the older nations as "remodernization", because their original modernization occurred during less rapid and integrated growth periods, as took place in Europe during the 12th and 16th centuries. However, to designate the countries which achieved early independence but whose social and cultural heritage was such that their culture and structures impeded modernization, he advocates the term "demodernization". The countries of Latin America which attempt to break down dimensions of the old structure in order to modernize are examples.

This recognition that modernization is not a single linear process prevents reckless generalizations about, and the extrapolation of, modernization and development policies from older Western nations to new nations. However, the recognition of these complexities should not preclude efforts to identify and investigate the features common to all modernization processes, irrespective of period or national context. The most significant attempt to measure modernization in this context has been that of Inkeles and Smith (1974) in their comparative study of six developing societies. As we noted in Chapter 1, Inkeles and Smith argue that modernization is essentially a social-psychological process through which a country becomes modern only after its population has adopted modern attitudes, values and beliefs. According to their conceptualization, a modern person is one who possesses the following traits (Inkeles and Smith, 1974:19–25):

1. openness to new experience;
2. readiness for social change;
3. awareness of the diversity of surrounding attitudes and opinions, and the disposition to form or hold one's own opinions;
4. being energetic in acquiring facts and information on which to base opinions;
5. time orientation toward the present and the future instead of the past;
6. a sense of efficacy or the belief that one can exert influence over one's own environment;
7. orientation to long-term planning both in public affairs and private personal life;
8. a basic trust in the calculability of the surrounding world, and that people and institutions can be relied upon to meet their obligations;
9. placing high value on technical skill and accepting it as a basis for the distribution of rewards;
10. placing higher value on formal education and schooling and aspiring to high levels of educational and occupational attainments;
11. respect for the dignity of others;
12. understanding the logic underlying production and industry.

In addition to the above characteristics which form part of their modernity scale (OM scale), Inkeles and Smith contend that two other dimensions characterize the "modern man", namely universalism and optimism. With respect to the first, the modern person believes that the rules or norms of society should be equally applied to everyone, irrespective of age, sex, friendship ties or relationships. Secondly, they argue that the modern person is one who is optimistic about his ability to control his destiny, and is not dominated by feelings of fatalism or the inevitability of events.

The important contribution made by Inkeles and Smith lies in their operationalization and measurement of modernity, and their contention that the components of the modernization variable are directly related to behavior which is typical of that found in a modern society. However, whether one describes modernity in terms of individual modernity characteristics, or at the societal level by terms such as rationalization, industrialization, or economic efficiency, there is an underlying commonality in meaning which fundamentally differentiates the "modern" society from one that is not modern. Although attempts to contrast the modern society with the traditional are fraught with difficulty (see our discussion later in this chapter), there is nevertheless an understandable tendency to see the modern society as evolving out of a more "closed", "traditional" or "premodern" social system. The precursor of the modern society and the modern person is one which is assumed to be opposite to the characteristics identified earlier, that is, closed to new experience, resistant to social change, unaware of the diversity of surrounding attitudes and opinions, and with a sense of fatalism about natural and social events.

Modernization and the notion of modernity have enjoyed wide acceptance in writings and research on social change and development. The variety and lack of consensus about its conceptualization has not deterred from its widespread use, particularly in the 1950s and 1960s. In trying to explain the theory's popularity, Tipps (1976) observed that:

> The popularity of the notion of modernization must be sought not in its clarity and precision as a vehicle of scholarly communication, but rather in its ability to evoke vague and generalized images which serve to summarize all the various transformations of social life attendant upon the rise of industrialization and the nation-state in the late eighteenth and nineteenth centuries. These images have proven so powerful, indeed, that the existence of some phenomenon usefully termed 'modernization' has gone virtually unchallenged (p. 62).

Insofar as education has been perceived as a major agent in producing the skilled manpower and the modern attitudes and values necessary for the existence of a modern society (as noted in Chapter 2), it is not surprising that modernization theorists and policy-makers have placed such considerable emphasis on it. It is thus to the relationship between education and modernization that we now turn in order to critically evaluate education's contribution to the formation of the "modern person", and in turn the "modern society". Our focus will be on individual modernity as manifested in attitudes, beliefs and behavior.

Education and Modernization

An essential preoccupation of modernization theorists concerns the process by which modernization occurs. Everyone agrees that there are many potential agents for the transmission of modern attitudes, for example, the school, family, media and work experience. However, what is of particular importance to our discussion is the extent to which schools function as a modernizing agent independently of the other agents.

In one of the early comparative studies of political participation Almond and Verba (1965) commented that: "Among the demographic variables usually investigated – sex, place of residence, occupation, income, age, and so on – none compares with the educational variable in the extent to which it seems to determine political attitudes" (pp.315–316). The formation of appropriate political attitudes, particularly those leading to political interest and democratic participation are, of course, important dimensions of the modernization process. However, education has been thought to exercise an even more pervasive effect on values, attitudes and behavior and thus act as a key agent in the development not only of the political, but of all dimensions of modernity.

There is considerable empirical evidence to support the above contention. In virtually every study available, it has been shown that exposure to schooling or level of school attainment is directly related to modernity-linked orientations. The raising of educational and occupational aspirations, less adherence to traditional customs and beliefs, an openness to new experiences, a willingness to migrate and a reduction in familism or family ties, are just a few such modern orientations which result from the school experience.

In one of the early studies of modernization, the documentation of the transition of Middle-East societies from traditional to modern, Lerner (1964) argued that a fundamental dimension upon which all modernity characteristics rested was what he called *psychic empathy*. Put simply, empathy is the ability which enables a person to adjust efficiently to continually changing environments, or in Lerner's words, "...to see oneself in the other fellow's situation" (p. 50).

Ultimately it is this psychic empathy which, according to Lerner, makes possible geographic mobility, the expansion of individual horizons and possibilities, and the creation of wider interests and opinions. In other words, phychic empathy, as a form of modernization, is "the infusion of a rationalist and positivist spirit" (p. 45), which is empirically manifest in many of the attitudes and behaviors found later in the modernity scale of Inkeles and Smith. More importantly, in a survey of Syrian respondents it was found that the presence of phychic empathy (as measured by an Empathy Index) was related to a number of individual factors, specifically age, sex, socio-economic status *and* education. With respect to education, 39 percent of the Syrian respondents who had at least a secondary education scored high on empathy, compared to 5 percent of the respondents who were illiterate. Conversely 74 percent of the illiterate respondents were non-empathic while only 19 percent of those with a secondary education were. The relationship between empathy and education was one of the strongest of those reported, and while education alone was not sufficient to produce a completely empathic population, it was nonetheless the most important factor (Lerner, 1964:436–437).

Numbers of subsequent studies in other countries have tended to support Lerner's early observations in Middle-Eastern countries. Using measures of modernity similar to those developed by Inkeles and Smith, Kahl (1968), for example, investigated the relationship between schooling and individual modernity in Mexico and Brazil, and found the correlations between the two to be 0.55 and 0.57 respectively.

The conclusions relating to Brazil were further supported by the findings of Holsinger (1974). Using three groups of Brazilian elementary school children in the third, fourth and fifth grades, it was found that exposure to schooling had a direct relationship with modernity, with the correlation coefficient between the two being 0.42. Furthermore, after the effects of other control variables were partialed out, the relationship remained virtually the same. In commenting on these findings, Holsinger stressed the importance of education for individual modernity:

> In light of this evidence and corroborating researches we conclude that for any child in Brasilia, the longer he is exposed to formal schooling, the higher will be his modernity score.... If a nation had no other resource than its schools, it could expect some modernization of its pre-adult population to occur (p. 44).

Similarly, in a study of 591 Nigerian 17-year-olds, Armer and

Youtz (1971) found that there was a direct relationship between exposure to Western-type schooling and individual modernity. Using a measure of modernity based upon six value dimensions such as independence from family, empiricism and future orientation, it was found that there is not only a strong positive relationship between schooling and modernity, but that the increase in modernity with schooling is a "linear" one, without sharp breaks. The figures showing this relationship are found in Table 4.1.

In exploring factors other than schooling which might explain the relationship, Armer and Youtz found that the impact of schooling persisted irrespective of family differences, exposure to the media, and other alternative modernizing agents. Furthermore, they argued that it is the curriculum of the Western-type school rather than its organization which accounts for modernity. In the case of Koranic schools it has been suggested that the use of traditional pedagogical techniques, particularly the emphasis on memory and rote learning without concern for understanding texts, inhibits further cognitive development and critical thinking even after students transfer to modern schooling. Although research has not clearly established whether the cause is pedagogical or social, exposure to Koranic schooling at an early age seems to inhibit later acquisition of modern values (Wagner and Lofti, 1980).

Since Koranic schools in some countries are organized and structured in much the same way as modern Western schools, then clearly the determining factor of traditional or modern values must lie in the curriculum, or some other aspect of the school process. Furthermore, the fact that Koranic schooling is stronger and better established in those countries which resisted the imposition of foreign (that, is, modern) values, such as in Morocco, Nigeria and Indonesia, suggests that its anti-foreign, anti-modernizing effect is recognized and intended (Wagner, 1985).

When Armer and Youtz (1971) analyzed students who had attended Koranic schools, they found that those who attended more than six years scored lower on the modernity scale than those who attended less than six years. Thus it is not simply formal schooling which produces modern persons, but formal schooling of a particular kind, namely that based on the Western model.

It is tempting to view formal educational influences as necessarily converging to produce a common set of attitudinal characteristics, and there may in fact be such convergences resulting from schooling in many areas of the world, but our evidence suggests that convergence is not necessary, that differences in perspectives can be fostered by different formal

TABLE 4.1. *Western Education and Percentage of "High" Individual Modernity among Nigerian 17-year-olds*

		Western education level								
	No education	Primary education				Secondary education				Total
	0	1–3	4–5	6	7	1	2	3	4+	
High individual modernity (N)	37.8 (312)	42.0 (50)	56.9 (58)	57.7 (52)	64.7 (51)	75.0 (20)	80.0 (20)	90.9 (11)	94.1 (17)	49.4 (591)

Note: Gamma (γ) = 0.45, p<0.001.
Source: Adapted from Table 3, Armer and Youtz (1971), p. 613.

educational systems, and that caution should be exercised in generalizing about the value-transition effects of unspecified formal educational systems (p. 622).

If the Western-type school exercises such a clear modernizing impact on attitudes and behavior in less-developed societies, then the effects should be apparent in the developed societies as well. There have been numerous studies in the United States, Britain and other Western countries which have documented the direct relationship between years of schooling and modern attitudes and behavior. One useful example is found in Stouffer's 1954 study of the attitudes and beliefs of Americans about Communism and civil liberties (1966). Tolerance toward nonconformists, a variation of modernity's "openness to change", was found to be directly related to education, irrespective of age. Thus, young respondents with university degrees were much more tolerant than young respondents with only a grade-school education. The young university graduates were also more tolerant than older graduates, suggesting that schooling alone does not completely account for tolerance. Stouffer, for example, suggests that external conditions associated with different age generations affect tolerance as well, and that on average a person "...is more likely to be more tolerant than his own parents" (1966:94).

The generation effects on attitudes identified by Stouffer are shown to apply also to the effects of culture. In the study of political attitudes and behavior in five developed and developing countries (United States, Great Britain, Germany, Italy and Mexico), Almond and Verba (1965) found that while education was strongly related to political behavior, there were nevertheless, variations between countries which were due to factors other than schooling. Thus 100 percent of the German respondents with some university experience indicated that they followed politics regularly or from time to time (a "modern" characteristic), while only 87 percent of the similarly educated Italians did so (see Table 4.2). On the other hand, the variation in political interest among those with a primary education or less ranged from a high of 69 percent for Germany to a low of 24 percent for Italy. Clearly, whether for cultural, political or social reasons, Germans with very little education are more "modern" than comparable Italians. Schooling alone, therefore, cannot completely explain level of modernity in a society, and there must be other non-school factors which explain these differences among the uneducated. Nevertheless schooling at higher levels, particularly university, whether because of educational exposure or selection, appears to considerably reduce the modernity gap across societies.

One possible insight into the multifaceted nature of the modernization process is provided by Cunningham's study of over 1300 students and their parents in a Puerto Rican high school (1974). His data suggest that while modernity, measured by the OM scale of Inkeles and Smith, was highly correlated with academic performance and

TABLE 4.2. *Percentage who "Follow Politics Regularly" or "From Time to Time" by Country and Education*

Country	Education level							
	Primary or less		Some secondary schooling		Some university		Total	
	%	N	%	N	%	N	%	N
United States	67	(339)	84	(442)	96	(188)	80	(970)
Great Britain	60	(593)	77	(322)	92	(24)	68	(963)
Germany	69	(790)	89	(124)	100	(26)	72	(955)
Italy	24	(692)	58	(245)	87	(54)	36	(995)
Mexico	51	(877)	76	(103)	92	(24)	55	(1007)

Source: Adapted from Table II.6, Almond and Verba (1965), p. 57.

the modernity of school peers (close friends), there was less association between the modernity of students and their parents. In general, however, the correlations were not very large, thus prompting Cunningham to observe that:

> Some [modernization] may come from parents, some from the school curriculum, and some from the school environment. But much of it must come from elsewhere, perhaps from sources outside the home and the school, such as the urban environment and mass media. If the school imparts modernity, the ways in which it does are not all identifiable (p. 218).

There can be little doubt, therefore, that factors other than schools contribute to the modernization process. For example, both the media and exposure to modern institutions such as the factory or even modern technology have been seen as having a modernizing effect on the values, attitudes and beliefs of individuals. In their study of modernization in six developing countries, Inkeles and Smith (1974) included these three basic modernizing influences, as well as other individual background characteristics such as age, occupation, possession of consumer goods, and urban experience. Based on samples of between 721 and 1300 respondents from Argentina, Chile, East Pakistan (Bangladesh), India, Israel and Nigeria, it was found that all three agents were significantly associated with the summary scale of behavioral modernity, with the school showing only slightly higher correlations than exposure to the mass media or occupational experience. The median correlations, as indicated in Panel A of Table 4.3, for the six countries were 0.52, 0.45 and 0.41 for education, media exposure and occupational experience respectively. The relative importance of each modernizing agent becomes more clear, however, when the interrelationships are partialed out or controlled for. In Panel B of Table 4.3 the beta weights (standardized regression coefficients) which, like partial correlations, take into account the simultaneous effects of other variables, show the "pure" or direct effects of each modernizing agent on the modernity scores. Here the pronounced importance of education for modernization is clearly apparent.

At the same time, however, it is also clear that exposure to the mass media or work experience each exercises its own independent influence on modernization. In effect, this demonstrates that any person can potentially become modern, even as an adult when the opportunities for schooling have passed. Nevertheless the six-country data firmly support the argument that schooling represents the strongest and perhaps the most viable policy-related individual modernizing agent and, as Inkeles and Smith observe, often far outweighs the other factors in importance.

> In all six countries, education emerged as unmistakably the most powerful force in shaping a man's modernity score. Indeed, judged by the number of points on the OM scale a man gained for each additional year of schooling, education was generally two or even three times as powerful as any other single input. In this, our conclusions are not new but rather confirm findings in several other studies of modernity. Occupational experience and mass-media exposure shared the second rank more or less equally (1974:304).[1]

However, it is one thing to document the causal relationship between education and individual modernity, and another to understand the process by which modernization occurs. What, then, is there about the school which enables it to have a modernizing effect on those who participate in it? One possible explanation is the so-called "hidden curriculum" of the school. By bringing young people together from diverse backgrounds and organizing their time according to set routines, the school may have the effect of broadening their views of the world and of learning the norms of tolerance, adjustability, the necessity of planning ahead and the importance of punctuality. Inkeles and Smith examine this aspect of schooling as a source of modernization and conclude that "...the

TABLE 4.3. *Correlation Coefficients (Panel A) and Beta Weights (Panel B) of Education, Mass Media Exposure, and Occupation Experience on Individual Modernity*

	Argentina (N = 817)	Chile (N = 929)	East Pakistan (N = 943)	India (N = 1198)	Israel (N = 739)	Nigeria (N = 721)	Median
Panel A							
Education	0.59	0.51	0.41	0.71	0.44	0.52	0.52
Mass-media exposure	0.57	0.46	0.38	0.56	0.38	0.43	0.45
Occupation	0.47	0.48	0.35	0.34	0.11	0.50	0.41
Panel B							
Education	0.41	0.34	0.32	0.56	0.33	0.32	
Mass-media exposure	0.30	0.24	0.20	0.20	0.30	0.22	
Occupation	0.22	0.31	0.27	0.17	0.08	0.30	

Source: Adapted from Tables 19-1 and 19-2, Inkeles and Smith (1974), pp. 266, 268.

answer lies mainly in the distinctive nature of the school as a social organization, something which has little to do with the curriculum as such" (1974:140). In further discussing this question, the authors single out several specific aspects of school organization which may have a modernizing effect, for example the reward and punishment process, the modeling behavior of students on teachers, the process of exemplification whereby the student learns to follow general and impersonal rules rather than personal ones, and generalizations of experience from one situation to others.

It is difficult to determine to what extent schools of necessity have a modernizing effect. We have already seen in the example of Koranic schools that it is possible to organize education so that modernization does not occur and that traditional beliefs and values are in fact reinforced. If modernization has Western connotations one seriously must ask to what extent is it a desirable by-product of schooling, especially in those societies which choose not to follow the Western model of development.

The investigation of this more complex aspect of the relationship between education and modernization is reported by Delacroix and Ragin (1978) in their study of modernizing institutions in forty-nine less-developed countries. Making the distinction between exogenous (from the outside) and endogenous (from within) modernizing institutions, the authors argue that the school is a domestically-based institution whereas the mass media may or may not be. The control of news sources by Western-based agencies and the dominance of Western culture through popular music and the cinema are common conditions in many less-developed societies. Thus Delacroix and Ragin contend that the school is able to modernize without "Westernizing", but the mass media, particularly when dominated by Western influence, are not. On the basis of their analysis of the relative contribution of schooling and cinema to economic growth, which they consider a form of societal modernity, the authors conclude that education furthers the economic progress of poor countries. Furthermore, they find that the contribution of education is stronger in "mobilizing regimes", that is, those countries with State-sponsored programs oriented towards participation and authoritarianism such as Algeria, Burma, Cuba, Egypt, Mexico and Tunisia. This, the authors argue, suggests that the school is "...an institution relatively free from the usual constraints of underdevelopment and therefore should be eminently responsive to voluntaristic intervention" (p. 145). On the other hand, the exposure to the cinema (measured in terms of attendance per capita) in general was found to have no effect on economic growth, and exposure to specifically Western films even appeared to impede economic growth. The overall conclusion of the authors is that while the school is an exogenous institution it can nevertheless be domestically controlled and therefore the deleterious consequences of exposure to Western influences can be mitigated.[2] Although the authors' definition of modernization as economic growth is a narrow one and departs considerably from that used by the individual modernization theorists such as Inkeles and Smith, they do provide evidence to suggest that schooling can contribute to societal modernization in a way which is not Western.

Education and Modernization: a Critique

It is clear that there is little agreement about the direct relationship between education and modernization or the process by which the relationship occurs. Apart from criticisms direcsed to the measurement of modernization itself, which have been discussed in Chapters 1 and 2, there are other difficulties with the education-modernization hypothesis which are more specific to the nature of education itself.

The cumulative research evidence leaves little doubt that education can be a powerful agent of modernization. Education broadens perspectives and mental horizons, it instils new values and beliefs supportive of modernization programs and goals, and promotes national unity and identity. Furthermore, it provides individual opportunities for upward mobility, develops skills and knowledge important for technological and industrial change, and in general helps overcome immobile ways of thinking and immobile systems of social stratification and differentiation. However, criticisms of the education and modernity thesis have focused particularly on two important assumptions whereby the two variables are linked. The first is that the effects of education are independent of measures of modernity, and the second that education exercises a direct causal modernizing effect on individuals.

With respect to the first, Armer (1977) contends that the standard measures of modernity, particularly as utilized in the Inkeles and Smith modernity scale, include knowledge items which are in fact the result of exposure to Western-style schooling. The questions in the scale relating to sources of news, the expected behavior patterns of workers in a factory, and the basis of political power are some examples. Thus it is argued that the findings which show a direct link between education and modernity are, at least in part, spurious. As long as conceptions of both modernity and schooling are based on

Western models this weakness in the education-modernity thesis will persist.

The second underlying assumption concerns the direct causal link between exposure to schooling and individual modernity. In virtually every society schooling is a selective institution. While the relationship between schooling and modernity as typically measured is well documented, there has been less evidence that schooling itself actually *causes* modernity. It could be that the variety of factors which contribute to school attainment also contribute to individual modernity. Thus, those students staying on longer in school may already be predisposed to modern values and beliefs. The direct effect of the school to this process may be less than normally assumed. The fact that students who attend non-Western-type schools sometimes do not manifest increasing levels of modernity does not contradict the observations made here, for those students are also products of a highly selective process. Nevertheless, irrespective of the configuration of causal factors, the strong association between Western-type schooling and modernity as currently measured cannot be totally dismissed.

However, more crucial perhaps than the link between education and individual modernity is that between modernity and development. If the contribution of individual modernity to the modernization of the entire society, particularly its social and economic development, cannot be demonstrated, then the contribution of education to societal modernization must be called into question. Does individual modernity, therefore, always lead to societal modernization, and ultimately to socio-economic development?

Modernization and Development

The general relationship between modernity, modernization and development is fundamental to the modernization hypothesis. As we have already noted, Inkeles and Smith argue that no society can hope to successfully embark on a program of social and economic development until it has "modern citizens". This statement begs several questions. Firstly, it assumes that only one kind of development is valid, namely the Western industrial model, and secondly, that the process of modernization which takes place through schooling will result in modern behavior. However, both of these assumptions can be challenged.

If a country chooses to follow a development strategy other than the Western industrial one, is it possible that the Western "modernity" of its population might actually prove dysfunctional to the attainment of development goals? For example, the agricultural model of development adopted by Tanzania and Papua New Guinea would not be aided by schools which produced adults who aspired to non-agricultural jobs and life in the cities.

Criticisms of the relationship between modernization and development have tended to focus on the dysfunctional aspects of modernization for society as a whole. Of central concern has been the presumed dichotomy between traditional societies, their values, norms and behavior, and modern societies. For example, Gusfield (1967) contends that there is no necessary incompatibility between some traditional values and beliefs and some modern ones (see Chapter 1). Indeed, according to Gusfield, there are at least seven major fallacies associated with the differentiation between "traditional" and "modern" societies: (1) that traditional societies are necessarily static societies, (2) that traditional culture is made up of a consistent body of values and beliefs, (3) that a society based on tradition has a homogeneous social structure, (4) that in changing societies, the traditional is necessarily replaced by the modern, (5) that the traditional and the modern are always in conflict, (6) that the traditional and the modern are mutually exclusive, and (7) that the process of modernization always weakens the traditional. Gusfield argues that in many contexts, the traditional and modern can exist side by side, as in the case of the syncretism of paganism and Catholicism often found in Spanish-speaking countries. Furthermore, the traditional may even support the modernization process, as in many countries where traditional status systems support modernization and economic development by providing legitimated manpower for the formation of new business classes.

Portes (1973), whom we also mentioned in Chapter 1, takes the argument further than Gusfield and contends that some traditional values are in fact more supportive of socio-economic development than many modern values. He likewise rejects the notion that all values in traditional societies necessarily impede the introduction of new forms of technology, or that the social organization of traditional societies necessarily gets in the way of the improvement of industrial or agricultural productivity. One only needs to cite again the case of Japan to show how traditional values, for example of the family, can be fused with highly productive technologies, as normally found in Japanese factories. Furthermore, it is indeed possible that modernization *might have detrimental effects* on the socio-economic development of a country. For example, when modernization has created a large segment of highly individualistic and highly trained manpower, certain behavior patterns may occur which are not in the best interests of the country in question. The "brain drain" of highly skilled and trained manpower from developing countries is a case in point. This phenomenon is often explained in terms of the achievement motivation which characterizes those who are educated to think of individualistic rather than collective success. In their study of the emigration of Argentine physicians, Portes and Ross (1976) argue that modernization can sometimes conflict with the interests of a particular society.

> Much harm has been done by the vast collection of writings which have preached modernity or 'westernism' to less developed countries as a solution to their problems (cf. Lerner, 1965; Inkeles and Smith, 1974). The syndrome of modernity-in-underdevelopment often has consequences which are the direct opposite of those originally intended. The reason is that important practices and values do not merely replace those that existed before, but interact with them in a process which leads to new and unanticipated results. Not incidentally, results of this dialectic, though frequently inimical to the weaker countries, have consequences favorable to the advanced ones. Thus, if we were to analyze who 'stands to gain' from premature modernization of the medical system we would have to rule out the frustrated professionals, the financially exhausted state, and the neglected population and choose, almost exclusively, the receiving countries which add substantial contingents to their professional manpower at little or no cost... The more success Argentine universities have had in modernizing their medical system in the absence of actual societal changes, the more they have produced physicians, whose proper realms of activity are the expensively equipped hospitals of the United States and not the modest clinics and dispensaries of rural Argentina (Portes and Ross, 1976:409).

Clearly in this example the modernization of health-training facilities has not fully contributed to the advancement of health care in Argentina. As Portes and Ross note, this negative impact of modernization occurs most often where one segment of a society modernizes more rapidly or in isolation from other segments, leading to serious disjunctures or even contradictions. Other examples occur daily in less developed countries throughout the world. Educated and professionalized teachers now refuse to teach in rural poverty-stricken areas, the attraction of entrepreneurial activity gives way to the security of a job in government or industry, and educated "modernized" youth migrate in droves to the cities in search of jobs in the "modern sector".

The above examples highlight a more fundamental criticism of modernization theory, namely its unilinearity and unidimensionality. There is little support for the notion that modernization represents one end of a continuum of social and psychological change, with traditional at the other end. The criticisms of the assumptions of unidimensionality by Gusfield (1967), Schnaiberg (1970) and Portes (1973) have recently been supported by Rau (1980). In a reanalysis of data from five countries, namely, Ghana, India, Brazil, Japan and the United States, Rau concludes that the concept of modernity has empirical validity, in particular with respect to its value component, but that there is little support for the notion that modernization is unidimensional. This means that the components of modernization can operate independently of each other and that it is possible for people to adopt modern values with respect to certain dimensions of their lives but retain traditional values with respect to others.

Indeed, even certain assumptions about the conceptual nature of modernization do not stand up to increasing knowledge about traditional societies. As indicated at the beginning of this chapter, modernization has often been defined in terms of the rationalization of the decision-making process. The assumption, of course, is that decision-making in traditional societies is not rational, and that any behavior which resists or impedes modernization is irrational. However, in a discussion of the resistance by African peasant tribes to economic change which, by Western standards, would be judged "modern" and "rational", Hutton and Cohen (1975) argue that resistance itself may be a highly rational response to economic threat. Where new economic structures are introduced, whose forms weaken the security of established peasant economic structures, a resistant response can be seen as rational. Hutton and Cohen contend that the African peasant, and indeed traditional people everywhere, must be understood in terms of their own "definition of the situation", which includes their own experience of the modernizing process. Thus resistance to change is part of the development process insofar as peasant farmers must protect their own vested interests when confronted by new, unknown, and potentially damaging economic structures. Thus, Hutton and Cohen call into question some basic assumptions of the modernization and development thesis.

> We are not likely to be helped by attitude surveys and cultural studies designed to test receptivity to modernization. Rather we need some understanding of the ways in which particular economies, social structures, and cultures are tied together, and

the impact on these of the experience of colonization and incorporation into a wider economy.... We do not want to suggest that peasant attitudes and opinions are irrelevant to the processes of economic development, nor to the success or failure of local projects, but we are arguing that such attitudes are unlikely as such to be important independent variables, and are themselves part of the development situations which require explanation. We should not then ask how we can change peasants' attitudes to more appropriately modern ones before we have answered the question, why do people hold the attitudes towards development which they do have? (p. 123).

Agricultural extension workers have had to realize that modern farming technologies are not always preferable to traditional technologies. Only gradually has the complexity of the traditional mentality and way of life been understood. The "bearer of modernization" is inevitably a "modern" person, and thus a stranger to the traditional. Modern technology often disrupts the balance of social relationships into which traditional technologies are imbedded. Finally, the promise of improvement, whether in productivity or life style, makes little sense to those who are doomed to low status and powerlessness, irrespective of whether they adopt modern technology. Thus only when the modernization of agricultural technology is seen in a wider cultural, social and psychological context can the resistance to modernization be understood. The reduction of the technology gap between traditional and modern, perhaps by promoting simpler technologies, the reduction of the social and intellectual gap between the modernizer and the traditional (by acknowledging the "wisdom" of traditional and uneducated mentalities), and reducing the emphasis on commercial benefits rather than status and power benefits, have been suggested as strategies for reducing the conflict between modern and traditional agricultural technologies (Rohrer, 1986).

Finally, the existence of an openness to change does not guarantee that modernization will proceed unimpeded. There are many examples where "breakdowns" or partial reversals in the modernization process have taken place. Eisenstadt (1970) argues that breakdowns in the modernization process are most likely to occur in those societies where adequate institutional structures do not develop in time to meet the needs brought about by the rapid changes in other social and demographic spheres of the society. Thus countries such as Indonesia, Pakistan, Burma and Sudan made considerable progress in health and education, but could not construct modern political institutions which could completely overcome the ascription-based elite structure of earlier traditional society. Thus, according to Eisenstadt, the political modernization of these societies was blocked and "reversed", leading to regimes which were less flexible and with lower levels of solidarity than those which existed at the outset of deliberate modernization. The implication of cases such as these is that the modernization of some sectors of societies does not automatically guarantee that all sectors of society will become modernized.

Thus while modernization may for the most part contribute to social and economic development, it is extremely important to clarify what kind of modernization and what kind of development is desired. The underlying orientation of the conventional concept of modernity is Western, capitalist and urban, and therefore its operationalization promotes a Western, capitalist and urban style of development. Some argue that the modernization process itself can create a form of colonialism and often operates in the best interests of the advanced societies rather than the less developed. However, the process of modernization in many countries, both capitalist and socialist, and developed and developing, may be a fact of life which is probably difficult to avoid and related to a world-wide diffusion of values. Yet, the highly complex nature of modernization and its potential link with a certain kind of development must be recognized. The fact that modernity may be undesirable in some countries suggests that care be given to the formulation of programs which may have modernization as their by-products.

Modernization, Quality of Life and Development

While the relationship between education, modernity and economic development may be somewhat problematic, a more specific question concerns the extent to which education and subsequent modernity contributes to an improvement in the quality of human existence. In recent years there has been a shift away from the notion that economic development is the single goal of development policy, to a notion which stresses the betterment of human social conditions. This latter goal is sometimes expressed in terms of meeting the basic human needs.

This shift was clearly stressed by Jan Tinbergen in his report to the Club of Rome concerning the need for a New International Economic Order:

> [There is a] ...need for new development strategies – national and international – defined and designed, not merely to meet the criterion of private or state profitability, but rather to give

priority to the expression and satisfaction of fundamental human values. Society as a whole must accept the responsibility for guaranteeing a minimum level of welfare for all its citizens and aim at equality in human relations.... It follows that the problem of development must be redefined as a selective attack on the worst forms of poverty (Tinbergen *et al.*, 1976:63, 66).

In this shift of emphasis to human needs it is important to understand that economic growth is not rejected as a viable strategy for development, but rather that the satisfaction of human needs is considered an equally important component for bringing about the social and economic development of society. There are two limits to economic growth: limits in natural resources and limits in human resources. According to most available evidence the known limits to natural resources are beginning to put severe restraints on the ability of societies to sustain their present levels of economic growth. On the other hand, it is clear that there is still considerable room for the mobilization of the world's human resources. However, the unequal distribution of material goods, the lack of adequate food, shelter and clothing has meant that large segments of the human population are able to contribute little or nothing to this mobilization in terms of human productivity.

The basic needs approach is not a development strategy *per se*, but it does direct attention to policy objectives which are development related. For example, the concern with basic human needs focuses on the consumption patterns of individuals and groups at the micro-level, and it also gives attention to the role of the allocation of public goods in national development policies (Weigel, (1986). In order that development occurs, therefore, not only is it imperative that there be a change in the attitudes, values and beliefs of individuals (individual modernity), but also that be an improvement in physical and social conditions. One recent study of basic needs statisfaction in Mexico concluded that level of literacy in the 32 Mexico states was highly related to the satisfaction of other basic needs, namely the eradication of infant child mortality, nutrition, clean water and health care. Furthermore, it was argued that Mexico would continue to lag behind other less-developed countries in per capita income until these basic needs were satisfied (Wood, 1988). The origins of the basic human-needs approach to development are foundamental concern about human resources.

The Human-needs Approach to Development

On May 1, 1974, the United Nations General Assembly passed a resolution declaring that the objectives of the "New International Economic Order" were to correct inequalities and redress existing injustices, to insure steadily accelerating economic development, and finally to maintain peace and justice for present and future generations. The significance of this resolution can be best understood if it is seen as the culmination of a long concern over the question of international poverty. To quote one writer: "The demand for humanity, justice and equity is as old as man and woman and as new as tomorrow" (McKay, 1977:2).

Research on poverty began in some European countries as early as the 17th century when social statistics were used as a means of describing social conditions (Chinapah and Fägerlind, 1979). By the mid-20th century many international organizations like the United Nations, the International Labor Organization, the World Bank and the World Council of Churches had become involved in international problems of poverty and the inequalities between nations. The resolution of 1974 marked the *official* shift in the concept of development, from the economic-growth model to one with a stronger emphasis on the material and psychological conditions of mankind.

The question concerning basic human needs is not simply one of inequality, although the rights of people and the satisfaction of their basic needs was certainly in the forefront of the Cocoyoc conference. But a central concern of the human needs approach actually appears to be related to a more subtle form of human capital theory. In his Nobel lecture, even Schultz emphasized the importance of population health, that is health capital, as part of the quality of a human population. Thus, it follows that the satisfaction of human needs is but a further extension of the desire to improve the quality of human stock, and which includes many dimensions of the human condition.

Probably the best statement of this broader view of human needs and their relationship to development is found in the Cocoyoc declaration:

> Development should not be limited to the satisfaction of basic needs. There are other needs, other goals and other values. Development includes freedom of expression and impression, the right to give and to receive ideas and stimulus. There is a deep social need to participate in shaping the basis of one's own existence and to make some contribution to the fashioning of the world's future. Above all, development includes the right to work, by which we mean not simply having a job but finding self- realization in work, the right not to be alienated through production processes that use human beings simply as tools (The Declaration of Cocoyoc, cited in Ghai, 1978:6).

In 1975 the Aspen Institute for Humanistic Studies (1975) differentiated between first-floor and second-floor needs. The first-floor needs consist of the minimum requirements to which every person should be entitled, namely food, health and education. Second-floor needs, on the other hand, consist of those needs defined by each nation-state for its own people. In a further development of the human needs concept, McHale and McHale (1975) argue that needs can be classified in terms of the biophysical and psychosocial, and that the former act as a means to achieve the latter. The biophysical needs are food, water, energy and shelter, while the psychosocial are education, security, recreation and communication.

Further dimensions of the human needs concept include those of equality and social justice. Equality refers to the distribution of goods among individuals. Those who espouse the human needs approach do not argue that every individual must have equal material resources, but that the range of variation between the social strata is reduced.

The question of social justice, however, is somewhat more complex. Galtung (1976), for example, describes the relationship between social justice and human needs in terms of group differences.

> There is another aspect to distribution: social justice. One way of conceiving of social justice is simply as follows: the level of need-satisfaction should not depend on sex, race, age, whether one lives in a city, town or village, whether one is employer or employee, who one's parents were, etc.... Social justice does not reflect level of satisfaction or equality in the population, but is nevertheless a very important dimension because it may express the degree of racism, sexism and 'agism' (discrimination of the young and the old by the middle-aged) in the population. What equality is to the difference between individuals, social justice is to the difference between groups (Galtung, 1976:263).

To some extent, the concern with social justice is independent of the concern with economic growth. Some would argue that even if the satisfaction of human needs made no contribution to economic growth, it nevertheless represents a viable strategy for the development of a society. They contend that the concern with basic human needs is as much a philosophical and moral issue as an economic one, in that fundamental necessities relating to biological existence, intelligence and sociality are inherent in the sociobiological nature of humans (Weigel, 1986). One of the criticisms of the economic-growth model is, at least in capitalist societies, that it leads to greater inequality and social injustice in a population. However, it is an open question as to what extent the concern with human needs can be effectively combined with an economic-growth strategy to produce a more comprehensive development model.

Of fundamental importance in the discussion of human needs is the question of how human needs are to be measured. Incorporating the human-needs concept into development policy requires that new indicators of development must be adopted, a process which is both empirical and political. Galtung (1976) argues that decisions regarding measurement involve a number of conceptual and practical questions which must be initially resolved. For example, he asks:

> What are in fact the human needs? What are the priorities in case of conflict? What are the trade-offs? Where are the cut-off points for the floor (the social minimum) and for the ceiling (the social maximum)? What would constitute a reasonable level of equality, of social justice – and along which dimensions? What are the units of self-reliance for the various human needs? What is the meaning of participation? What are the minimum and maximum limits for our responsibility to future generation [s]? (Galtung, 1976:264–265).

However, the measurement of basic human needs is only part of the task of converting the concept to policy directives, for human needs are both a quantitative and a qualitative phenomenon. Before basic needs can be measured quantitatively, it is essential that decisions of a qualitative, even definitional nature be made. For example, what is food? How does one define shelter? What counts as education? So far in general discussions about human needs these fundamental questions have not been dealt with, except at philosophical, moral and political levels. In spite of the volume of printed matter on the subject, empirical research has been virtually non-existent. Furthermore, there is little research evidence which confirms the link between human needs and changes in attitudes, values and behavior. This does not mean, however, that the eradication of poverty and disadvantage would not produce or make possible such changes.

In many ways, the new focus on the meeting of basic human needs as a viable development strategy parallels the many notions of modernization and individual modernity discussed earlier in this chapter. Similar to modernization theory, the human-needs approach focuses on changes in people, but unlike modernization, these changes are primarily in improving physical, social and political conditions. Modernization, in the sense we have used it, refers to social-psychological change. Nevertheless the two processes are closely related in that social-psychological change becomes possible when human needs are met. Indeed, it has been suggested that this shift in attitudes, values and behavior regarding our understanding of basic human needs and economic development will constitute something of a "moral revolution". As Weigel (1986) commented: "Could it be that observers in the 21st century will view the global maldistribution of resources with the same disdain that we presently hold for the institution of slavery" (p. 1432). Both approaches, then, are concerned with the improvement in general quality of life, and both place considerable emphasis on education as part of that improvement.

Education, Modernization and Development: a Summary

Apart from the discussion of basic human needs, there is little doubt that the process of modernization as experienced by individuals has brought about increasing control over, and the rationalization of, many aspects of the human condition. Moore (1979), for example, argues that modernization represents the first global process of social change experienced by mankind, and that improvement in the conditions of birth, health and life expectancy have and continue to diffuse throughout all countries. OECD statistics record much of this "convergence" of modernity in some of the more advanced countries of the world, but even within the limited range of OECD countries wide divergences exist. In 1985 infant mortality varied from a low of 5.9 per 1000 live births in Japan to 14.1 and 17.8 in Greece and Portugal respectively. Telephones per 1000 inhabitants varied from highs of 890 and 832 for Sweden and the Switzerland to lows of 67 and 180 for Turkey and Portugal. (OECD, 1987 : 24) Parallel to these figures, full-time school enrollments for children aged 15–19 ranged from highs of 99 and 96 percent for the United States and Japan to lows of 42 and 47 precent for Turkey and Portugal (World Bank, 1988).

Clearly the variation in these indicators of technological modernity (especially infant mortality and telephone availability) correlate with participation in the educational system. However, as with much of the empirical data regarding education and modernity, it is difficult to adequately differentiate between cause and effect. It may be true that educational attainment correlates highly with other indicators of modernity, but the demand for and participation in education is itself an indicator of modernity. Furthermore, as has already been discussed, it is the type of schooling which is most closely related to Western-style modernity which suggests that the desire for and selection of schooling assume, *a priori*, a predisposition or openness to the modernity process. It may be that modernization is a global process which proceeds by diffusion between societies, but, as we have seen, its rate and character are contingent on numerous other factors such as culture, natural resources and political condition.

Finally, it is important to recognize that indicators of modernity, the means whereby modernity is diffused, and even the appropriate indicators of human needs and the quality of life, differ from society to society. In particular, systematic variations between capitalist and socialist, industrial and non-industrial, and developed and less-developed societies in the modernization process require that caution be exercised in order to prevent overly simplified generalizations about a process which is inherently complex and diverse. To this extent, the role of education, the characteristics of modernity, and the development strategies to bring about modernization are themselves conditioned by and in turn differentially affect societies of varying structural properties. This consideration has received little or no recognition in most previous and current research on the modernization process. We examine some of these structural properties in greater detail in later chapters. Our immediate attention, however, turns to another dimension of development, namely the political, and examines its importance in the process of change and socioeconomic progress.

Notes

1. Of equal significance in the findings of Inkeles and Smith were those factors which did *not* have an impact on individual modernity. Among the most important were the urban experience (measured by city size and cosmopolitanism) and ethnic identity. See their discussion in Chapter 15: "The Quantity and Quality of Urban Experience" (pp. 216–229).
2. The authors recognize that some schools in Third World countries were established through Western contact and may in fact transmit Western values. However, they argue that in contrast to the cinema, schools are more likely to be influenced in some way or another by the political system and therefore are more likely to serve the interests of the State. See, for example, their footnote on p. 128.

5

Education, Political Mobilization and Development

THE link between education and the political system is not unique to current interests, and both Plato and Aristotle were concerned about the interrelated effects of these two social institutions. This concern is best illustrated by the following common-sense sayings about the school and the State cited by Coleman (1965:6): "As is the state, so is the school", and, "What you want in the state, you must put into the school".

Social philosophers, social scientists and educationists have generally agreed that formal education is both determined by and a determinant of the political system. In specific terms it is usually asked to what extent education promotes the mobilization of and participation in political activities, for example through voting and other forms of political behavior. Conversely it is also asked to what extent the political system affects, and indeed controls what goes on in schools.

Elites have always recognized the relationship between education and political power, both in terms of control and legitimation and as a potential source of political discontent. But apart from these more obvious "political" concerns about education and politics, there is the more specific concern about the link between education and political development. As in previous chapters, we must first address ourselves to the question of political development itself, particularly its conceptual and operational meaning.

Political Development

As with other concepts relating to development, the notion of political development is broad and not easily defined. Perhaps the most widely accepted definition is that put forth by Coleman (1965) in the following passage. For Coleman, political development is:

...the acquisition by a political system of a consciously-sought

123

and qualitatively new and enhanced, political capacity as manifested in the successful institutionalization of (1) new patterns of *integration* regulating and containing the tensions and conflicts produced by increased differentiation, and (2) new patterns of *participation* and resource distribution adequately responsive to the demands generated by the imperatives of equality (p. 15, italics ours).

The key concepts are clearly those of integration and participation. Integration refers to the extent to which a society is able to create unity and solidarity among its people, and to bring about a sense of national identity over and above that generated by family, tribe, village or region. At one level, the processes of political integration incorporates the process of political enfranchisement and the bestowal of citizenship. As such, politically integrated individuals, or citizens, are those who enjoy political legitimacy and possess both rights and duties toward other citizens and toward the political state of which they are members. In many developing societies the problem of integration relates to the creation of independent nation-states where none previously existed, and where colonial or other ethnic or social identities had previously prevailed. For the developed societies, the problem of integration may be different, but no less real.

The concept of political participation is almost self-explanatory. The underlying assumption here is that a population in which there is extensive political mobilization, either through voting, interest in, or reading about political matters, is preferable to one in which the masses are politically inactive or stagnant. Some, of course, may disagree with this assumption and contend that if political participation leads to political instability, then it is difficult to argue that development has taken place. The notion of participation and integration suggest a harmonious system held together by individual rights and duties based on consensus. Yet we would argue that participation, irrespective of outcomes, is always preferable to non-participation as a component of political development. This perspective, of course, falls within the structural-functional paradigm and has dominated the thinking of political scientists for several decades. The notion of political development within the conflict perspective takes a somewhat different form.

Conflict theory in general sees political development in terms of conflicts of political interests within the society. Struggles for power are seen as part of the everyday scene of political processes, and conflict theory focuses on the extent to which these processes occur in an open and equitable context. Dependency theory, a variant of the conflict approach, views political development in terms of political liberation from influences outside the country, be they neo-imperialistic or neo-colonial. Political integration and participation are important components of this perspective, but so are self-determination and autonomy.

Following our framework, one must also keep in mind the difference between notions of political development in Western capitalist and socialist countries. The perspective put forward here is clearly the former. The socialist ideology perceives development in terms of the class struggle and the greater political (working class) control over the forces and means of production. Nevertheless national integration (and perhaps a national consciousness) remains important for political mobilization and development even in this context.

The question to which we first turn concerns the extent to which education leads to greater political participation, and furthermore to the impact of societal structures on the relationship between the two.

Education and Political Development

> The educated individual is, in a sense, available for political participation. Education, however, does not determine the content of that participation (Almond and Verba, 1965:319).

The optimism regarding the effect of education on political participation has paralleled that regarding the effect of education on economic growth and modernization. This optimism has generally been of a conservative nature, and stems from the conviction that "...all national educational systems indoctrinate the oncoming generation with the basic outlooks and values of the political order" (Key, 1963:316; cited in Zeigler and Peak, 1971:212). However, it is also generally agreed that education acts as a change agent to the political system, and as Coleman argues, the educational system can be viewed "as the master determinant of all aspects of change" (1965:3).

As a conserver of the political system, and a contributor to political development, education has been regarded as serving three main functions: (1) as the main agent for the political socialization of the young into the national political culture, (2) as the primary agent for the selection and training of political elites, and (3) as the main contributor to political integration and the building of national political consciousness. For each of these the formal school, in the Western sense, is seen as the educational mechanism through which these functions take place.

(i) Political Socialization

The concept of political socialization is generally defined as "the process by which a person internalizes the norms and values of the political system" (Massialas, 1969:20–21). This process of intergenerational continuity in political values and behavior obviously is due to many factors, the family and peer groups representing two important ones. However, the school, because of its institutional autonomy from other factors, has been regarded as the prime arena within which this process of political socialization takes place. Regarding political socialization Hess and Torney have stated that "the public school is the most important and effective instrument of political socialization in the United States" (1967:200).

Yet the empirical data supporting this contention is not without controversy. The question concerning the transmission of political values and behavior, in particular the relative impact of the home and the school, is still not completely understood. In the important study of civic education in ten countries, Torney *et al.* (1975) concluded that the faith that governments placed on schools to prepare the young for citizenship is only partly justified because of competing influences from outside the school. Furthermore, because of the hierarchical nature of the modern Western school, it may not be a suitable institutional setting for the teaching of all civic values, least of all those relating to democracy. More recently Torney-Purta and Schwille (1986) contend that no industrialized country has had complete success in the teaching of civic values, and suggest that many desired values may in fact be incompatible, for example the support for democratic values (tolerance and equality) and the support for the national government (national patriotism and trust in government).

In the ten-country study Torney and her colleagues found that affective outcomes of civic education are less explainable by means of home and school factors than are cognitive outcomes, that is the factual aspects of civic knowledge. Furthermore, they found that the actual school practices, such as patriotic rituals, and less stress on drill and rote learning, and more sterss on independent thought are likely to increase democratic value support (1975:289). Finally they contend that there are at least five stages of political socialization:

Stage 1: Very vague, inarticulate notions, with emergent images of one or two institutions, e.g. the police.
Stage 2: What may be called the 'sheltered' view, in which primarily the harmonizing values and processes become established.

Stage 3: An intermediate stage of growing awareness of social conflict, of economic forces, of the U.N., of multiple institutional roles, etc., but essentially still with a sheltered orientation.

Stage 4: The sophisticated or realistic view, with less stress on fairmindedness and understanding, clear awareness of both the cohesive and divisive functions of many institutions, of overlap between institutional functions, of social bias, low participation, oppressive potential, etc.

Stage 5: Scepticism, a general contempt for institutions and lack of belief in their efficacy, an emphasis on discordant functions, unfairness and class bias, denial of participation and of improved understanding (pp. 318–319).

The importance of early childhood experiences in the acquisition of political orientations was well documented by the early 1960s. For example, Levine (1963) pointed to studies showing that "effective and evaluative orientations toward political authority roles precede the acquisition of factual knowledge about the behavior involved in role performance" (pp. 286–287). As early as age 7, children were found to label themselves as Republicans or Democrats, apparently following the practice of their parents, long before they had any knowledge or understanding about political parties. Thus it is of considerable importance to keep in mind that before the child ever steps into a schoolroom, the basic foundations for political socialization by the school are, at least in a moderate sense, already in process.

There is much difference between countries in the civic values which are desired. For example, in many English-speaking industrialized countries such as the United States and Britain, the value on individual success is emphasized, while in Japan, Greece, and many German-speaking countries security is seen as important. In the United States individualism and freedom are highly valued, whereas in the Soviet Union emphasis is placed on service to the community and the country (Torney-Purta and Schwille, 1986). Although all countries have had less success than desired in the inculcation of civic values through schools, the less-developed countries represent a unique situation in this regard.

Levine (1963) argues, for example, that in new nations the local political culture might have greater impact, through family and peer groups, than the national culture. Thus the political values of children entering the school might have a different frame of reference, and the interaction with the school could clearly take a different form. According to Almond and Verba (1965), schooling is related to civic knowledge and competence, in both developed and developing countries, but the level of overall knowledge and competence appears to be greater in the developed than the less-developed countries.[1]

One could thus argue that the need and indeed the possibility for political socialization through the schools is much greater in less-developed than developed societies. In the first place, the possible impact of alternative socializing agents is not as great simply because their participation in the political culture of the new nation-state is not as extensive, or in the case of emergence from neo-colonial status, would require a re-socializing into the new independent political culture. A second reason is that in less-developed societies, the political culture and a sense of nationalism may even have to be created through the schools by breaking down the values and orientations based on the local, tribal or political structures. Finally, in many less-developed countries the new political values being taught in schools may conflict with the political values of authority and duties in traditional cultures, as Harber (1984) found in his study of the Hausa in Nigeria. This latter point will be developed further in a later part of this chapter.

(ii) The Selection and Training of Political Elites

In all societies, whether developed or less developed, capitalist or socialist, industrialized or agriculturally based, the stability, survival and effectiveness of the political system depends on those who constitute the elite and hold positions of power. Since classical times, social philosophers have had an interest in those whose destiny in life was to lead others, and of particular concern were the characteristics which set these elite apart from the masses. For Aristotle, the main characteristics required for the elite were that they be men of virtue and excellence, and who put the good of society ahead of their own interests. Other significant political and social thinkers, such as Pareto, Mosca, Michels, Lasswell and Mills, have discussed elites in more specific contexts. For example, C. Wright Mills argued that the United States is controlled by an elite "in command of the major hierarchies and organizations of modern society" (cited in Massialas, 1969:83).

Our main concern, however, is to determine the extent to which schools contribute to the recruitment and training of political elites. Furthermore, we also want to make clear that the filling of elite positions is not always a conservative process as "new" elites sometimes initiate a considerable shift in the trends of the political order. Thus it is not enough to demonstrate that schools produce elites, but that these elites have a direct impact on the political and economic development of a society.

There is virtual consensus among social scientists about the strong relationship between education and political leadership. Empirical studies have generally shown this to be the case in both Western developed societies as well as non-Western developing societies. At the same time, however, it is also recognized that there are other avenues to political power, for example religious, economic and the military (Massialas, 1969).

The documentation for this positive relationship between education and elite recruitment is most extensive in the Western societies. Studies in the United States, Britain, France and Australia have all shown that either level of schooling or the type of schooling differentiates the ruling elites from the masses. In the case of the United States, higher education seems to be the key to elite attainment, with lesser importance on type of institution, though among the latter, institutions such as Harvard, Yale or Princeton do play a significant role (Warner *et al.*, 1963). In Britain, the public schools have long been recognized as serving the same function, as have the French *lycée* and the German *gymnasium* (Frey, 1970; Bourdieu, 1973). A study of Australian elites has produced similar results, not only with respect to educational attainment but also to the role of elite schools (Higley *et al.*, 1979).

Although these patterns are also found in less-developed countries, they are sometimes contingent on cultural and historical factors. In Papua New Guinea Latukefu (1988) argues that a traditional elite, based on knowledge about deities, mythology and folklore, always existed before the formal education system was established. The modern elite, on the other hand, are products of modern, sometimes elite, schools and have played an important role in the move to Papua New Guinea independence. The modern elites and their children follow a lifestyle modeled on the Europeans, and the gap between them and the rest of the population is widening. Elite schools, by passing on modern knowledge, ensure a claim to future elite status (Smith and Bray, 1988).

It has been argued that following independence or a revolutionary war, the elites are likely to be recruited from among those who were important in the struggle for independence. Thus, because of charismatic leadership, military prowess, or some other criteria, it is possible for a relatively non-educated elite to hold power. Such was the case, for example, in Jamaica, where all the political elites were more educated in 1958 than in 1954, a pattern which continued after independence. As one author observed, over time the characteristics of the elite in less-developed countries begins to approximate that in developed countries (Massialas, 1969). This pattern holds true for other elite charasteristics as well. In Turkey, Frey (1965) found that the over-representation of urban elites began to decrease over time. Overall these changes point to an increased "openness" of the political system and to some suggestion of participatory democracy, and thus political development.

However compelling the above evidence might seem, the link between education, political recruitment and political development can be highly problematic. Even in societies where an established and highly restricted educational system exists, elites sometimes are drawn from the relatively uneducated. Such was the case in traditional Ethiopia prior to World War II. Under a system of traditional elites, the ruling classes were often illiterate but were attended by scribes who constituted the educated elite. Milkias (1976) observes:

> This does not in any way imply that because they were illiterate, the kings, princes and noblemen were ignorant. On the contrary, they were men who excelled in political intrigues and maneuvers. *It does indicate, however, that education was not a prerequisite for political power, at least not in the direct exercise of it* (p. 82).[2]

Naturally in this context, the scribes had considerable influence, even though they did not occupy positions of power. For this reason, they were very much feared by the general population as having "magical powers" and being spies. It was only after the traditional system of education was taken away from the church in the 1940s that Western education began to be valued by the ruling classes. Even though Western-type schools were widely established by Haile Selassie following the Italian occupation, it appears that their intended function was to provide a core of bureaucrats to serve a strong and centralized State. This educated elite, however, had no access to political power nor did they contribute to the modernization and development of Ethiopia apart from that allowed by the Emperor. It was only during the 1970s, with the overproduction of secondary-high-school graduates and their frustration over the slow pace of modernization and their own lack of opportunities, that they began to challenge the political elite (Wagaw, 1979; Sjöström and Sjöström, 1982).

Other considerations concerning education and political recruitment must be kept in mind. If the recruitment process is such that the characteristics separating the elites from the masses is too great, the "communication gap" may lead to forms of political instability (Massialas, 1969:111). Frey (1970), on the other hand, has pointed to the importance of "release" from political power as well as recruitment to it. Recruitment is but one side of a dual phenomenon; of equal importance is the flow of personnel through the system, and the extent to which elites become "entrenched" in their elite positions. As Frey has pointed out, this has been a neglected aspect of the study of elite recruitment and education.

A recent study in Zambia is illustrative of how educated elites can block radical school reforms aimed at breaking precolonial ties. Starting in 1969 through 1982 the Zambian government made three attempts to remove British practices in the Zambian educational system, only to have the entrenched elites block these radical reforms in favor of a slower incremental change (Lungu, 1985). The Zambian example is important because it indicates the importance of elite power, even in a country where the government identifies with socialist principles. Clearly, Frey is correct in advocating more research on the role of elites in educational and development decision-making in different political contexts.

Although much has been written about the importance of education for elite recruitment and training, many questions remain unanswered. For example, little is currently known about the conservative and change aspects of this relationship, and why some recruited and trained elites turn out to change rather than maintain the system. Furthermore, it is often difficult to identify those features of elite rule which can be said to promote political development. Education can just as easily serve to maintain a totalitarian and backward political regime, as was intended by the Ethiopian Emperor, as it can influence greater participatory democracy and thus political development. There is much descriptive material but little theoretical and analytical sophistication which would enable the prediction of outcomes in any given educational and political context. As we shall argue later in this chapter, education's link with political development is problematic, and must be seen within specific social and cultural contexts.

(iii) Political Integration and the Building of National Political Consciousness

A third, and perhaps the most important, contribution which education makes to political development is in the development of the nation-state itself, by legitimating the process of center-formation and the creation of a national culture. One of the major prerequisites for the creation and stability of a nation-state is the establishment of consensus regarding political values and the conformity of the population to those values. As we have seen earlier, the process of political socialization represents a key mechanism through which it is hoped that the creation of national consensus and the formation of loyal citizens takes place. In addition, national consensus and loyalty are fostered through the use of national symbols such as the flag, a national song or anthem, a consitution, a monarch, a religious person, and other similar symbols which legitimate national physical and cultural boundaries. Formal education, or more specifically schools, have been seen by some as social institutions whose main task is to break down local or regional identities and loyalties, and replace them with national identities and loyalties. Indeed, Cohen (1970) forcefully argued that the emergence of schooling as a separate institution was itself related to this boundary-maintenance function.

There has been considerable debate among political scientists and educationists about the meaning of political integration and the importance of consensus and conformity for the stability of a political system. It has been argued, for example, that the formation of consensus is more important in new or developing nation-states where intra-societal tensions and cleavages continue to exist after political state-formation has taken place.

However, it has also been argued that nation-states which suppress conflict are basically unstable, and that the tolerance of diversity of interests and values may, in the long run, strengthen the national bond. A political system which is open to a plurality of demands "... is said to be in a state of dynamic equilibrium, or stable". Rigidity or unresponsiveness in a political system must require either highly efficient political socialization in schools (already shown to be problematic) or the use of some form of coercion, which by definition is incompatible with political development. Thus it has been said of conflict that "... regardless of the perspective from which it is approached, widespread social conflict is imperative for the vitality of democratic political systems" (Zeigler and Peak, 1971:215). Following this line of argument, then, it could be said that ethnic and cultural diversity may, in the long, run, be preferable to forced homogeneity. Where, then, does this leave the question of education's contribution to political integration and the consolidation of the nation-state?

To begin with, education serves as an important legitimating agency for establishing the legal jurisdiction of state authority, and above all for defining the criteria for membership in the State, i.e. the bestowal of citizenship. To this extent, the education system, in particular mass education, has been called a baptism "in a national history, a written language, national culture, and the mysteries of technical culture" (Meyer and Rubinson, 1975:146). The expansion of education is therefore seen as inherently political and ideological. According to Boli *et al.* (1985) the emergence of mass education can be explained historically as the incorporation of the individual into expanding rational societies and states, which both legitimate the individual and contribute to the strengthening of the nation state and its institutions.

However, there is evidence which calls into question the ability of education to serve as a viable integrating and consolidating agent. This seems to be particularly true in new developing states where the education system represents the work of outside, pre-independence interests, and to a large extent continues to promote the inequalities of those interests. An example of this can be found in Nigeria where ethnic differences have been exaggerated and aggravated through the "colonial" education system, with the result that the impact of education has been said to be disintegrative rather than integrative (Chukunta, 1978).

Historically, Nigeria from colonial times to the present has been an ethnically and culturally divided country. The Muslim northern part of the country was considered to be inhabited by "advanced communities", while the southern was seen as a land of "primitive tribes". Thus the strategy of British colonial rule was to educate the South, largely through Western-oriented missionary schools, while the North was left culturally intact with schools compatible with Muslim culture. Although the Westernization of the South produced behavior sometimes defined as reprehensible and intolerable, the Christian South came to have a larger number of educated who later formed the basis for the political elite of independent Nigeria.

> As the north was shielded from much missionary activity, it did not have the 'benefit' of widely diffused education, and its stock of educated people was severely limited. This disparity was later to become a disintegrative factor in Nigerian society as corrective measures in employment had to be taken, which drew charges of discrimination by the south (Chukunta, 1978:71).

Proselytization and the production of low- and middle-level clerical staff to service the missionary – colonial organizations were the primary goals of colonial education in the South. The long-term political effects of colonial education became only too apparent following independence with the Biafran war. In spite of overt gestures to national integration through education, there is little evidence that this has occurred. Indeed, it is ironically the education system which helps to maintain and segregate these regional differences. As Chukunta (1978) observes, it is:

> ... the increased availability of educational opportunities that makes it possible for a Nigerian to obtain all of his formal education – even up to the doctoral level – without leaving his state of origin and, thus, without interacting with a large number of other Nigerians (p. 74).

The tendency for educational access and attainment to discriminate unequally along ethnic, racial, regional or other boundaries can create obstacles to political integration, and in some cases lead to disintegration.

A slightly different example of the disintegrative effects of education can be found, though to a lesser degree, in Kenya. Also largely due to its colonial experience, Kenya displays "severe" regional imbalances in resources and services. For example, there is one medical practitioner per 84 people in Nairobi Province, but one per 2219 in Nyanza Province. Kenya's strategy for minimizing discontent resulting from these disparities has largely depended on symbols of national unity, for example the concept of *Harambee* and the role of the schools themselves. The official 1972 policy statement of schools and the attainment of national goals states that "education in Kenya must foster a sense of nationhood and promote national unity" (cited in Court and Prewitt, (1974:111)). Indeed, evidence has shown that the schools have had a homogenizing effect with respect to the national economic system, as there has been considerable consensus across regions about job aspirations and the jobs perceived as important to national development. On the other hand, there is considerable variation between regions in student political attitudes regarding government policies in the allocation of national resources. As Court and Prewitt argue: "When the number of elite roles begins to fall behind the output of qualified candidates, and individual mobility is correspondingly curtailed, collective concern with regional equality of opportunity is likely to increase" (1974:115).

This perspective is shared by Evans (1977) who concluded, following a study of secondary-school students, that increasing unemployment among educated Kenyan youth with high occupational aspirations represented a potential source of political instability. In his view, education has successfully fostered national economic goals and aspirations among youth, but the political system is not adaptable enough to undertake policies for the radical redistribution of resources. Thus Evans concludes that "... one may expect a period of intensifying social and political violence and unrest in Kenya" (1977:48).

There are other examples to suggest that the role of education in political integration and nation-building may be problematic. As education expands to include various interest groups both in and outside the political elite, the challenge to the established political system may come precisely from among the educated. There has been much writing, for example, on the causes and effects of student activism and demonstration. Theoretically, according to the model put forward above, the more educated should be the most integrated into the national culture and its political values. However, even in Asia and Africa, many students experience frustration as they perceive their paths to upward mobility blocked by leaders who are less well educated than they themselves are (Hanna, 1975).[3] Students have engaged in political protest for a variety of reasons. A study of student riots in the 1950s and 1960s concluded that the causes were government interference in universities (Buenos Aires), lack of government funding for universities (Paris), church-state relations (Barcelona), and government international relations (Tokyo) (Bereday, 1983). Although the causes varied, in each case the protests reflected student discontent, "an expression of disapproval", "a reaffirmation of (an) idealistic stance", and a demand for "intellectual independence" (p. 181). There is thus sufficient evidence to suggest that education at any level may be dysfunctional to national integration and nation-building, and that these negative effects are found in all types of societies, both developed and less developed, capitalist and socialist, and industrial and non-industrial. The dilemma which this empirical fact poses for policy-makers is a serious one, for on the one hand political development, in terms of greater political participation and national integration, cannot occur without an educated population. On the other hand, the educational process itself potentially sows the seeds of disintegration and can place obstacles to further integration, and thus to political development.

The contradictions in the education-political development linkage may be inherent in the educative process itself. The same tension, for example, is apparent in the role of education as both a promoter of social change as well as a vehicle for the reproduction of social structure. Hanf and his colleagues (1975) confront this contradiction and suggest that in some countries, a freeze on educational expansion might be a viable policy alternative. For ultimately, in their view, "as long as educational expansion exceeds the expansion of jobs, the interaction between the educational and the political system tends to destabilize the latter" (p. 84). If one considers the popular demands for education and the limits to economic expansion as constants, then the only alternative in dealing with this expansion is in the character and structure of the education system itself. In other words, education must both respond to popular aspirations and at the same time remain "profitable" both to the individual and to society. There have been a number of attempts to reform educational systems in this manner. Vocational schooling and the "ruralization" of education are two such examples which will be examined in greater detail in a later chapter. What is clear here, however, is that the tendency to regard education as a panacea for political stability and development is no longer tenable without considerable qualification. However, to regard education as inherently destabilizing would be equally erroneous.

The Impact of Political Systems on Educational Structures

We now turn our attention to the other side of the coin and examine the ways in which the political system influences the educational system. No one would deny that, at least in some countries the structure and operations of an educational system are influenced in a direct manner by many other institutions, for example the family, religious organizations, local community groups, and so on. These organizations often have an input into matters such as the curriculum, the use of various kinds of assessment and class punishment, and even the extent to which children remain or participate in the school system (Frey, 1970).

The effect of the political system on education is of concern since, as we have already shown, the potential impact of the school on politics is significant. In other words, the relationship between the two is a reciprocal one, and the extent to which political development takes place at all depends on the compatibility between the two systems.

The type of political system is important in determining the nature of its impact on the schooling process. In many ways, the differences in education between capitalist and socialist regimes, developed and less-developed countries, and rural and urban societies are due to the effects of the political systems themselves. Bronfenbrenner's (1974) investigation of childhood and schooling in the United States and the Soviet Union is a good illustration. Schooling in the United States reflects a competitive, individualist orientation which is suitable for the demands of a capitalist system (see Bowles and Gintis, 1972, 1976) whereas the collective and less individualistic competitive schooling process found in Soviet classrooms is more geared to life in a socialist system. Yet, ironically enough, at another level the schooling systems reflect in their selection processes the stratification systems of both societies. The middle- and upper-class bias of American schools is legitimated by an "IQ ideology" (Bowles and Gintis, 1972), whereas in the Soviet Union, where a similar bias seems to exist, the justification is in terms of "... the selection of those who will be able to make the greatest contribution to social and economic development" (Dobson, 1977:263).

Colonial and post-colonial political systems often exert considerable influence on educational systems such that the stratification structure of society is efficiently preserved and maintained through a stratified school system. Between the 16th and 19th centuries the education system in Peru reflected the continuing attempt by the Spanish conquerors and their descendants to impose their worldview and technology on the remnants of the Inca empire and civilization. As such the history of Peruvian society and education has been one long series of introductions of foreign ideas which only partially and imperfectly have been superimposed on earlier forms. Thus the conflicts between the indigenous Indians and the conquistador culture were preserved largely through the education system, "... an institution completely by and for the non-Indian element", and which "perpetuates a colonial and colonizing spirit" (Paulston, 1971:21). From the Spanish conquest in 1532 and through both the Colonial and then in 1825 the Republican Period, education in Peru always served the ruling elite. Furthermore, education was organized in such a way as to support an export economy, dominated in virtually every respect by foreign interests. The native population, the Indians, were given just enough education to assimilate them into the lower levels of the wage structure and thus avoid the possibility of future class conflicts (Carnoy, 1974). Even today at the top of the social hierarchy are the "Blancos", the Spanish and "other" European elite who attend elite private schools in Lima and abroad, and who often complete, or at least attend university. They are followed by the Mestizos, who are generally part Spanish, and who are found in the managerial, professional and other white-collar occupations. The Mestizos generally attend lesser private schools and almost certainly complete secondary schools, and sometimes attend university. The Cholos are largely indigenous, attend government public schools, and sometimes attend secondary schools. On the bottom are the Indians who live in rural villages or haciendas as farm laborers and herders, and who "may" attend a few years of the Indian schools of the Sierra or "jungle schools". The Peruvian education system is stratified in such a way that the division between the classes is maintained, in spite of occasional efforts at democratic reform (Paulston, 1977b:415).

Until the entry into power of the Peruvian Revolutionary Government in 1968, education was influenced by an entrenched neocolonial political system. The subsequent efforts of the Peruvian Educational Reform Commission in 1970 reflected the overt efforts of a new political system to change the educational structure.

The statement in the General Report of the Education Reform Commission clearly indicates the political role of education in implementing reform:

... as the character and orientation of any national development policy depend basically on the character and orientation of the State's efforts, the final content of any educational policy will depend on the State's general policy. Consequently, the scope and goals of all educational reform processes will revolve around two main factors, both of decidedly noneducational nature: on the one hand the national development policy and on the other the State's political orientation. Therefore, it follows that if the policy and educational activity of a revolutionary régime are to be authentic, they must faithfully reflect the essential character and nature of this régime. Considered in this light any educational reform in Peru must contribute to transformations which the government has set as the objectives of structural change. Therefore it must fit the Peruvian model of revolutionary policy (cited in Bizot, 1975:1–2).

The development strategy of the Peruvian revolutionary government incorporated economic, political and social reform through a "transfer of power" from oligarchies to the people. At the economic level this included, among other things, the nationalization of all aspects of the petroleum industry, the defense of national sovereignty and dignity, agrarian reform, worker participation in industry, and finally the move towards self-supported industrial development.

The educational reform reflected these socio-economic and ultimately political goals. In particular the educational strategy followed a program of "conscientization" (see Chapter 2), based upon participation by the individual and the community. Education was seen as a tool for forging a sense of national identity where none previously existed, for the eradication of group inequality, and for fostering regional relevance by the decentralization of educational administration. The correspondence between development needs and educational reform is clearly reflected in the following words by the Peruvian Minister for Education in 1969:

We are convinced that there is an enormous disparity between our present education system and the needs arising from the social situation in Peru. For this reason reform must be total, that is to say, there must be changes in education from its very foundations to its operative aspects, such as infrastructure, curricula, methodology and teacher training (cited in Bizot, 1975:16).

It is not our purpose here to discuss the long-term results of the Peruvian educational reform strategy or to evaluate its effectiveness. This is another issue which merits attention in its own right. However, as a case study it provides an excellent example of the close relationship between the political system and the educational system, and illustrates the direct influence of the political on the educational.

To be sure, other equally relevant examples exist. Several decades ago, Bereday and Stretch (1963) observed that "all societies indoctrinate", and that the school is a major agent in this process (p. 9). Indeed, in a comparison of political exposure in American and Soviet Union schools, Bereday and Stretch found that in grades 5 to 12, almost 46 percent of American school time was devoted to some form of political and social education, compared to 38 percent for grades 5 to 11 in Soviet schools. Apart from attempts to explain these difference in terms of effectiveness and the political needs of the two societies, namely a plural democracy versus a monolithic ideology, the authors regard their findings as indicative of the impact of political systems on educational structures.

Studies have also documented more subtle aspects of political intrusion into education. Cary (1976), for example, has shown how Marxist-Leninist ideology is reflected in the content of school subjects such as History, Geography, and Social Science. After analyzing seventeen textbooks in grades 4 through 10 of Soviet general education schools, he found that while all subject textbook curricula showed patterns of ideological intent, there was considerable variation between them; history apparently makes a major contribution in the indoctrination process, and the intensification increases between the middle and senior grades.

Another dramatic example can be found in the case of Cuba where the form and structure of education before and after the Revolution differs sharply. The transformation of Cuban education occurred in accordance with the goals of the Revolution: to increase productivity, to eliminate economic, political and cultural dependence on the United States, to eliminate the rigid class structure of capitalist Cuba, and to create a "new socialist man" who would participate in the transformation of work into a challenging and creative activity (Bowles, 1971). It is not as though the school in pre-Revolution Cuba was unaffected by the political system. In fact, when asked in Italy "Is the school in Cuba an instrument of the State?", the Cuban Minister of Education replied, "Yes, of course, just as it was before the triumph of the Revolution, and as it is in the present day in Italy" (Carnoy and Werthein, 1977:573).

Before the Revolution in 1959, Cuba had one of the highest illiteracy rates in Latin America with less than half of the primary-school-age children attending school. The condition of Cuban education under capitalism between 1925 and 1959 has been described as "educational stagnation" whereby the participation rates in primary schools actually *declined* from 63 percent in 1925 to 51 percent three decades later, and was still in decline at the time of the Revolution (Bowles, 1971).

A number of educational reforms were initiated immediately following the Revolution which reflected and supported its political and economic goals. Perhaps most impressive was the literacy program which relied on a quarter of a million *alphabetizadors*, literacy teachers which included both students and professional teachers. By the end of the campaign in the early sixties, illiteracy had fallen to 3.9 percent, the lowest in Latin America. In addition, Cuban reform emphasized the educational value of productive labor through the *escuela al campo* program ("the school to the country"), whereby urban students spent as much as twelve weeks a year in the countryside, in part to augment the agricultural supply, and in part to break down the rural-urban cultural and social differences. The integration of schooling with productive work life was further promoted by the creation of the *circulos de interes*, or "interest circles", whereby students participated in "extracurricular" activities in science and technology, such as animal science, soil chemistry, and the like. In 1973 there were 20,000 such circles with a membership of over 300,000 students. The goal of these activities was to stimulate interest and commitment to careers in applied science and technology, and also to bring together students and professionals who shared a common interest. Finally, as part of the reform objectives to break down the elitism of Cuban education, participation rates at all levels of schooling, including university and other tertiary institutions, were increased considerably between 1953 and 1973, and the educational level of the population currently reflects this. In 1953 only 6 percent had secondary schooling compared to 20 percent in 1973. For university attainment the figures were 2 and 10 percent (Carnoy and Werthein, 1977:581).

In Cuba, the eradication of the vestiges of capitalism and the creation of the "new socialist man" through education have not been without difficulty. The heavy costs of school reform at the expense of alternative development investments is one such dilemma; another is that the eradication of class divisions is not an automatic result of higher school participation rates. Furthermore, there is some evidence that interaction between the political goals and educational reform has had its impact on the political structure itself, with pressures toward "dismantling the paternalistic state apparatus that has existed since Revolution" (Carnoy and Werthein, 1977:585). Finally, Castro himself has recently suggested that educational expansion may have taken place at the expense of educational quality, and has urged new reforms which include improvements in teacher quality, raising testing standards, and even the creation of new elite schools (Richmond, 1987).

The examples from Peru, the Soviet Union and Cuba, showing the pervasive impact of political structures on the forms and processes of education could be repeated, although in somewhat less dramatic manner, in similar analyses of most societies. Other societies, however, which have attracted much attention have been The People's Republic of China and Tanzania, where contrasts between "before and after" the ascendancy of new political regimes have been most dramatic. What is most apparent in all these examples is that both the content and structure of schooling reflect the structure of political power and domination, and as such serve the programs and goals of political regimes. Yet it is important to keep in mind that the relationship between education and political mobilization is a reciprocal one, and just as the political system imposes its imprint on the educational system, so too does the reverse also occur. To some extent an educated population has the potential to collectively act independently of the political system, and thus at the very least imposes certain restraints on that system.

Conclusion

Any assessment of the contribution of education to political mobilization and development defies oversimplification and is contingent on the particular development goals of the society. Furthermore, as should be clear from our discussion in this chapter, education is only one of several social institutions which both affects and is affected by the political system. There is fairly consistent evidence that in capitalist societies committed to democratic processes, schooling *does* socialize the young into the system, instil in them greater political awareness and recruit political elites. But other social institutions such as the family and the media perform the same task, and to some extent might do it more effectively.

But schooling in capitalist societies is not unique in this regard, as similar relationships occur in socialist societies as well. It is difficult to avoid the conclusion that the political impact of schooling corresponds to the prevailing ideological goals of the political system, whether those goals be overt or covert, that is, part of the official or the hidden curriculum. Where the goals of the system are political mobilization in the capitalist sense, then it is likely that those goals will be achieved, at least in part. However, it should also be noted that to educate for political mobilization may also mean educating for political apathy and even political discontent, and may generate support for alternate structures (Barbagli and Dei, 1977).

There is no reason why the process should be any different for a revolutionary or a socialist society, where, as we have seen, schools operate in much the same way but in support of a different set of development goals. Schooling for urban or rural life, or in the context of developed or developing societies, follows much the same process; only the political goals are different.

One of the principal difficulties in research on the relationship between education and the political system has been the concentration of much of that research in capitalist societies. To this extent, the content of the findings relating to political socialization, political participation and political recruitment are mostly limited to Western capitalist systems, although the processes are clearly more general. Schooling does contribute to political mobilization and development, but the specific form and content of that mobilization and development are contingent on the ideology of the political system involved.

Notes

1. One example would be in the degree of knowledge about the government. Whereas 65 percent of the United States sample could name four or more party leaders, only 5 percent of the Mexican sample could do so. Yet in both countries education was directly related to both civics knowledge and political competence (Almond and Verba, 1965).
2. Italics have been added.
3. Cohen (1970) argues that student unrest and activism, at least as manifested in Western advanced societies such as the United States and France, was in fact a conservative boundary-maintaining effort. The protests were largely against the empirical expansion of the centralized State, not against policies which would further integrate and develop the nation-state itself. Cohen's comment illustrates this twist very well:

   Perhaps those who vigorously condemn our schools for failing in their roles in instilling patriotism and nationalism have misplaced these criticisms. Perhaps our schools have succeeded only too well (p. 147).

PART 3
Policy and Practice

6

Strategies for Educational Reforms

SOCIETY-wide reforms usually mean major changes in the economic, social, ideological and political structures of a nation. They usually take place after revolutions or violent political takeovers, but they can also happen more gradually. In this chapter we focus our attention specifically on the question of educational reforms. The term "reform" is frequently used in a vague and diffuse way and is usually defined as an attempt to change things for the better in a country or a part of a country, particularly its population. In contrast to innovations in the field of education, which seldom have economic, social, ideological or political implications, important educational reforms always involve a political process with implications for the redistribution of power and of material resources (Paulston, 1976:1). Educational reform as we define it refers to a thorough change in the structure of the educational system of a country. It means a fundamental alteration in national educational policies, causing in turn major changes in some or all of the following:

1. the national allocation of resources to the field of education;
2. the allocation of resources within the existing educational system to other levels of the system;
3. the percentage of students completing different levels of the educational system;
4. the percentage of students from different social strata or the percentage of female students that complete different levels of the educational system;
5. the aims of the curricula and their content.

Educational reforms can also take place outside the formal educational structure. Other agencies like religious, political, and economic organizations can in a formal or informal way educate varying proportions of a population. Like the educational system, these agencies can also initiate fundamental changes in their own

145

structures, thus affecting the goals and character of their educative impact on a population.

It is thus important to remember that in spite of very thorough educational reforms the formal educational systems of today do not have a monopoly on education itself. The Polish sociologist Jan Szczepanski (1980) has described what the calls "the Total Educational System" which extends from birth to post-school adult age. If we look at the secondary-school stage only, the family, youth organizations, mass-media, peer-groups, sport, tourism, libraries, cultural institutions, films, theatres, museums, medical and social services are all educative and modify the educational impact of schools. When we discuss strategies of educational reform it is important to keep in mind these constraints on the potential impact of the reform itself. However, when speaking about the future forms of educational systems Szczepanski comments:

> The idea of the 'educative society' will be an important factor in shaping the future organization of formalized schooling, and I would not be surprised to see some kind of formalized division of labor between the school systems and extra-school educational institutions (p.37).

Theories of Educational Reform

Insofar as reforms are usually the result of struggles between groups with different political, economic and ideological interests, it can often be difficult to reveal *the* theory behind any given reform. Earlier, in Chapters 1 and 2, we presented the major theories of change and development which have influenced the interpretation and shaping of social structures. Many of these theories have been fundamental in guiding educational reforms and can also be used in the evaluation of the effects of these reforms. An overview of theories related to educational reforms can be found in Paulston (1977a).

Paulston contends that by and large the unique character of any particular educational reform effort can be explained at least in part by the theory of change, or more fundamentally, the theory of education and development which prevails in a given society. In Table 6.1 we present typologies of educational reform strategies and outcomes for some of the theories of development which we have considered in earlier chapters.

We see in this attempt to relate theory to reform that there are striking differences between the theories in the character of the reform processes, as well as in the desired outcomes. For example, if the development strategy in a particular society is based on Western-

Theories	Preconditions for educational reform	Strategies for educational reform	Outcomes of educational reform
Evolutionary and neo-evolutionary	Education system no longer adequate to meet the needs of society as it moves toward a new stage of social or economic development	Promote the adaption of education to fit the new needs of society, i. e. curriculum change, increased participation and specialization	Greater adaptation and "goodness of fit" between education and other societal institutions
Modernization	Pre-modern values, attitudes and beliefs which are seen to constitute obstacles to social and technological development	Promote the expansion of a "modern" educational system, including high participation rates and standard curriculum for needs of the future direction of societal development	The creation of a population of modern individuals, able to cope with the demands of rapid social change and the needs of modern institutions
Dependency	Economic, social and cultural dependency; not only dependent institutions but dependent psychology; schools producing "lumpenbourgeoisie"	Educational and curriculum reform stressing nationalism, self-reliance, and technologies appropriate for the development needs of the society	The formation of individuals committed to national development, collective-orientation, and with technological skills appropriate to the development needs of the society
Marxist—Socialist	Education system subordinate to the needs of capitalism; the formation of docile workforce; increased awareness for change	Education for consciousness and awareness of needs for structural change; preparation for participatory democracy	The formation of the "socialist man"; elimination of educational and social privilege and creation of an egalitarian society

TABLE 6.1. *Some Theories of Development and Educational Reform.*

type modernization, then the educational reform strategy will aim at "institution building", and be based on Western institutional models and technologies. In Third World societies this means the imitation of Western schooling with appropriate levels of educational technology and educational outcomes, for example high academic achievement and the inculcation of modern attitudes, values and beliefs. Mass schooling can be looked upon as a way for society to stimulate progress through the combined efforts of capable, motivated individuals acting as effective citizens politically, economically and technically (Boli, 1989).

On the other hand, if the development strategy follows a more Marxist or neo-Marxist theory of change and development, then educational reform, particularly in a new socialist state, will more likely be directed toward the restructuring of the school system such that the social relations in the school correspond to the social relations of production in the new social structure. In effect, part of the reform measures will be directed to the elimination of privilege and elitism in the school system as well as in society. In each case, the theories underlying the reform strategies assume that educational systems are intricately linked with other dimensions of the social structure, and that reforms in education will have an impact on the society as a whole, but also must be supported by those other structures.

Some studies referred to and criticized by Simmons (1980) would contend, however, that educational systems are comparatively independent of economic, political and cultural/ideological forces. These studies argue that if the educational system of a country should be changed, it is more a matter of technicalities which determines whether the reform will be successful or not. Efficient and well-trained teachers, good school-buildings, new curricula and different kinds of technical equipment are the important prerequisites needed for a successful reform.

We do not, however, agree with this point of view. Instead, we contend that the educational system is dependent upon, but also influences, the economic, political and cultural/ideological dimensions of the society. (A further discussion of our position will be found in Chapter 9). We believe that historical studies of educational reforms are essential in the understanding of what is currently taking place in all societies where major policy changes have been initiated. In saying this we do not wish to imply that history repeats itself, but rather that it is important to study how the different structural fields interact when educational reforms are introduced and how contradictions and goal conflicts arise within and between various institutions.

In the following section, we examine in detail the long-term educational reforms in one country where they have been well documented, studied and to some extent also evaluated. In this presentation we raise questions about educational reforms today and point to similarities and differences between yesterday and today. Finally we summarize what we feel are major dimensions of educational reform, particularly for development, and suggest of both limits and possibilities of such reforms for the attainment of development objectives.

An Historical Example: Educational Reforms in Sweden 1527–1977

The decision taken in 1527 by the Swedish parliament to introduce Lutheranism as the State religion also had a fundamental impact upon education in the country. One of the goals of Protestantism was that all people, not only the priests, should be able to read and understand the gospel. This was also theoretically possible, as the New Testament had been translated into Swedish in 1526.

At the time of the Reformation almost every major town in Sweden had a school (Brandell, 1931) and a university had been founded at Uppsala in 1477. The schools had been funded by the Church, and when its economic and political power was diminished, the university was closed and many schools gradually became deserted. In 1530 the King complained to his council about the low school attendance and in a letter written in 1533 he observed that "where there used to be two or three hundred students, there are now only fifty, or perhaps none at all" (Sjöstrand, 1958:85–86). After this statement he urged people to send their children to school.

But why was it considered necessary for children to learn to read and write when many of the jobs formerly offered by the Church, where these abilities were important, were no longer available because of the decline of Church power? The goal set at the Reformation that as many as possible should be educated to read the gospel was very difficult to achieve, and as an example of educational reform the Reformation can be considered a failure. One reason was that no financial resources were allocated by the King or the Church for the schools. Nevertheless, some important results were achieved by the reformers that later on would pay dividends. The entire Bible was translated into Swedish in 1541, and the Catechism of Luther in 1537. Together with the hymn-book the Catechism formed a book of

1000 pages, not too expensive for common people to buy (Johansson, 1977:18). For future educational reforms in Sweden, it was of great importance that there was a written literature in the Swedish language.

Education of the Elite

At the first part of the 17th century Sweden was rapidly becoming one of the more important countries in Europe, with political and economic control over land all around the Baltic Sea. Economically these times were also good for Sweden, as trade was flourishing and exports were increasing. Sweden's copper production furnished 70 to 80 percent of the world's supply; iron and steel production was also significant. Several trading companies were established in Sweden, mainly by foreign families moving into the country. As Sweden was growing both economically and geographically, it was considered important by those in power to develop and centralize its administration. Consensus concerning religious matters was also regarded as being essential, as the Lutheran State Church was the means by which State decisions were carried out at the local level. It was necessary to educate civil servants both for the central and the local administration through a formal school system.

From 1623 to 1648 funds were made available by the State to establish and maintain thirteen upper secondary schools – *gymnasia* – in different parts of the country (Brandell, 1931). In the 1620s the University of Uppsala, which had been re-opened in 1566, received a donation of 350 farms from the State. In order to "Swedenize" other parts of the country new Swedish universities were opened in Turku (Åbo), Finland, and in Dorpat, Estonia. At the end of the century the number of university students in the whole country was about 2000, compared with only about 300 in Denmark. The University of Uppsala had about 1000 students.

The old aristocracy usually did not make use of the formal educational system. Instead, their children had their private tutors with whom they were sent abroad to foreign universities after the age of 12. The new upper secondary schools and the universities were thus attended by middle-class and farmers' children, as well as a few of the very poor. The schools made it possible for these children to climb the social ladder. Most became ministers or civil servants at the central or local level. Some also became administrators at the central level, and, if they reached a high position,they were usually appointed noblemen. This new elite was well rewarded for its service to the State in forms of land and the right to tax farmers in the area where they had their estates. As a result, whereas in the beginning of the 17th century more than 50 percent of the peasants owned their farms, only 30 percent did so 50 years later.

The educational reform of the 17th century was successful in building up to the administrative framework of the education system. Schools were built and the system functioned well. During this period a teacher/student ratio of about one to 20–25 was achieved. The curriculum was well defined and centrally decided upon. However, when it came to methods of teaching and the preparation of textbooks, very little was done. Frequent complaints were made by educational commissions about the poor teaching found in the schools. To help improve this situation, the Moravian philosopher and educator John Amos Comenius was asked in 1638 to come to Sweden to prepare new school texts. He finally arrived in 1642, but when he did present an outline of a textbook, most of the political administrators and bishops making up the educational commission were hesitant. The 16-year-old Queen Christina seems to have been among the few interested in his work. As Comenius belonged to a Protestant sect far more democratic than the Lutheran State Church, the bishops of the commission found him dangerous and they persuaded the group to decide to send him out of the country, accusing him of not being a "good Lutheran".

The educational reform in 17th-century Sweden was successful in many respects. Thanks to huge allocations of State money a stable educational system was established. This system was the core for producing a new Swedish elite education during several centuries. The system gave rise to social mobility, as the new elite to a great extent came from other social strata than the old feudal land-owning nobility. Quite a stable administrative system of civil servants was also established through the new elite. The inequalities that arose from the too generous awards to them had to be resolved at the end of the century by expropriations by the State. However, as representatives of the political power and together with the State Church, where only one religion and one way of thinking was permitted, the new elite used its power to oppress other groups financially and intellectually. All this was possible even if what was going on in the classroom was not entirely perfect from an educational point of view. As a sorting device the educational system of the elite-school was useful to the country.

The Literacy Reform

During the 17th, 18th and well into the 19th century the Lutheran

Church was the ideological apparatus of the Swedish State. Religious and civic education of the masses was carried out by the ministers of the Church. Attendance at religious services was in most parts of the country compulsory and, if people did not attend, various types of punishment were used, such as sitting in a certain pew in the rear of the church (Pleijel, 1970:21) or isolation from the community except one's own family. In this way it was possible for the Church to reach and control everyone in the society. However, ministers and bishops complained that most people did not follow in practice what was preached by the Church. This was the situation when the Church in a law of 1686 initiated a reform with the goal of establishing a literate population.

The main goal of the law was to make the population more orthodox in its Lutheran beliefs and practices, and the law stated that every head of household was responsible for the teaching of reading to all his family and servants. Children, farm-hands and maid-servants should "learn to read and see with their own eyes, what God bids and commands in His Holy Scripture" (Johansson, 1977:11). If the head of the household could not read himself, he had to find somebody who could do so.

The most important tool used to realize this educational reform was the Catechism of Luther, published in a new, more modern, translation in 1689. This book was used for more than 100 years in most Swedish homes. A very important part of the Catechism was a collection of words from the Scriptures called the *hustavla*, which set out the rules of the social order in society (Pleijel, 1970:30–52).

The Church law of 1686 led to the setting up of organized examination registers in all parishes of the country. The bishops instructed the clergy to conduct annual examinations of all their parish members. The examinations were held in small groups, with a few households gathered. The social pressure not to fail in this public event must have been great! Reading ability, as well as knowledge and understanding of different parts of the Catechism, was recorded in the examination registers. At the beginning of the reform, reading was recorded as *"cannot* read", "has *begun* to read", "can read *a little"*, "can read *acceptably"* and *"knows* how to read". In later years a five-point scale was used (Johansson, 1977:26, 47). To make the ministers better in transmitting the message of the Church, they were also brought together in small groups once a year by the bishop who tested them on their knowledge of a longer version of the Catechism.

What were the actual results of this reform? As most of the examination registers are still available, the development of reading ability in Sweden can be studied even quantitatively. A research group at the University of Umeå has found that the reading campaign was a success, although it took about sixty years for the majority of the population to become literate. In the early stages, it was only the upper classes who knew how to read. Among the farmers, men learned to read before the women, although when women did learn, they usually achieved better results than men, probably because they also taught the children how to read (Johansson, 1977). Even though the program was successful, literacy spread slowly. Over and above the examinations, other social pressures and controls were used. For example, young people who wanted to marry but had not learned how to read, had to postpone their marriage until they were able to do so. Admission to Holy Communion was also made contingent on the ability to read.

While the goal of making people literate was accomplished almost without formal instruction, it was subsequently much more difficult for the State and the Church to maintain complete control over the use of literacy, and particularly to ensure that the whole population remained "good" Lutherans.

From the point of view of the Church and the State there was a risk taken in teaching everyone how to read. Some began reading books that were banned, and also to read those books to others. In 1726 a new law was passed stating that it was forbidden to read religious books to people outside the family. According to the *hustavla*, the rules of the social order in society, the clergyman was the only one who had the right to read and preach to people outside his own family. The penalties for breaking this law were fines for the first conviction, very high fines or jail for the second, and for the third the culprit was sent out of the country (Pleijel, 1935:307). Those attending forbidden religious meetings at which religious books were read, were also fined. The aim of this law to preserve the purity of the Lutheran Orthodox religion and to reserve the transmission of religious and civic ideology to the State Church.

However, in spite of the risk of punishment, people gathered to read religious books and laymen continued both to read and preach. Some were fined, and from the protocols of the courts it can be seen that at the beginning most of the law-breakers were found among the well-educated, but as the ability to read spread to lower social strata, these people also began to break the law.

The ideological message transmitted by most of the forbidden literature was that of the Pietistic movement. For the Pietists, religion was seen as a personal matter between an individual and his God, something that could not be "administered" by a State Church. The individual was responsible for his own salvation, and man was made to feel free in relation to the Church as an institution. Only the individual, not the minister of the Church, was responsible for the salvation of his own soul. The Pietistic movement, which originated in Germany, was perceived as a great threat to the established order. The State tried to control the printing and importation of books, but nothing helped. Sometimes young ministers joined Pietistic movements. When this was found out, they were usually sent away to another parish. However, instead of dying, the new ideas spread.

In the beginning of the 19th century a rapid population growth, combined with land-reform, produced a landless proletariat (Winberg, 1975). Under the land-reform, previously common grazing land was divided up for cultivation, with the result that the subsistence economy was partly broken. Formerly, cheese and butter produced on this land were the only things sold by the farmers, but now as England established her manufacturing industries and began to keep sheep where grain had formerly been grown, Swedish farmers could sell grain to England. Farmers with large holdings suddenly had money to buy more land from the small landholders. In this way a landless proletariat emerged, whose members were useful as farm hands on the bigger farms in the planting and harvesting season but who had to find work elsewhere and in other ways when the farming season was over. To some extent they could be used in the growing industries. The new proletariat owned no land, *was literate*, and began to challenge the authoritarian structure of the society as transmitted by the State Church. As the parents had to be away from the home during long working hours, religious education and other kinds of upbringing in the home decreased. The members of the new proletariat were likely to be more receptive to new ideas other than those preached by the ministers.

Although it was still forbidden to read other than the authorized books, in some parts of the country a large percentage of the population was influenced by a new Evangelical movement of Pietistic origins. These people were called "readers", as they read and discussed the Bible and other books together. In his novel *The Emigrants* the Swedish writer Wilhelm Moberg describes how groups of this kind, when punished, sold all their belongings and left for the United States. There are examples of parishes where a high percentage of the population left in this manner.

In 1830 in Paris, students and the new middle class revolted against an authoritarian regime where King Charles X and the government had tried to re-establish the power of the nobility and the Church. Radical movements arose in many European countries, and in Sweden a liberal opposition formed which worked against the conservative government. The liberals in Sweden consisted of a new class of merchants, owners of industry, and some noblemen who abolished the feudal system on their estates and started more capitalistic ones, with wage workers.

The growing proletariat was a problem, and at parliamentary sessions in the 1830s possible solutions to the problem of the poor were discussed (Fredriksson, 1942:219). One idea was to establish a formal educational institution, a *Folkskola* (elementary school), for the children of the masses. Charity schools had already been established in some cities to keep vagrant children off the streets (Sandin, 1986:267). The debate concerning these proposed elementary schools lasted over several parliamentary sessions. Of the four estates making up parliament, the liberal owners of industry and the merchants were in favor of the idea, while most of the conservative noblemen were opposed to it. The cleargy was split in two groups: the conservative was against the proposed educational system, while a more liberal group wanted it. This latter group could see the reform as an opportunity for the Church to regain its power. The farmers understood that they would be the ones to pay for the reform, and when one of their proposals of a state-financed elementary-school system was abolished, many of them were hesitant.

In 1839 the liberal-leaning Crown Prince Oscar anonymously published an article in a Stockholm newspaper, where he expressed the view that the new elementary school would be valuable for the whole nation, both for the rich and the poor. He dismissed the conservative view and instead argued that "... in America the rich people view this (compulsory education) as the only way to keep their wealth against the vulgar demands of the masses". He also suggested a blueprint of how the new school system should be organized. After long discussions at the parliamentary sessions of 1840 and 1841 a bill was enacted in 1842 that every parish within five years should establish at least one school, that every school should have a qualified teacher, and that the head of every school board should be the parish minister (Fredriksson, 1942:312–317).

The Elementary School Reform

In a time of great economic change the four estates making up parliament had decided upon an educational reform mainly intended to improve the situation of the groups in society not represented in parliament. It was compulsory for each parish to build and maintain a school, although attendance was not compulsory. However, education could still be carried out within the framework of the family. As the teaching of reading had been a task for the family since the late 17th century, it was assumed that children would know how to read when entering school. In this way the informal and formal educational systems were tied together. The Church saw the formal school system as an opportunity to strengthen its power: Catechism was the most important subject, while reading and writing were also compulsory. It is important to note that through the informal system writing was not learned, and therefore it was through the formal elementary-school system that the ability to write developed in Sweden. Mathematics was a compulsory subject for boys, but girls could also learn if they wanted.

As school registers and diaries were kept in many parishes, school attendance during this period can be studied. Gerger and Hoppe (1980), for example, have studied attendance in a small and very poor parish in southern Sweden. They show that school attendance among children living far from the school or belonging to the landless or the poor was very low in contrast to the children of the fairly well-to-do farmers living close to the school. As the distances to the school were great, the parish was divided into different districts between which the teacher moved. In this way the school-days per year offered to each child were around 50. Children of the wealthy classes usually had their own tutor or went to private schools leading directly to elite institutions.

To organize a formal educational system proved to be a daunting task. However, the administrative framework of the school reform was not so difficult to establish; schools were built, and teachers were trained and allocated to these schools. Even if the children of the proletariat did not attend to the extent anticipated, the number of students coming to school often was quite high. In some schools there could be more than sixty students of different ages in the same class. After about 10 years school attendance began to decrease. Some visitors to schools described the classroom situation as being very poor, and many children found it difficult to learn anything in school.

The insufficiencies of the new school system soon called for changes. Preparatory schools were established, and school inspectors who were to visit and evaluate the quality of instruction were appointed. Types of complaints from inspectors could be as follows: the schools needed repair, non-literate children were not to be taught with the literate, irregular school attendance was common, Bibles instead of proper reading books were being used, and more than one teacher was needed (Gerger and Hoppe, 1980:50).

Schoolbooks were centrally produced. A new translation of the

Catechism with a more modern language was published in 1878. Readers, including topics from different subjects like history, geography, and the natural sciences, were published. Also books developed for writing and spelling were printed. Most books published during this era were nationalistic and had a religious overtone. Around 1880 school attendance was made compulsory for 6 years beginning at the age of 7.

The primary schools were administered by the Church. The school boards were dominated by the rich and very seldom were members of the poor represented (Gerger and Hoppe, 1980:46). If the Church as a representative of the State thought it would secure its power through the new school system, it was mistaken. Instead, a new institution arose that competed with the Church. The schoolmaster enjoyed high prestige in the local community and was often active and a leader of organizations, such as the Evangelical free cruches, the teetotaller movements like the International Order of Good-templars, and liberal-thinking political parties. These organizations were growing very rapidly in the later part of the 19th century and were also spreading a new and more democratic ideology, not least through books and periodicals. As an example, the Evangelical movement *(Evangeliska fosterlandsstiftelsen)* in a five-year period from 1856 to 1860 had sold 1 1/2 million books at a time when the whole population was only 3.3 million (Isling, 1980:138–139, 178). The goals of the new organizations were different from the leading ideology of the State and the Church. Frequently conflicts arose between the schoolmaster and the religious and political leadership. With new and more democratic community laws on local government in the 1860s the teachers often were elected to the governing bodies. They were usually much more liberal in their thinking than the representatives from the Church and the establishment. When the social democrats appeared, teachers were interested in their ideas. One of the liberals was Fridtjuv Berg, who proposed a comprehensive six year elementary school for all children. These ideas were considered very dangerous, and even the elementary teachers' union founded in 1880 banned the spread of the pamphlet at their general meeting in 1883. It took between 70 and 80 years for this idea to become acceptable at a time during which the country changed from a comparatively backward agricultural society to an industrial nation. During this period both the elementary and the elite system changed. However, it was not until the 1950s that the first comprehensive schools appeared, and in 1962 a 9-year comprehensive school was introduced in the whole country.

**Economic, Political and Ideological Background to
the Comprehensive School Reform**

At the end of the 19th century, Swedish industry began to expand
rapidly. In 1870 it employed 15 percent of the labor force, and in 1900
28 percent. When the world-wide depression hit Sweden in the early
1930s, 35 percent of the work force was found in industry. After
World War II there was a new expansion and by 1950 43 percent were
employed in industrial work, the figure reaching 45 percent in the
1960s. While more than 70 percent were occupied in agriculture in
1870, only 14 percent remained on the farms in 1960, and by 1978 this
figure was down to 5 percent. Since the 1950s there has been a rapid
growth in the tertiary sector. By 1978 a majority of the labor force
(58 percent) was employed in the provision of services. The proportion
of people employed in industry had diminished to 37 percent by the
end of the 1970s. Employment in trade and other private services
increased modestly during the 1970s, while employment in the public
sector grew rapidly (National Central Bureau of Statistics, 1979).

In 1870 Sweden was a comparatively poor European country, while
a century later it was among the richest in the Western world. The
Swedish economist Assar Lindbeck (1974) describes the economic
development in the following way:

> Growth and industrialization in Sweden during the last one
> hundred years is an example of successful export-led or
> 'export–based' growth in the context of a private enterprise
> economy with a remarkable innovative capacity of private
> entrepreneurs and with a rather 'liberal', market-oriented
> economic policy – combined with an elaborate, publicly
> operated infra-structure in transportation, education, health,
> etc. – and later on a rather comprehensive social security system
> (p. 7).

The move from an agricultural to an industrial and then to a
postindustrial society also meant a change from rural to urban life. In
1980, 87 percent of the Swedish population lived in urban areas
(World Bank, 1980b).

With the growth of the economy the shortage of workers became
severe, especially in industry. One solution was to employ women for
jobs that previously had been male-dominated. Women were
employed in industries as truck drivers, crane operators, sprayers,
carpenters, painters, inspectors, and outside the industries they were
found, for example, as bus and taxi drivers. However, this was not
enough to fill workforce needs, and a large number of immigrants
were brought in.

Traditionally, there has been, throughout history, a significant migration of people of Finnish origin to Sweden. According to the balance of the labor market in the two countries the number of Finns working in Sweden has fluctuated. By 1980 the number was about 300,000. In the 1960s, manpower was brought in especially from the Mediterranean countries. Sweden has absorbed 50,000 Yugoslavs, 20,000 Greeks, 17,000 Turks and 10,000 Italians. Thousands of immigrants have come from Spain, North America, and the Middle East.

Refugees have also come from different countries in successive waves; 30,000 have come from the Baltic states, 30,000 from Poland and other East European countries, and 10,000 have come from Chile or other Latin American countries. By 1980, Sweden, out of a population of 8.5 million, had about 425,000 foreign nationals and 340,000 who had recently attained their Swedish citizenship. The children of immigrants in 1980 numbered 350,000 and were found in most schools and classes (Widgren, 1980).

As Sweden was transformed from an impoverished agrarian to an industrialized community, the political structure also gradually shifted. Important to the country was also the ability to keep out of wars, and by 1980 Sweden could look back on almost 170 years of continuous peace. In 1866 a new bicameral parliament replaced a *riksdag* of four estates. Suffrage remained highly restricted until after World War I, when in 1918 male and female suffrage was adopted for both chambers. It was the Social Democratic Party and the Liberals who were winning the struggle against the Conservatives at the same time as the fall of the German Empire. During the depression the Social Democrats took power in 1932 and were able to stay in government as the leading party until 1976. During this period of reformist policy the Swedish model of "labor peace" became famous, and the change of the country to a welfare society took place. During the whole period of Social Democratic government there were no great changes in ownership of industry, of which approximately 95 percent is still in private hands.

Before the economic boom of the 1960s the Swedish population was homogeneous in matters of language, ethnic factors and Protestant religious affiliation. Between 1880 and 1920 the popular movements, like the "free churches", the teetotallers' organizations, the workers' unions, and the producers' and consumers' cooperatives, grew rapidly and their participants were trained in democracy in their many small units that were spread all over the country. The democratic ideology of these organizations has been of paramount importance. In 1920 the free churches had 300,000 members. In 1910 the teetotallers reached a peak of 350,000 and in 1920 the unions had 400,000 and that number has been continuously growing (Isling, 1980:177).

Founded in 1889, the Social Democratic Party very soon moderated its original Marxist views and worked for pragmatic rather than doctrinaire ends in economic development (Paulston, 1968:9). Its ideology to maximize both equality and efficiency was of great importance, especially after World War II. Being able to stay in power alone or in coalition with other parties for more than 40 years, the Social Democrats could place their party members in many important positions in the growing bureaucracy.

The radical changes in the structure of Swedish society originating from changes in methods and conditions of production did not take place without conflicts. However, changes have mainly occurred through compromises between the owners of the industries, the unions and the pragmatic technocrats of the growth-conscious bureaucracy (Heidenheimer, 1978:3). As the society changed, so did the formal educational system.

The Merging of the Elementary and the Elite School Systems

After World War II most interest groups in Swedish society agreed that changes in the formal educational system were called for. In some cities the compulsory 6-year elementary school had already been prolonged to 7 or 8 years. After what had happened in Central and Southern Europe during the war it was also considered to be important that the school should produce democratic individuals. A blueprint for the development of the future Swedish school system was submitted in 1948 by the School Commission, a committee established in 1946. Its first chairman was the Minister of Education, Tage Erlander, who from October 1946 was Prime Minister of the country for a period of 23 years. The proposal was for a compulsory 9-year comprehensive school that would replace all schools catering to students from 7 to 16 years of age (SOU, 1948:27).

In 1950 a 10-year program of experimentation was enacted by parliament (Marklund, 1980a, 1980b). According to the blueprint every school was to be an "experimental" school and every teacher should try his own ways to improve pedagogical methods. During the first year of the experiment fourteen communities took part, while 10 years later the number increased to 367. Almost half of all students in the relevant age groups also participated (Isling, 1974:101). Some groups in the society, like the Secondary School Teachers'

Organization (LR), were opposed to the undifferentiated secondary school. The teachers of the elementary school, however, favored the new comprehensive school, as did the workers' union (LO) and the white-collar federation (TCO).

Considerable research has been directed to an evaluation of the consequences. In one such study by Svensson (1962), published just before parliament voted for a 9-year comprehensive school, it was shown that students who were in undifferentiated classes in the later grades had achievement levels the same as students who were in the selective academic school. The study took advantage of a unique situation, where the city of Stockholm was divided into two sectors. In the southern part of the city no separation of students took place during the first six grades and in some districts not until the ninth grade. In the northern sector the dual system was retained and there the students transferred to the selective elite schools after the fourth grade. Social background and initial ability, measured by tests and school marks, were kept under control in the 5-year follow-up (Husén, 1978).

Curriculum studies surveying the knowledge and skills required of the individual in Swedish and mathematics, both as holder of an occupation and as a citizen, were performed by Dahllöf (1960). Similar studies were conducted for physics, chemistry and in the social sciences.

Already when the 10-year program of experimentation was decided upon many resources were made available. One reason why more and more communities decided to join the experimental program was that favorable loans were made possible for school buildings, the only condition being that State norms were followed. The teacher salaries were also provided by the State.

All over the country new large schools of good quality were built. The idea was that technical facilities and program options would be better in bigger schools, and for this reason many small village schools were closed. After municipality amalgamations the students were brought by bus or taxi to the centrally located schools. The enlarged municipalities were intended to have the population as well as the financial resources to maintain bigger schools.

A comprehensive school bureaucracy grew up, both at the national and the local level. New central curricula were defined and developed. Almost all textbooks had to be revised, and teacher training was provided in new Schools of Education. The optimism was great, and the big problem of "individualization within the framework of the class" would be solved by using new teaching facilities and materials tested and developed through research and development projects (Husén, 1986).

Soon teaching practices in the new schools were very similar to those before the reform. Abstract verbalism dominated, and to a large extent the parents decided to let their children follow academic tracks. Students with educated parents completed school with better grades and achievement than their less advantaged counterparts. However, in international comparisons Sweden has the highest national homogeneity of schools, when student achievement is used as a criterion (Passow *et al.*, 1976; Marklund, 1980).

On the whole, the school reform was successful in producing new buildings and bureaucracies. The standard of the new textbooks was high, but the school reform had great difficulties in creating changes in the classroom. On the whole, the new system worked in a manner similar to the old, and the optimistic view of formal education as an agent to a more equal society was not fulfilled.

In an evaluation of the school system it was found that the biggest problem at the end of the comprehensive school was the negative attitudes of the students against the school (Comber and Keeves, 1973:107; Husén *et al.*, 1973:162). In spite of this, an increasing percentage of any relevant cohort continually sought entry to the *gymnasium,* and thus for more education. Traditionally, the *gymnasium* had been a school leading to university studies and civil service jobs. For centuries only a few percent of an age group passed through this kind of school. By 1945, 8 percent of the relevant cohort attended the *gymnasium*. Technical and vocational schools were not included in this figure. In the late 1950s to the early 1970s the demand for non-compulsory secondary education increased rapidly. Starting in the 1971 academic year, all schools for the age range 16 through 19 were merged. The new school inherited the traditional prestigious name *gymnasium/gymnasieskola,* but was no longer as highly selective. At the end of the 1970s about 90 percent of all 16-year-olds continued to this school. The twenty-one programs are divided between vocational and academic ones. Students in vocational and academic lines can have up to 12 hours a week together. However, in most of the classes they are taught with students enrolled in their own program. In order to remove the distinction between "academic" and "non-academic" education it was legislated in 1972 that students from the "vocational" 2-year lines, in some cases after supplementary studies in Swedish and English, should be eligible for university admission. At the same time, it was decided that work experience along with marks obtained in the *gymnasium* could be used for admission to higher education. Today, adults of 25 years of age, with at least 4 years of work experience, can enter institutions of higher education, which, especially at the undergraduate level, tend to be more vocationally-oriented and specialize in courses useful for future occupations (Marklund and Bergendal, 1979:37). In the late 1980s however, there has been a trend to strengthen the situation of young students. Examples of such policy measures are: quotas for young students, less value for work experience, and introduction of entrance examination tests for students from municipal adult education programs (Abrahamsson, 1988).

The reform of tertiary education enacted in 1977, according to recommendations by the Educational Commission of 1968 (U68), can be seen as a continuation of the intentions behind the changes at the *gymnasium* level. Education has been looked upon as a lever of social improvement for both the individual and the society as a whole. The owners of enterprises, the unions and not least the Social Democrats (the political party in power during the reform period) believed that the reforms would benefit their own interests. However, the three groups were very different. The industrial concerns found the young, educated generation to be more critical and pretentious than earlier generations. Young people were not willing to take the hard, dirty, or simple jobs and they did not like to work on assembly lines. Whether the school reforms were one of the causes of the fall of the Social Democrats in 1976 has also been discussed. In the OECD review of educational reforms in Sweden (OECD, 1981a) it is stated: "There are, in fact, signs of some alienation of the young from the Social Democratic Party which was in power between 1934 and 1976; they tend to identify it with big industry, with life in the city, with high taxes and bureaucracy" (p. 18). This reaction by the young educated is consistent with our observations in the previous chapter that political systems cannot completely control the output of schools and other educational institutions.

However, several goals of the reforms at the tertiary level have been achieved; 38 percent of the relevant age group now enter higher education (World Bank, 1985). New universities and university branches have been founded with the result that a higher percentage of students from the areas where these new institutions are situated go on to higher education. They also recruit substantially higher proportions of students with working-class backgrounds (OECD, 1981a:29). However, considerable social-class differences between social groups in the choice of secondary and higher education remain (OECD, 1981a; Reuterberg and Svensson, 1983).

Age and sex distributions have changed considerably in higher education. In the middle 1970s, 39 percent of those registering for higher education were above 25 years of age compared with 10 percent a decade earlier (OECD, 1981a:31) and in the mid 1980s more than 50 percent of the university students were older than 25 (Statistics Sweden, 1986). Extensive programs for changing traditional sex roles through education have been drawn up by the authorities. Although more girls enter higher education today than they did previously, traditional ideas about male- and female-dominated subjects and occupations have been difficult to change.

All post-secondary education is, at the beginning of the 1980s, part of a unitary system administered through two central administrative agencies. An extensive bureaucracy has been built up both at the central and local levels. Researchers have complained that a model of governance and administration applied uniformly to all institutions of higher education is not applicable to research or graduate studies (Husén, 1976:419; Segerstedt, 1974). It is argued that research needs more substantial autonomy than can be found in a bureaucratic system, an argument, which is not new, but through the centuries saved the Swedish universities from rigid State control (Svensson, 1987).

As we have seen in this chapter, the educational reforms in Sweden have a long history. What can be learned from the Swedish experience which could be applied to other societies contemplating similar reform measures?

1. The establishment of the elite-School in the 17th century was of great importance for the country. In many respects this was a successful enterprise with significance for several centuries. Inequalities are easily created through an elite educational system even if such a system can give rise to some social mobility.

2. The Literacy Reform during the 17th century is significant as it was successfully instrumented without school-buildings and almost without formal instruction. The importance of books and literature which are easy for everyone to read was apparent in this example. Books were available in practically every home. The reform would not have been a success if the State Church had not been well organized and had not had powerful sanctions. It is important to remember that it took about 70 years for the whole population to become literate.

3. It took a period of approximately 50 years for the Elementary School Reform to reach all Swedish children. The intention was that the school would help the children of the poor, but the fairly well-to-do were the ones who benefited most.

4. Through the centuries it has been fairly easy to establish new administrative systems, to build schools, to recruit teachers and to

make curricula decisions. To change what happens in the classroom has proven to be much more difficult.

From the mid-1950s to the present day, Sweden has been in the forefront of educational reform. Few countries have been able to change their school systems in such a systematic and planned way as has Sweden. Many of the goals set up by the decision-makers have been achieved; others have been much more difficult to achieve.

The State Church, and later also other important organizations within the country, have looked upon the formal educational system as an agent to establish their own power. Over the centuries this has been difficult. One reason for this is that many forces of economic, political and ideological origin influence the educational system.

Educational Reform and Societal Development: some General Observations

The case of Sweden presented here provides useful guidelines for understanding further the possibilities and limits of educational reform as a means of promoting the social and economic development of a society. The history of Swedish education does not consist of one, but rather many educational reforms (see Table 6.1). The literacy campaign was motivated primarily by religious considerations, and can in many respects be interpreted within the context of the neo-evolutionary model. In the 19th century, the move toward compulsory education was based largely on a desire to mobilize Sweden's human resources, and thus stemmed from an implicit modernization theory. Finally, the 20th-century move toward comprehensive schooling apparently reflects the desire, still current in Sweden, to utilize educational reform as one of the means to eliminate inequality in Swedish society. Although inspired by Social Democratic policies, the underlying theoretical assumptions approximate those found in the Marxist-Socialist model. In each case of educational reform, the implementation of policies resulted in unforeseen consequences – as in the example of the literacy movement and the ability to read "forbidden books" – which either had to be endured or used as a basis for further educational change. Furthermore, the effects of reforms cannot occur overnight, but do take time. Nevertheless it seems apparent that throughout the period of educational development there existed among the decision-makers a deep conviction that education represented a key to bringing about other changes in society. While we do not argue that the rapid industrialization of Swedish society in the late 19th and early 20th centuries was due entirely to education, it would be reckless to dismiss the possibility of significant effect altogether.

The limits of educational reform originate from the inter-relationships between education and other dimensions of the social system. Even to the extent that some reform measures may originate among groups which are not part of the ruling-class structure, because of these interrelationships the reforms will inevitably be changed into a product acceptable to those in power (Carnoy, 1975a:366). Thus education alone probably cannot change society, or even modernize it, a point we made in Chapter 4. However, combined with other reforms in other sectors of society, it can make a significant contribution to societal development. In Sweden, the success of educational reform was due, in large part, to the overall policies of the Swedish Parliament and Church, which not only endeavored to reform education, but other sectors of society as well.

There is a lesson here for those concerned with development in the Third World. Perhaps part of the disillusionment with education as a viable development strategy which began to emerge in the early 1970s may have been due to the simple fact that education *alone* was expected to provide the development impetus. However, it would be equally erroneous for any development strategy to ignore education, for in so doing not only would a major potential support for development be lost, but the non-reformed educational system would then become a force working against reform in other sectors. Speaking about the importance of schooling as a source of restructuring American society, Carnoy states:

> Nevertheless, we think it is a mistake to imply... that we should ignore schooling in restructuring society. If we begin to change income distribution through political action, we must also change the distribution of schooling, and especially its hierarchical structure and the way it transmits knowledge, or else we will not change one of the important factors contributing to the old structure of income (Carnoy, 1975a:370).

Educational reforms, when linked with reforms in other sectors of society as part of a consistent and compatible development strategy, represent a potentially powerful force for changing society in a desired direction. The case of Sweden clearly illlystrates this.

7

Women, Education and Development

Now that we have examined aspects of educational reform and national development, we will turn our attention to one of the neglected development policy areas: the inequality between girls and boys, and women and men. In all three dimensions, the economy, modernization and quality of life, and political participation and mobilization, women lag far behind men in many countries of the world. Since all three dimensions have been shown to be crucial for the development process, it follows that the exclusion of women represents a serious violation of justice and human rights, and a major loss of potential human resures for any society which places high priority on improving the quality of its population and making more equal the distribution of its standard of living.

The indicators available show the dramatic differences between women and men throughout the world. Some of these were summarized in the Nairobi Women's Conference in 1985 and which closed the United Nations Decade for Women (Convergence, 1986). Women form a third of the world's official labor force, but are more vulnerable to unemployment than men. In the agricultural sector, women grow almost half the world's food, but own hardly any land. In many countries women cannot obtain loans or own property, and often are not included in agricultural development projects. At the same time, women perform most of the world's domestic work, which means that many women work a double day. Women provide more health care than all health services combined, yet outnumber men among the world's illiterates, and in almost all countries of the world they have less formal education than men. Even in industrialized countries, women continue to be excluded from equal political participation. They have gained voting rights in several countries only within the past two decades, but remain under-represented among political leaders and in elected political assemblies. Economically, socially and politically, women exercise less control and power than men, and in many countries are actively discriminated against.

In this chapter we identify women as a group which has hitherto

167

been invisible in nation-building efforts and examine the extent to which they compare with men on a range of development indicators, including education. After briefly discussing the major social theories of gender roles, we will examine the educational participation and performance of women and men, and their unique socialization experiences in educational settings. We will then link the educational disparities between women and men in economic, social and political spheres, followed by a discussion of contradictions, tensions and constraints on women as participants in the development process, and suggest possible policy strategies to overcome them.

Social Theories of Gender Inequalities

One of the characteristics of the modern world is the better understanding of the relative importance of biological and social factors in explaining variations in gender roles, and the disparities in participation and attainments in various sectors of society. No one denies that there are fundamental biological differences between women and men. Clearly women's biological role in the reproduction of children places constraints on their ability to participate fully in other activities at certain stages of their lives. However, whether these biological differences are related to metabolic differences which influence other behaviors and abilities is more controversial. If women are perceived to be weaker, more passive, and more emotionally oriented than men, it is due to cultural rather than biological differences. Ultimately it is the ways that women and men are defined – the attitudes, values and beliefs about the biological differences – that determines variations in their roles in societies.

There is no single social explanation for the consistent economic, social and political disparities between women and men across societies. During the last 20 years a number of theories have emerged, many in feminist and sociological writings, which have attempted to link gender inequality with wider social structures and characteristics.

Acker (1984) divides the major social theories of gender inequality into two categories, the fundamental and the implementary. The first is concerned with explaining why women are subordinate to men, while the second focuses upon the processes and practices which maintain this subordination. Fundamental approaches include the functionalist, Marxist-feminist and radical-feminist approaches.

The functionalists argue that gender roles are a consequence of the relationship between biological differences and the needs of an increasingly differentiated society. Thus functionalists attribute the sexual division of labor to society's needs to organize and maintain the production and distribution of resources, as well as to ensure loyalty to social rules and norms. As we described in Chapter 1, functionalists focus an social order and consensus, and therefore argue that differentiated and unequal gender roles serve to maintain an integrated orderly society through consensus.

The Marxist-feminists attribute the subordination of women to the needs of capitalism to have both a domestic labor force and a "reserve army of labor" which will further the interests of the capitalist class. Thus women reproduce the labor force biologically (childbearing) and socially (childrearing), they act as consumers for the products of capitalism, and they serve as a source of psychological and material comfort for male workers in the capitalist enterprise. Women's subordinate social position is due to the class conflict and oppression which is generally characteristic of a capitalist economy.

The radical feminists differ from the Marxist argument, in that instead of capitalism, patriarchy is seen as the major source of women's subordination. Patriarchy assumes the superiority of men, and it pervades all aspects of the cultural and institutional life of society. Thus the radical feminists maintain that throughout history men have struggled to exercise power over women. Instead of economic oppression, the radical feminists argue that patriarchy represents an enduring form of oppression which is found not only in capitalist societies, but all other economic systems, including the socialist, and across all social groups and classes. The socialist feminists combine the Marxist and radical view, in that they include both capitalism and patriarchy as the source of gender inequality.

The implementary approaches concentrate on the social processes which explain how women come to attain their subordinate positions. Rather than structures, implementary approaches focus on the socialization processes whereby women acquire attributes which make them unsuitable or inappropriate for certain social positions and economic activities in society. Thus these approaches are concerned with the ways that masculinity and femininity are constructed and reconstructed throughout a person's lifetime. Girls are socialized into traditional personality traits of their societies, which in turn restrict their choices and options. Within this framework the way girls and boys are raised in the home, taught in the school, and encounter wider society become important for explaining gender inequalities throughout the life course.

A theoretical perspective which extends the analysis for understanding gender inequalities in education and development, and which may be useful for developing policies and strategies to eradicate this inequality includes the role of the State. For ultimately, the State determines which collective benefits and services should be made available to individuals and groups (Stromqvist, 1987).

In the functionalist ("liberal feminist") approach, the State is seen as responsive to pressures from interest groups, and through various measures, for example education, can institute reforms designed to bring about greater gender equality. The greatest source of criticism of this view is that in spite of reforms in many societies, there has been an underestimation of the power of structures and oppositional interest groups which have inhibited progress in this respect.

The Marxist feminists argue that the class structure itself is responsible for women's inequality, and that short of a radical restructuring of the economy, the most that can be expected from the Capitalist State is lip-service to greater equality but passive tolerance to the continued existence of gender inequality. Marxist feminists are confident that in the new Socialist State, gender inequality will be eradicated.

A more complex view is held by the radical and socialist feminists who agree that the State plays a role in the enforcement of male patriarchy. For those in these approaches, even socialist states support gender inequalities, for it is not enough to eradicate capitalism to bring about equality. Patriarchy must also be abolished.

Stromqvist (1987) links women's inequality to the role of the State in the control and production of knowledge. She sees the control and production of knowledge as related to the family. According to her argument, because women are seen as responsible for the moral upbringing of children, the State, through its explicit and implicit policy behavior, ensures that women will be imbued with a commitment to the traditional social and sexual division of labor. It will not support educational policies that will question the family, or the existence of gender differences in society.

Conversely, the education of men as breadwinners is continually favored. Each of these perspective highlights aspects of gender inequality which have empirical substance, at least in some cultures and some societies. However, each has weaknesses which are worth noting. The functionalist position, for example, fails to take into account the dysfunctions to society of gender inequality, particularly through the wastage of talent and the inherent conflict produced by some forms of gender inequality which may result in social instability rather than stability and integration. The Marxist-feminist position does not, and cannot address the pervasiveness of gender inequality in non-capitalist societies, whether traditional or modern. The radical feminist position is on firmer ground in that patriarchy, its central explanatory factor, is possible in all cultures and societies. However the origins and maintenance of patriarchy are assumed and not well explained, and the radical feminists fail to acknowledge ways in which women sometimes possess power over men, even in overtly patriarchial societies.

Those who adopt one of the implementary approaches do focus on the mechanisms of construction and reconstruction of gender inequality, but tend to neglect the origins of, and exceptions to, these processes. In general, none of the dominant theoretical approaches takes into account various forms of resistance to gender inequality and male dominance, or forms of female power in otherwise male-dominated societies. Nevertheless, they have in common the recognition of male dominance in most societies, and represent efforts to theoretically explain the apparent pervasiveness of gender inequality in all societies.

One important factor of these perspectives for a discussion of the implications of gender inequality in education and development strategies is that they, all at least implicitly, identify the State as a key institution in explanations for the source of gender inequality. If this is the case, then the consequences of these theories is that either the State initiates programs designed to bring about greater gender equality, or the State itself must be changed. This is a question to which we return at the end of this chapter.

Educational Inequalities

There are a number of levels at which one can approach the question of educational inequality between women and men. The most basic concerns access, or what some call equality of educational opportunity. Access understood in this way refers to both the opportunity to participate in education and the availability of facilities which in many countries are not distributed equally, for example in the different facilities available in rural and urban areas. The second level of inequality is in participation, or the extent to which individuals and groups enrol in and attend formal educational activities. The distinction is important, because enrolment and retention figures, which already reveal group variation in most countries, are not necessarily good indicators of actual attendance and attainments in schools or classes. For example in many parts of the world attendance is affected by the planting and harvesting of crops.

A third level of educational inequality is in treatment and academic performance. We know that not all students or groups of students are treated equally by teachers and administrators. Streaming, curriculum tracks, attention-giving, and stereotyping are all forms of differential treatment received by students. These treatments are one factor which lead to variations in academic performance. Finally, inequalities occur with respect to the effects of education on adult life. It can happen that the value of education for the attainment of jobs, income, political power and social networks may be different for women and men, even though the type of education may be the same.

It is difficult to obtain data on the equality of girls and boys in access to schools in all parts of the world. It could be assumed that material facilities, wherever they exist, provide opportunities equal to both sexes. However, we do know that in families in some countries, boys are favored with access to schools while girls are expected to contribute to domestic chores. More explicit is the case where girls are deliberately excluded from some kinds of schools, for example, single-sex schools, or schools conducted in areas where coeducation is not allowed and decisions are made in favor of boys.

In some countries of the world, the statistics indicate that girls enrol in schools to the same extent or more than boys, at least at the lower levels. However, this is not true in most less developed countries where boys dominate in school classes. At the tertiary level women participate less than men in all regions of the world. Although the gap is closing, in 1980 much improvement in the enrolment of women was still necessary if complete equality was to be reached. Projections to the year 2000 suggest that these inequalities will remain in many parts of the world. Overall figures concerning the enrolment rates of women and enrolment ratios for the three levels to the year 2000 are found in Table 7.1.

If we focus first on the proportion of females to total enrolments, we see that at the primary level by 1980 the developed countries (and some of the developing regions, namely Latin America and East Asia) had almost reached the 50 percent level, that is, girls made up one-half of all school enrolments, which is what we would expect under conditions of equality. South Asia had the lowest percentage, with 41 percent females. However by the year 2000 it is estimated that in almost all regions, except perhaps in South Asia, primary level female enrolments will approach 50 percent. As one might expect, female percentages lag further behind at the secondary and tertiary levels. Again by 1980 girls constituted 50 percent of secondary enrolments in the developed countries and Latin America, but only 36 percent in South Asian countries. The percentages are lowest at the tertiary level for all regions.

TABLE 7.1. *Percent Females of Total Enrolments and Total Enrolment Ratios (in Brackets)*
For Country Groupings: 1960 to 2000 (projected)

Region	Primary			Secondary			Tertiary		
	1960	1980	2000	1960	1980	2000	1960	1980	2000
Developed Countries	49 (106)	49 (107)	49 (105)	49 (55)	50 (78)	50 (87)	35 (12.8)	46 (30)	48 (37.6)
Developing Countries	39 (60)	44 (86)	46 (96)	28 (13)	39 (31)	44 (49)	24 (2.0)	34 (7.4)	39 (11.8)
Africa	36 (44)	44 (78)	47 (93)	29 (5)	38 (21)	44 (43)	17 (0.7)	27 (3.2)	32 (6.4)
Latin America & Caribbean	48 (73)	49 (104)	49 (109)	47 (14)	50 (44)	50 (67)	30 (3.7)	44 (14.3)	45 (25.9)
South Asia (a)	36 (62)	41 (93)	45 (93)	29 (15)	36 (31)	41 (47)	26 (2.2)	31 (6.7)	37 (10.1)
East Asia (b) (China)	48 (98)	49	49	47 (31)	48	48	21 (1.8)	31	40

(a) Afghanistan, Bahrain, Bangladesh, Bhutan, Burma, Cyprus, Democratic Kampuchea, Democratic Yemen, East Timor, India, Indonesia, Iran, Iraq, Israel, Jordan, Kuwait, Lao People's Democratic Republic, Lebanon, Malaysia, Nepal, Oman, Pakistan, Philippines, Qatar, Saudi Arabia, Singapore, Sri Lanka, Syrian Arab Republic, Thailand, Turkey, Vietnam, United Arab Emirates, Yemen.

(b) China, Democratic People's Republic of Korea, Hong Kong, Japan, Mongolia, Republic of Korea. Female enrolment ratios, in brackets, are for China only.

Source: UNESCO, *Trends and Projections of Enrolments by Level of Education and by Age: 1960–2000 (est in 1982)*, Division of Statistics on Education, Office of Statistics, March 1983, Table IV in Annex I for Percent Females, and Tables 3 and 9 (pp. 19 and 35), and Table III, Annex I for Total Enrolment Ratios.

The total enrolment ratio, that is, the proportion of boys and girls enrolled in schools of the relevant age category (in brackets), gives us a further indication of the educational disadvantage of women because it shows that in some countries, the percentage of girls is from an already low total enrolment ratio. In 1980 virtually all males and females were in primary school in Latin America (104 total ratio with 49 percent female), but in Africa the primary enrolment ratio was only 78 with 44 percent of that 78 percent female. At the tertiary level, the figures are much lower, with 1980 enrolment ratios of 30 in the developed countries to a low of 3.2 for Africa, of which 46 and 27 percent respectively were female. These gaps are projected to continue through the year 2000.

By and standard, then, the educational participation of women lags far behind that of men in many parts of the world, and this condition is likely to persist to the year 2000. In itself, this raises serious equity and human rights issues. However, the question here is whether closing this gap by furthering the education of women makes a significant contribution to economic development, or put another way, whether the returns to the education of women warrants such an effort. In reviewing research from 61 countries, Psacharopoulos (1985) found that the rates of return to the educational investment on women exceeds that of men, particularly in the developing countries. In percentage terms, the average return, for all levels of education combined, was 15 percent for women compared to 11 percent for men. This differential prompted Psacharopoulos to comment that "expanding the provision of school places to cover women is not only equitable but socially efficient as well" (p. 592).[1]

Academic Performance Inequalities

Is getting more girls into schools sufficient to promote the further social and economic development of a society? Can their disadvantage be overcome by getting them into schools? These questions turn our attention to the differential academic performance of girls and boys. Few topics have received more attention than this in the educational literature.

In most developed countries the data suggest that at primary school girls perform at the same level as boys, but at the secondary level they begin to do more poorly. This variation appears partly related to subject, for girls continue to do as well as boys, sometimes even better, in reading ability and language learning. However, they invariably fall behind in mathematics and science, which in most countries are more highly valued and lead to more prestigious and better paying jobs. In the comprehensive set of international surveys conducted by the International Association for the Evaluation of Academic Achievement (IEA), a higher performance by boys over girls was found to be persistent across countries and within countries (Kelly, 1978). In the most recent IEA survey of science achievement in 17 countries, it was found that boys scored higher than girls at all levels, and that the gap increased from the 10-year-olds to the 14-year-olds. Although there was variation in subject area, and also between countries, overall the preliminary report observed that "...since 1970, there would appear to be little change in the superiority of boys over girls at the 14-year-old level and Grade 12 level" (IEA, 1988:4). An example of the persistence of male dominance across countries in science achievement is found in Table 7.2.

TABLE 7.2. *Sex Differences in Science Achievement, 14-year-olds, Seventeen Countries*

Country	Boys	Girls	Difference
Australia	18.44	17.12	1.32
Canada (Eng)	19.51	17.69	1.82
England	17.59	15.87	1.72
Finland	19.18	17.81	1.37
Hong Kong	17.17	15.41	1.76
Hungary	22.18	21.49	.69
Italy	17.43	15.95	1.48
Japan	20.92	19.43	1.49
Korea	18.98	17.01	1.97
Netherlands	20.96	18.65	2.31
Norway	18.85	16.99	1.86
Philippines	11.92	11.11	.81
Poland	18.91	17.34	1.57
Singapore	17.38	15.51	1.87
Sweden	19.28	17.50	1.78
Thailand	17.39	15.76	1.63
U.S.A.	17.36	15.53	1.83

Source: International Association for the Evaluation of Educational Achievement (IEA, 1988); Table 16, p. 64.

In order to correctly assess these gender differences, several details need to be pointed out. First of all, for 14-year-olds, boys performed better than girls at all levels. However, the average difference in scores varied considerably, the largest being in the Netherlands (2.31), the smallest being in Hungary (0.69). There seemed to be no pattern indicating that these differences are related to levels of development. However, it is important to note that girls in Hungary performed better than boys in all other countries except their own, and girls in Japan, on average, did better than boys in all countries except

Hungary, Japan, Netherlands and Canada. Clearly, then, the explanation for sex differences is not necessarily a development-related issue in causal terms, but the persistent domination of boys in academic performance in some "important" subject areas does raise issues related to the education of women and subsequent social and economic development.

The reasons usually given for gender-related differences in academic achievement include opportunity to learn, support systems for learning and the absence of appropriate role models (Finn *et al.*, 1979). For example, in the first IEA study of mathematics achievement (Husén, 1967) it was found that even where interest levels were identical, boys still outperformed girls, leading to the conclusion that "exposure" to mathematics might be one of the explanations for gender differences. This does not necessarily mean differences in science and mathematics enrolments, but more importantly the different emphases on learning and the amount of interest by teachers given to girls in science and mathematics classes. Social support, in the form of encouragement and actual assistance seems as important, particularly where cultural factors mediate against the education of girls in non-traditional subjects. Finally, it has been argued that the absence of female role models directly inhibits girls' achievement in non-traditional subjects. Although the sex of teacher may not completely explain differential treatment and expectations between girls and boys (men and women teachers may in fact hold similar expectations about the appropriate subjects and performance levels of girls), the data suggest that girls in single-sex schools with women teachers do better than girls in coeducational institutions.

Human rights considerations alone require that women have the opportunity to perform to the best of their ability in schools. However from a development perspective, the utilization of human resources and talent make it imperative that raising the educational participation of women alone is not sufficient, but maximizing their ability to perform is essential if the full benefits to them and to society are to be obtained.

Inequalities in the Labor-Market

The increasing participation of women in the paid workforce and the important changes that have followed, have been called "one of the most remarkable features of this century" (ILO, 1985:201). Although the increased educational participation and achievements of women in schooling is desirable purely in terms of the extension of human rights, the subsequent mobilization of human resources which education accomplishes adds to the social and economic development potential of any society. The increased participation of women in the workforce has changed the perception of women's roles in most societies, and has resulted in major transformations in the nature of work for both men and women.

The contribution of women's work to social and economic development is not easy to calculate. In the first place, much of women's unpaid work, largely in family labor and household work, clearly makes valuable contributions to families and society, but it is rarely acknowledged as such. Nor can the contribution be easily computed in economic terms, much less be included in national accounting (Rogers, 1980; Tinker, 1987). In the second place, in the paid workforce, women often do not receive wages equal to men, even in the same occupations and skill levels. Thus their economic contribution is likely to be underestimated. Nevertheless in all countries of the world, these contributions cannot be ignored any longer.

At the global level, women have entered the paid workforce in dramatic numbers, although it has varied between regions. By 1980 women accounted for over one-third of the world's labor force, but this varied from a high of 48 percent for East European nonmarket economies to a low of 5 percent for the high-income oil exporting countries (World Bank, 1983). Not only has the female percentage of the paid labor force changed over the decades, but the participation rate of females has also increased. This too has varied, and has been more true of the industrialized countries than the less developed countries. The data in Table 7.3 give these participation rates from 1960 to 1980.

TABLE 7.3. *Female Labor Force Participation Rates: 1960–80,*
by Country Group

Country group	Female labor force participation rates		
	1960	1970	1980
All Developing	27.6	26.6	26.2
Low-Income Developing	31.5	29.9	29.5
Middle-Income Developing	19.5	19.6	19.7
High-Income Oil Exporters	2.5	2.7	3.0
Industrial Market Economies	27.0	29.6	32.5
East European Non-Market Economies	45.9	45.1	46.1

Source: World Bank, (1983), Comparative Social Data: 148–149.
These figures are based on the nearest available dates; For example, the 1960 figures include those for 1959 and 1961 for appropriate countries. The compilers argue that because of the stability of these figures over time, a spread of one or two years is not important.

The regions which were high on female participation were also high on female composition of the labor force. For example in 1980 the highest participation levels were found in the East-European non-market economies, 46.1 percent, while the lowest were found in the high income oil exporting countries, 3.0 percent. In some parts of the world, namely the less developed countries, the participation rates of women have actually declined, due to the decrease of women working in the agricultural sector. So in these latter countries, female participation dropped 1.4 percent. Conversely, the main increase in participation rates has occurred in the industrialized countries, both the capitalist and the socialist. The increase in the former was particularly large, being 5.5 percent between 1960 and 1980, most of which was in the service sector.

An indication of the general shift from the agricultural sector to the industrial and service sectors is found in Table 7.4. Clearly the decline in the agricultural sector has been a world-wide phenomenon, and has affected both women and men. Nevertheless most agricultural workers are in developing countries, and in 1980 two-thirds of all female workers in these countries were engaged in agricultural activities, mostly farming. Of their female counterparts elsewhere in the world, only 7.7 percent of women workers in the industrialized capitalist countries and about one-fifth of the women workers in the socialist countries were in the agricultural sector. Conversely, two-thirds of the working women in the capitalist countries, and almost one-half in the socialist countries work in the service sector. In evaluating these data, one must keep in mind that

TABLE 7.4. *Composition of the World Labor Force,*
by Sex and Sector of Activity
(1970 and 1980) (in percentages)

| | | Agriculture | | Industry | | Services | | Total | |
		1970	1980	1970	1980	1970	1980	1970	1980
Developing	F	73.6	66.3	12.5	16.3	13.9	17.4	100.0	100.0
Countries	M	62.8	55.7	17.7	21.6	19.5	22.7	100.0	100.0
Industrial									
Market	F	11.4	7.7	25.4	25.8	63.2	66.5	100.0	100.0
Countries	M	12.0	8.5	44.6	45.9	43.4	45.6	100.0	100.0
Industrial									
Centrally	F	31.7	21.5	29.6	33.1	38.6	45.4	100.0	100.0
Planned	M	27.7	19.4	44.2	50.3	28.1	30.3	100.0	100.0
Countries									
Total	F	54.3	47.8	17.9	20.8	27.8	31.4	100.0	100.0
	M	49.2	43.5	25.7	28.8	25.1	27.7	100.0	100.0

Source: ILO, **World Labour Report–2**, adapted from Table 13.1, p. 205.

many of these changes have also affected men, particularly the shift way from agriculture. However, the labor force composition does differ between the industrial and services sector in the indusrialized countries.

What are the consequences for education and development of these characteristics of changing female participation in the labor market? To begin with, the concentration of women in the agricultural sector in developing countries means that for the most part women are working in difficult low paid jobs with long hours. In addition, they must carry the responsibility for domestic chores, and it is estimated that a rural woman's typical day includes from 12 to 16 hours of work (ILO, 1985:204)

At the same time, it is precisely the agricultural jobs which are under pressure by improved technology and the rationalization of the agricultural sector. Men get the improved technical jobs while women get pushed into the residual less well paid jobs. Because of this, many rural women have been forced to migrate to cities to take equally low paying jobs in the industrial and service sectors, such as in the "female industries" of textiles, clothing, electronics, and the food and beverage industry. Although it could be argued that these jobs are necessary for the continued development of many countries, the pressures on them, from technological changes, and the lower skill of women in them, means that women's participation in the workforce is constantly under threat from possible retrenchment and replacement by men. Many women work at jobs below their productive capacity.

The problem of female labor market inequalities is not limited to the less developed countries. In the industrial capitalist societies women constituted about 40 percent of the labor force and about 25 percent of the industrial labor force in 1980. Many are increasingly found in the capital-intensive industries such as electronics. Studies in both Canada and the United Kingdom have shown that women's jobs are more affected by technological changes and automation than men's, and their hold on employment is much more fragile. In the service sector where almost two-thirds of all women work, similar difficulties exist. Most of the women's jobs in the service sector are in occupations such as sales personnel, nursing, teaching, and secretarial. Studies in the Federal Republic of Germany and the United Kingdom have predicted job losses in these areas: 25 percent and 36 percent of office jobs in the private and public sectors accordingly are predicted for Germany, while it is estimated that 170,000 secretarial jobs in the United Kingdom will be lost due to new electronic technologies by 1990 (ILO, 1985:211).

The highest concentration of women in the workforce is found in select industrialized capitalist and socialist countries. Both France and Sweden rank high in the former, while the latter ranges from a high of 50 percent of the labor force in the Soviet Union and a low of 30 percent in Czechoslovakia. They are distributed in almost all occupations in the industrial sector, but are concentrated in the light industries. Of all the groups of countries in the world, it has been observed that women in some socialist countries, notably the Soviet Union, do enjoy reasonably good working conditions. In the service sector, again women are distributed throughout, and constitute up to two-thirds of all workers. Finally, about one-half of all agricultural workers are women, some of whom are found in specialized positions, for example as agronomists and veterinary experts.

The picture which emerges points to clear gender inequalities regarding participation in the paid labor force. If women do represent a development resource, then that resource is most utilized in the developed countries. In the less developed countries, even though women are largely concentrated in the agricultural sector, it would appear that they do not enjoy good working conditions even where they are productive and make important contributions to the economy. The inequalities of the labor market are related to inequalities in education. As the education of women in all societies more closely approximates that of men, so too will the pressures for a more equitable distribution of women in the workforce.

**The Contribution of Women to Economic,
Social and Political Dimensions of Development**

In one of the earliest studies of women and development, Boserup (1970, with Liljencrantz, 1975) argued that the problem of women's unequal participation in the development process began with the shift from family production for subsistence to the specialized production of goods and services. In the former, women's contribution was central and substantial, but as their contribution became replaced by economic activities outside the home, they were given less opportunity to contribute to new ways of production. Boserup further argued that colonial domination exaggerated this process of increasing women's disadvantaged position in the production process. In many ways, development strategies have made things worse for women, rather than better.[2]

We have already seen from research that the economic benefits to society for the increased education of women is substantial. However, this view is not always shared by decision-makers, neither in developed nor in developing countries. In Uganda, for example, the rural-to-urban migration of women for employment reasons during recent decades has led to the displacement of women from traditional jobs and their exclusion from, or inability to find, jobs in the modern sector. In order to discourage this migration, attempts were made to create the impression that women who migrate to cities have lost their dignity and morality.

> However, the general attitude that still prevails in East Africa is that urban migration is bad for women because it corrupts their virtue, leads to marital instability and erodes traditional norms. This leads to the weakening of the family structure, an increase in juvenile delinquency and violent crimes. But the worst perceived influence of the towns is the idea that prostitution is encouraged among women. This seems to be the rationale for the preoccupation of the public and the law and policy makers with the problem of female migration (Obbo, 1980:28).

Although this example may appear extreme, it does reflect the fact that women are given less priority in the competition for jobs, and that a wide range of strategies is used to inhibit access both to education and to occupation. In many developing countries the prospects of women gaining access to education and occupations is inextricably linked with social class, and "family strategies" for survival and upward social mobility. Papanek (1985) found how, in two countries at different ends of the development continuum, Egypt and Bangladesh, the constraints on women were a function of education and job opportunities, cultural expectations, marriage prospects, and an already perceived valuable contribution to the informal economy and family mobility opportunities through traditional means. In Egypt the increase in female participation in the labor force is largely due to the increased employment of better educated women. In rural areas decisions regarding schooling favor males simply because the range of employment opportunities for them is greater. Ironically this further deters the employment prospects of women, as illiteracy is much more a liability for females than for males. Generally, however, women at all levels entered the workforce not for employment alone, but out of economic necessity.

Papanek has documented a much more extreme situation in Bangladesh where she found a strong "culture against women". As she observed, "... females are socialized to sacrifice their health, survival chances, and life options" for males (p. 336). Not only did most women work because of economic pressure, but improvements in education were accompanied by the risk of lower marriage opportunities, especially in rural areas. Ultimately, according to Papanek, the relationship between education and employment for women not only varies by gender and class but is closely linked with "family strategies". The investment in education and pursuit of employment is part of a wider calculation of the benefits to the family, either in the form of supplementary cash income or the possibility of the improvement of marriage prospects, and thus upward family mobility.

The complex relationships between class and gender in educational and occupational destinations is found in Biraimah's (1987) study of 500 students at the University of Ifo, Nigeria. Biraimah found that although females represented about 22 percent of the students, they were much more likely to have had high status origins than their male counterparts. However the data showed that while the educational and occupational expectations of all students were "relatively inflated and unrealistic" (57 percent of males and 33 percent of females expected to earn doctorates), those of males were higher than females for all socioeconomic groups except the lowest. Likewise, the same pattern was found regarding career expectations: males, regardless of socioeconomic status background, held higher career expectations than even the high status females. Like Papanek, Biramiah concluded that traditional role expectations and limited financial resources exercise a "crippling effect" on the life chances of Nigerian women, even those from elite backgrounds (1987:582).

These observations from the developing countries are not unique – they are found in varying degrees in all societies. Basically, even though the economic benefits to the investment in the education of women can be demonstrated empirically, the forces resisting that investment are entrenched in cultural, familial and ultimately the social practices which discriminate against them. In some contexts (for example, Bangladesh) the resistance is seen mainly in economically beneficial terms, the result of "family strategies" to maximize gain and avoid risks, while in other contexts (for example, Uganda) it is seen as competition against men and the loss of traditional female roles and behavior. Nevertheless, as a resource potential for the further development of society, the education of women is of such high priority that Psacharopoulos and Woodhall state that "... with a better qualified female population, national development is likely to be fostered through the changes that can be expected in the nature of labor force participation and through the gains in family welfare, family planning, and health and child care" (1985:245).

Thus apart from economic benefits, the education of women contributes to social development and a rise in the quality of life of a country. In many developing countries, efforts to improve standards of living are swallowed up in population growth. We saw this previously in the case of literacy campaigns, where the proportion of literates may increase, but at the same time the absolute numbers of illiterates can also increase due to population growth. (See Chapter 2.) Research has shown that there is an inverse relationship between level of education and fertility and population control, and the relationship is stronger for women than men (Cochrane, 1982). Likewise it has been shown that women are more influential in maintaining the health and nutrition standards of children, and that the higher the education levels of women, the higher these standards are. Finally research in many countries, developed and less developed alike, have identified the educational level of the mother as being more important than father's education in explaining the educational attainments of students. This is particularly true in the preschool preparation of children for schooling (Selowsky, 1982).

The importance of the education of women for political mobilization and political development has not been widely researched. However, there is no reason to believe that raising the education of women would not also contribute to the political development of a country. As persons largely identified with the transmission of cultural and moral values of society, including those underlying political behavior, a better educated female population is likely to contribute not only to a more politically active adult population, but also to the transmission of political values as well.

Recent research has found that there is a close relationship between organizational mobilization and participation in a wide variety of activities. In Kenya, most participants in the literacy campaign were women, and most of the women were members of women's associations (Carron, 1988). Although the direction of causality is not clear in this case, the relationship between literacy and other forms of political participation has been well documented. Thus one can easily argue, even in the absence of clear documentation, that the contribution of investment in the education of women seems to benefit the political development of a country as well.

Apart from human rights considerations, and contributions to the economy and labor force productivity, there are clearly many "non labor market" development-related benefits to be had by countries in programs aimed at raising the level of female education. There is justification, therefore, in the recommendation governments give strong priority to appropriate programs aimed at furthering the educational levels of women (Kelly, 1987 b).

Contradictions in Education
and Development Programs
For Women

All development strategies involve trade-offs whereby decisions are made on the basis of political and pragmatic priorities. The attainment of some priorities may work to the disadvantage of others. This contradiction or dilemma is particularly true in the case of programs directed to the eradication of all inequalities, particularly the inquality of women. As we saw at the outset of this chapter, sex division of labor in societies are imbedded in cultural, religious and economic values, such that equalizing the participation of women, and thereby opening up for them more widespread participation ino ther sectors of society, will inevitably affect cultural, religious and economic norms. Programs aimed at reducing the educational inequalities of women may bring about, as a consequence, widespread changes and possible disruptions and conflicts in society, and at least in the short term, a level of social disorganization. Two cases will illustrate these contradictions and problematic outcomes.

(i) The Education of Women
in Islamic Countries

In many Islamic countries, some of which are rich oil exporters, the education of women lags behind that of men, and the participation of women in the labor force is the lowest in the world. (See Table 7.3.) In spite of the inequalities judged by these criteria, it has frequently been argued that the status of women in Islamic societies is very high and that they enjoy a prestige which is different from, but equal to that of men. Al-Hariri comments that "It is easy to infer that the Quran and the sayings of the Prophet are clear in stating that men and women are complementary to each other, and in their full cooperation and harmony lies the very purpose of life" (1987:51). All Muslims, male and female, are to be educated and female children are to be treated equal to male children.

Yet, in spite of these commitments to equality of the sexes, the Islamic countries are among the lowest in the education of women. For example, the female ratio for primary school enrolment in 1980 for the high-income oil exporting countries was 73.1 percent. This was lower than the comparable female ratio for low-income developing countries, which was 79.3 percent, and far behind the universal primary education of females in the industrialized countries. The figures at secondary level are more encouraging, but only with respect to comparisons with developing countries. The secondary female enrolment ratio for the high-income oilexporting countries was 36.2 percent compared to 25.7 percent for all developing countries but 86.0 percent for the capitalist industrialized countries (World Bank, 1983).

These figures may be interpreted in a number of ways. Perhaps they simply indicate that the current high-income oil exporting countries lagged behind even the poorest of the developing countries when their oil resources were discovered, and that in time the gap will decrease. They might also indicate more deeply entrenched cultural beliefs and practices by which males and females are treated differently. Al-Hariri (1987) points out that although Islam guarantees males and females equal access to education, "... it does insist on keeping women in a position that ensures their stable family life" (p. 52). For this reason in Saudi Arabia, at least, the free intermingling of males and females is frowned upon, including integrated education, and a separate system of education for girls has been created. Included in this system is a curriculum for girls education, "... based on scientific thought, and with consideration of the nature of women and what society needs from women's services" (p. 53). Thus women in Saudi Arabia are receiving an education which is deemed appropriate for their place in Islamic society, and those who have reached higher levels have done so in acceptable fields, such as the humanities and languages.

Although the sex-segregated education of most Islamic societies may eventually result in equal educational attainments for women, there remains evidence that in practice the education of boys will be favored. A study of 26 Pakistani married women living in a Scottish town confirmed the enduring hold of traditional Islamic values (Siann and Khalid, 1984). There was consensus that the education of boys should be favored over girls, but not because of lack of aspiration for girls. Among this sample of Islamic women, the criterion of family honor, of *Izzet*, was considered much more important than individual social mobility, and the way women behave has a strong affect on family honor. In their view, the family structure and culture of Pakistani Islamic society provided a safety net for women such that they could always return to their parents if their marriage did not succeed. Thus family honor rather than economic success was considered the most important consideration in the treatment of

Islamic girls. Although it could be argued that because these women were living outside a Muslim country that their views were distorted, it should be noted that their views were often made with explicit comparisons with Scottish (Western) women.

One should be cautious about generalizing too much from these examples, as there are wide variations between Islamic countries. If we examine the percentage of females of the total student enrolments for each level, we find the following projected figures to 1990. At the *primary level* the high is 49 percent female of total enrolments for the United Arab Emirates compared to a low of 29 percent for Pakistan. At the *secondary level* Bahrain and the United Arab Emirates are high with 48 percent compared to a low of 25 percent for Pakistan. Finally at the *tertiary level* Iraq is high with 44 percent compared to a low of 23 percent for Bangladesh (UNESCO, 1983a). Thus irrespective of the overall enrolment ratios of Islamic countries (that is, what proportion of children of any age group are actually in school) the *balance* between males and females for some Islamic countries is equal to that of many developed and less developed countries. Likewise, the low female enrolment rate for some Islamic countries indicates considerable inequality and thus room for improvement in educational and national development strategies. Indeed, for Saudi Arabia the improvement of education for females is a specific education policy, although females continue to lag behind males in enrolments (Wagner, 1985).

For Islamic countries, then, the education of women involves a strategy touching the cultural and religious core of the societies themselves. Just as there are wide variations between Islamic countries in the interpretation of and adherence to Islamic law and practice (for example, with respect to the *purdah*, or the wearing of the veil by females), so too is there variation in efforts to give males and females equal educational opportunities. What must be clear, however, is that the education of women will bring about fundamental changes in the role and status of women in Islamic society, and will affect the role and status of males as much as females.

(ii) The Education of Rural Women
in Asia and the Pacific

As we have seen in Table 7.1, the educational enrolment ratios for women in South Asia is between that of Africa, with a low ratio, and that of Latin America, with the high ratio. However if we broaden our perspective to the wider region, we find that the case of illiterate or poorly educated rural women represents another dilemma for understanding the dynamics of education and development linkages.

When we focus on the Asian-Pacific region as a whole, we find that it shelters 75 percent of the world's illiterate population of 15 years of age and above. It has been estimated that in the region there are 100 million primary school-aged children who have never been enrolled in schools. Furthermore, even though considerable progress in educational expansion has been made since 1960, the actual number of illiterates has actually increased in the last 15 years, from 537 million in 1970 to 555 million in 1985. More importantly for our consideration is the fact that this increase is due entirely to the increase of female illiteracy, from 390 million in 1970 to 415 million in 1985 (Sakya, 1987). The combination of female illiteracy and rural illiteracy, largely overlapping, prompted Sakya to observe:

So the message is very clear. If the countries which have a serious problem of illiteracy and primary education could address themselves to the problem of girls and women education and other disadvantaged populations, the goal of achieving education for all will be easily achieved (Sakya, 1987:6).

Ironically, this concentration of mainly female illiteracy is found in what has been called the "globe's most dynamic economic region". Although we cannot discuss all countries of the region, the following observations will pertain to Afghanistan, Bangladesh, Bhutan, China, India, Nepal, Pakistan, Papua New Guinea, and Thailand.

The variations in total educational enrolments and the education of women vary considerably in this country group. For example two countries, China and Thailand, have virtually reached universal primary education, with the lowest level of total enrolment being Bhutan, with 15 percent, and Afghanistan, with 36 percent. However, the disparities in the education of girls is equally varied. The largest disparity in terms of male-female enrolment ratios are Nepal with a 98 percentage gap, followed by Pakistan with a 48 percentage gap. The lowest disparities are found in Thailand with 5 percent and Bhutan with 9 percent (UNESCO, 1986). It should be apparent that disparities between male and female educational enrolments do not necessarily relate to total enrolments except when universal education is reached. What is to be noted, however, is the fact that all these countries endorse, in principle, equal education for boys and girls, and all acknowledge the importance of education for girls as a contribution toward national development. How, then, can the disparities be explained?

The evidence from cumulative research provides a partial answer which also highlights the dilemmas and contradictions which surround the education of females. Firstly, in many of these countries, marriage customs are *virilocal,* that is all benefits of the woman go to the husband's family. Any investment in females is seen as a loss for the family of the bride and a gain for the family of the husband. Thus there are pressures to make greater investments in the education and training of males, for these investments will remain in the family, and may even serve to attract a better suited bride (Nelson, 1979).

A second deterrant to the education of females is the belief that an educated female will no longer want to carry out the expected duties of rural women, since many of these ordinary tasks, such as working in the fields, would be lost to the village. Thirdly, where modern technologies have been introduced, the women have often been left more deprived and isolated than before. The notion of "negative modernization" has been used to describe the increasingly disadvantaged condition of women in some circumstances, such as those observed in countries where *purdah* is practiced (Pastner, 1974).

Very often the education of females is impaired by mothers working in the labor market. As already noted, much participation in the workforce in poor countries is by those in difficult economic conditions. Ironically, by working, mothers impair the education of their daughters who must remain at home to cook and care for children. Finally, the education of females is often resisted by males who see this as a threat to their own control over women's lives and activities in rural areas.

Overall, the social factors related to the inequalities of female education in many developing countries are complex and difficult to overcome simply by the introduction of government policies to encourage the education of girls. The dilemma arises when the education of girls brings about consequences which have a negative effect on other aspects of family and village life. It is for this reason that programs aimed at a better sex balance in education should not only involve the girls themselves, but boys and the total village community. In the Asian and Pacific region, programs have not only included the provision of specific facilities, curricula materials, and more women teachers, but also programs to educate village adults who must understand better the condition of women and why their education is important not only for justice reasons, but also for their own benefits and those of the country as well (UNESCO, 1986).

Conclusion

The equal education of women in all countries represents an important development objective, but one which is often neglected. Even in the developed countries where enrolment rates are almost equal, other more subtle inequalities exist, as in educational performance and attainments. In the case of many less developed countries the attainment of these goals may involve costs in the form of changes in traditional cultural and social patterns of behavior. For the developed countries equally important changes may also occur, but perhaps in a more subtle manner. The general issue of gender inequality poses a particular challenge for countries to come up with suitable policies and programs designed to eradicate them.

As was pointed out at the beginning of this chapter, the role of the State in these policies may be crucial. Yet, for some countries the endorsement of equal rights may not be sufficient, for discriminatory practices may be passively tolerated and allowed to continue. Even the establishment of separate schools for girls must be carefully considered in the context of what Stromqvist (1987) calls the "control and production of knowledge". The education of females, by controlling their access to some forms of knowledge, may just as successfully exclude them from the mainstream of economic, social and political life as no education at all. Furthermore, as Kelly (1987 b) notes, access to schools is only part of the solution: conditions need to be provided so that girls will be able to remain in school, and ultimately have an equal opportunity to participate in productive activity. Whatever the costs may be, however, it should be clear that the inequality of women represents a violation of human rights and a neglected development resource, and have high priority in all educational and development policies and programs.

Notes

1. In actual fact, there was some disparity in rates of return to women between levels. For example at the primary level the percent return is 19 and 17 for men and women respectively, 16 and 21 percent at secondary level, and 15 and 14 percent at the tertiary level. Psacharopoulos (1985) warns that because of the increased probability that educated women are more likely to participate in the labor force, and that because women tend to earn less than men for the same jobs, the rate-of-return differentials in favor of women is likely to be underestimated.

2. Boserup's pioneering contribution to the study of women and development remains central to discussions today, in spite of the critiques annd evaluations of her argument (Beneria and Sen, 1981). The literature has now become extensive, and readers might wish to begin by also consulting bibliographies such as that produced by UNESCO (1983). Although this chapter focuses mainly on women in the developing countries, it should be clear that similar issues exist in the developed countries.

8

Evaluation of Education in Development Policy

UNDERNEATH most concerns about the relationship between education and processes of change and development is some kind of potential for reform. Even if a school system is achieving its desired educational objectives, there is always the possibility that the task can be done more effectively and more efficiently. As we have seen in chapter 6, specifically in the example of Sweden, educational reform is directed to the attainment of goals which are seen to affect the entire social structure. Absolutely crucial to any kind of reform, however, is the ability to evaluate or determine the extent to which it has accomplished what it set out to accomplish. One reason why much confusion and controversy prevails in the discussions concerning the relationship between education and development is that, until recently, very few educational policies have been carefully monitored and evaluated.[1] The analysis of educational phenomena *ex post facto*, for the most part, is less desirable than a careful strategy of monitoring and evaluating of a program from its beginning. In either case, however, any form of evaluation is desirable to none, and those who are in decision-making positions but who ignore the results of empirical evaluation research do so at the risk of failure or, conversely, of not knowing about the success of their efforts.

Evaluation Research and Policy

Stated most simply "an evaluation is a process by which revelant data are collected and transformed into information for decision-making" (Cooley and Lohnes, 1976:3). Evaluation is comparative, is concerned with standards, involves value judgements, and is directly oriented to decision-making processes (House, 1980). As such, evaluation is an extension of pure research, with one important exception. Pure research is expected to produce new knowledge which is generalizable, while evaluation research produces

191

knowledge specific to a particular context. Pure research does not necessarily lead to action, but the success of evaluation research is contingent on the extent to which it has been relevant for policy-making (Wolf, 1987). More important for evaluation success, however, is the extent to which evaluation research rigorously conforms to the accepted standards and norms of research itself. Policy decisions, programs and reforms are only as good as the quality of the research upon which they are based.

Evaluation research can be directed to the analysis of specific programs as well as to the performance of entire systems. For our interests this means anything from the evaluation of the effectiveness of experimental literacy programs to the societal impact of accelerating enrolments and the increase of participation rates for all levels of schooling. Likewise evaluation research can and should cast its net wide. Not only are the effects of specific educational inputs, organizational contexts and outputs legitimate evaluation targets, but so too are the assumptions, ideologies and theories underlying educational practices. Evaluation research is just as likely to be critical of current practices as it is confirmatory. Ultimately evaluation research represents a type of "demystification" of the taken-for-granted and the assumed. Cooley and Lohnes (1976) correctly observe that:

> For far too long the values that have guided educational practice have been determined by custom or politics alone. Their validity has gone unchallenged by educational research. Values have had some transcendental existence ascribed to them (p. 10).

Evaluation research cuts across theoretical paradigms and research methodologies. Literacy programs guided by the "conscientization" process of Paulo Freire are suitable targets, as are the expansionist schooling programs based on theories of human capital. Likewise the highly technical approach of Jencks *et al.* (1972, 1979) in the examination of the determinants of inequality in the United States represents one form of evaluation, while Bereiter's (1973) more theoretical and critical evaluation of schooling represents another. Evaluation research can be comparative, as for example the studies of the International Association for the Evaluation of Educational Achievement (IEA) which, since 1959, have investigated student performance on standardized tests in subjects such as science and mathematics in many countries (Postlethwaite, 1987). Evaluation research more typically focuses on the evaluation of education policies within one country, such as the evaluation of the Follow Through Program in the United States, which is sometimes regarded as the beginning of large scale evaluation in that country (Popham,

1987). Even decisions to pursue radical educational practices require an information base and a continual information flow, derived from specific and rigorous research plans.

The assessment of education's contribution to any social change, and particularly to development policy, is contingent on research suitable for such evaluative judgement. To this end it is essential that relevant questions, for example the specific policy goals sought, the means to achieve the goals, and the larger social, economic and political consequences of the pursuit of those goals, are adequately addressed in evaluation research. At the same time, however, there are dangers which must be recognized in evaluation research. The subjective bias of the evaluator may seriously affect the judgement concerning the program or project evaluated, for example when the evaluator has sympathetic or critical attitudes towards the political goals of the host country or whatever is being evaluated (Elzinga, 1981).

Further limitations of evaluation research include the fact that it normally applies to programs in one locale, it assumes that program outcomes are static, when they normally are constantly changing, and it often identifies the problems of programs but may not clearly identify the solutions to be followed in improving them (Wolf, 1987). Finally, a major limitation in evaluation research lies in the extent to which its findings are accepted and utilized by policy-makers. Because policy decisions reflect social and political interests, the results of evaluation research may not conform to the interests of the policy-makers, and therefore are often ignored by them (Husén, 1984).

The Underlying Assumptions of Education and Development Policy

In the 1960s and 1970s the provision of educational facilities and the formation of national development strategies were regarded as desirable, valued, and as goals to be sought. They were seldom, if ever, questioned. The international economic recession of the 1980s, along with the increasing costs of educational and development policies, has forced policy-makers to scrutinize more closely the consequences of these policies. It is in this context that evaluation research has become important, for it addresses questions such as: Who benefits from educational reforms and programs? and Who decides which programs and reforms should be adapted, and who implements them? (Cooley and Lohnes, 1976; Weiss, 1977; Apple, 1978; House, 1980).

An often neglected dimension of planning decisions, and indeed of the evaluation of planning, has been the realization that all such activities are ideologically grounded. This is another way of saying that the underlying assumptions upon which plans are based are as much political as they are scientific. In fact, it should by now be evident from our overall discussion of education and development that the scientific is often very much confused with the ideological, such that the true picture of the relationship may be forever obscured. No assumption should be immune from challenge or criticism.

At the heart of all decisions for educational expansion and reform is the conviction that schooling is preferable to no schooling, and that a government has the right to intervene in educational matters. However, the limited evidence currently available suggests that these assumptions may not, at least in every case, hold true. With regard to the first, it cannot be taken for granted that schooling processes, that is factors related to learning, are the same for all societies. Both educational policy and empirical research have generally assumed a standard model of educational inputs and outputs based on our knowledge in Western industrial societies. It has been said, for example, that learning behavior appears to share common mechanisms across cultures and that the burden of proof rests with those who question this position.

The implications stemming from this assumption are far-reaching, and indeed if learning does occur differently across societies, then expenditures on inappropriate school systems may represent massive wastage and inefficiency.

We do know that much learning takes place outside schools, and that some forms of cognitive development may not be school-specific. A study by Fahrmeier (1975) of Nigerian children between the ages of 6 and 13 showed that while the children who attended schools attained higher levels of cognitive ability over a given time-period, those who did not attend schools made cognitive gains as well. Most surprising in Fahrmeier's research, however, was the finding that the gap in ability between the schooled and non-schooled children remained constant for each age group during the test period. One obvious interpretation of this finding is that differences in cognitive ability already existed before schooling for some began, and indeed may have been a selective factor in school attendance itself.

In citing this example we do not suggest that schooling makes no contribution to learning whatsoever. Indeed, Sharp and Cole's (1974) study of 446 Mexican individuals between the ages of 14 to over 60, including both schooled and unschooled, concluded that schooling exerted a "profound effect" on the development of cognitive abilities and skills. There is an emerging consensus that the learning which takes place outside of school differs from that in the classroom. Wagner and Spratt (1987) identify research which suggests that schooling does affect cognitive skills such as logic, reasoning, memory and certain perceptual skills. On the other hand, there is evidence that many people who have little or no schooling can perform complex everyday tasks with the use of cognitive tools such as number tables, calculators, etc. Resnick (1987) cites as an example unschooled Brazilian bookmakers who use task-specific probability tables to operate a very complex lottery system, involving combinations of bets and payoffs, without knowing anything about the calculations involved. Clearly, schooling makes possible the learning and development of certain skills, but other skills, often more practical, can be learned through everyday experiences. The issue is that at present we still know little about the relative impact of the school experience across cultures and societies, and to assume a model of learning as though it were universally valid, particularly when educational planning and expenditures are concerned, may render the best intended policies and programs quite useless, or at least less effective than they might otherwise have been.

Closely related to the question of learning models is that of mode of cognition itself. Often education programs assume that the objectives of schooling are more or less standard across societies and that the learning of particular skills to a specified level of competence is possible in any culture. What is often overlooked is the possibility that modes of cognition may vary systematically between cultures, societies, ethnic and racial groups and the sexes. The debate concerning modes of cognition has entered the discussions of school achievement particularly between the sexes and racial groups in the United States. It has not been taken into account in the macro-level debates about the matching of forms of schooling with development policies across countries. Ultimately it may be that development goals modelled on Western industrialized countries may require cognitive and technical skills inconsistent with modes of cognition dominant in a particular culture. Examples of research on differing modes of cognition can be found in Gay and Cole's (1967) study of mathematical ability among the Kepelle in Liberia, Gladwin's (1970) study of navigation among the Puluwat Islanders in the South Pacific, and Horton's (1968) discussion of modes of African thought. In each case the arguments put forward challenge the conventional assumptions that thought processes are universal, and that the extrapolation of educational forms across societies can be expected to produce similar results.

Conflicts and tensions produced by the extrapolation of educational and development models across societies is another neglected area for evaluation research, for there seems to have been in the past the conviction that the benefits of education far outweigh the costs. However, there is increasing evidence that for some societies and cultures, education in its formal Western model is not desired, and in some instances even resisted. The reasons for this resistance are not difficult to grasp. One explanation focuses on the disruptive influence of schooling on traditional family cohesion. In Venezuela, for example, Guajiro Indian parents saw the school as potentially alienating their children from the family and village, such that attendance at school was regarded as a prelude (a causal one) to the eventual migration from the village altogether (Watson-Franke, 1974). Likewise research in Ghana has identified deliberate resistance to schooling because of its deleterious effects on traditional ways of life. As long as education in development programs is accepted entirely in its Western form, these conflicts and tensions can be expected to occur (Blakemore, 1975).

As we have discussed in Chapter 4, such reactions to schooling need not be irrational. The ethnocentric bias of modernization theory tends to regard perceived anti-modernization attitudes as stemming from the entrenchment of traditional norms and as obstacles to development and progress. Yet studies of peasants' reactions to innovations in agricultural technology have shown that resistance is often highly rational and calculated (Hutton and Cohen, 1975). What has been said about the acceptance of new agricultural technology can also be said of schooling in traditional contexts. The long-term unknown outcomes of schooling, in particular its Western form, can often be seen as questionable, the acceptance of which appears to constitute high risk. It is important to point out that the kind of resistance we have been describing is not restricted to less-developed societies, as similar reactions occur, although in different forms, in Western industrial societies. The debates over curriculum, teaching methods and school organization often can be divided into two camps: those who promote innovation and those who resist it. Unfortunately the failure of policy programs sometimes rests on the inability of those responsible to conceptualize and understand the rational validity of differing points of view. "Modernization and development" programs are "truly modern" only to the extent that they are perceived as such by the participants.

What we are arguing here is that basic assumptions concerning education, schooling and development policy should be subjected to careful scrutiny and evaluation prior to the final formulation and implementation of any program. The basic assumptions are many; here we identify three which we feel should be examined in any education-development strategy: (1) that the learning of some skills and abilities only takes place within schools constructed according to the Western industrial model, (2) that cognitive processes and modes of rational thought are identical across all societies, and (3) that schooling in its Western form is rationally desirable and all resistance to it represents irrational behavior based on traditional anti-modernization values. Evaluation research must include some recognition of assumptions such as these, and if nothing else, lead to the clear articulation of the value-positions of policy. Thus the political and the scientific will, to some extent, be less obscure and more openly stated and recognized. Presumably the formulation of education and development programs will then be more relevant and realistic.

The Specification of Desired Outcomes and Goals

The next step in the utilization of evaluation research in the formulation of viable development programs is the clear specification of development goals, and more precisely the role of education in the achievement of these goals. The decision regarding goals is more than academic, and must take into account the natural and human resources available to a particular society, as well as the political goals of those in decision-making positions.

What then are the desired goals and outcomes of development, and how should they be measured? Educationalists and policy-makers have often disagreed about the most desired outcomes of schooling, but generally the most important can be classified into three groups: (1) cognitive outcomes, which include various kinds of knowledge, skills and problem-solving abilities; (2) affective outcomes, which involve the growth of personality characteristics and emotions, and finally (3) psycho-motor learning, which include such skills as balance, hand and eye coordination, relaxation and perception of body abilities and image. While it is impossible to draw clearcut distinctions between all three outcome groups, most research generally focuses on one, and most often this is the first, that is cognitive outcomes.

The Evaluation of Cognitive Outcomes

Although cognitive outcomes are usually identified in terms of achievement scores of some kind, for example mathematics, reading or science, they also include the whole range of attitudes, values and aspirations which are seen to be highly related. Thus in attempting to investigate the relationship between education and modernization, researchers have focused on attitudes and values as outcomes of schooling rather than academic achievement (see Chapter 4). Unfortunately in research attempting to investigate the relationship between education and socio-economic development these kinds of measures are rarely, if ever, used. The result has been that while we have considerable information about schooling, modern values, attitudes and modern behavior, we know little about the impact of academic achievement on these phenomena.

External examinations, such as the *baccalaureat* in France and the CSE (Certificate of Secondary Education) examination in the United Kingdom, are forms of evaluation of cognitive outcomes which were originally intended to guarantee objectivity and egalitarianism in educational rewards and selection. This form of evaluation has come under increasing criticism in many parts of the world because of its influence on curriculum development (Lewin, 1984) and its tendency to reduce the meaning of certificates and other awards to that of "meal tickets" for high status occupations or for selection to tertiary institutions. It is partly for these reasons that some regard such examinations as irrelevant for less-developed countries (Kiros *et al.*, 1975).

Educational testing at the national level through the use of standardized tests developed by agencies such as the ETS (Educational Testing Service) in the United States, or the NCUEE (National Center for University Entrance Examination) in Japan, is becoming increasingly popular to assist in evaluation and selection (Heyneman and Fägerlind, 1988). The standardized tests developed and used by the International Association for the Evaluation of Educational Achievement (IEA) represent an attempt to evaluate the cognitive outcomes of schooling at an international level.

Cross-cultural differences in test-taking ability have been well documented, and to some extent differences between the developed and less-developed countries could partly be explained by factors such as these. Even with utmost care, the transferability of test items from one language to another cannot be guaranteed, and thus the validity of the results may be called into question.

The IEA studies in the early 1970s have provided documentation of the discrepancy between developed and less-developed countries in academic achievement. The analysis of these studies further suggests that the difference between these two groups of countries prevails across a variety of dimensions and that, at least from simple correlation analysis, there is a direct relationship between level of economic development and academic achievement. These findings are presented in Table 8.1.[2]

TABLE 8.1. *Country Rank Order Correlation Coefficients between Level of Economic Development and Achievement, IEA Countries*

Achievement	Population I (10-year-olds)	Population II (14-year-olds)
Aggregate achievement	0.62*(N=12)	0.45(N=13)
Science	0.37 (N=15)	0.26(N=17)
Reading comprehension	0.55*(N=13)	0.44(N=14)

*Significant at 0.05 level
Source: Adapted from Passow *et al.* (1976), Table 3.2, p. 174.

In the mid-1980s the IEA conducted a second study of science achievement in 24 countries, half of which are less-developed. Preliminary results suggest that with the exception of Korea and Hong Kong, the relationships reported in Table 8.1 will be repeated (IEA, 1988). There are several explanations for these differences in performance between developed and less-developed countries. Human capital and modernization theorists would argue that additional emphasis on education should help equalize educational outcomes and thus help close the gap in socio-economic development. Differences in achievement therefore are attributable to (1) lack of familiarity with the testing procedures; (2) curriculum deficiency, that is, less opportunity to learn in less-developed countries; (3) the poverty of school resources; or (4) the disadvantaged backgrounds which larger proportions of children in less-developed countries experience (the social deprivation theory) (Inkeles, 1979).

It is interesting that there have been few attempts to explain achievement differences between the developed and less-developed countries using radical explanations. The possible inappropriateness of Western models of schooling or the presumed universality of certain highly valued and desired educational outputs have largely been taken for granted rather than critically examined. Radical and neo-Marxist explanations for achievement differences, however, would regard the latter considerations as central to understanding the continuing discrepancies between developed and less-developed countries. The very concern with measuring achievement across societies reflects, in their view, the centrality of Western capitalist and industrial hegemony over countries in the developing world. Thus differences in achievement on Western-styled tests are not, in themselves, seen as very meaningful, but the extent to which these differences are utilized for policy decisions represents an attempt to continue the presumed cognitive dominance of Western capitalist societies over the less-developed countries, and further, to justify Western intervention in educational policy. From the radical perspective, this activity is seen ultimately to serve best the interests of Western capitalist societies. In many ways, the use of standardized achievement tests cross-nationally attains ideological significance in much the same way that the use of IQ scores to evaluate students has been regarded as an ideological apparatus in support of the dominant bourgeois classes in the United States (Bowles and Gintis, 1976).

Unfortunately evaluation studies have not tended to examine the implications of variations in school outcomes, and in particular to the contribution which the different types of outcomes have on social and economic development. Ultimately all evaluation rests on a political or ideological base and only has meaning as long as the underlying assumptions are recognized and taken into account in the design, execution and interpretation of evaluation results. Once the political goals are clearly articulated, and the expected contribution and consequences of schooling to student cognitive achievement are determined, evaluation can assess the efficiency of education programs intended to achieve these goals.

The Methodology of Evaluation Research

Even the best data can fail to provide an evaluation and understanding of the performance of an educational system if inappropriate methods are used, or if the results produced by particular methodologies are misunderstood or misinterpreted. There is no single appropriate evaluation methodology; rather the methodologies are appropriate to any given set of evaluation goals and data. The work of Cooley and Lohnes (1976) provides an instructive example, as their discussion of evaluation research in education focuses on statistical procedures and includes factor analytic techniques, canonical analysis and regression analysis. House (1980), on the other hand, has identified eight different evaluation models and a wide range of evaluation methodologies. He suggests that in addition to the quantitative analysis of census or survey data, the use of case studies, in-depth interviews, observation, reviews by panels and self-studies may, given appropriate evaluation goals, prove to be suitable methodological procedures. Benson and Michael (1987) argue that one of the most powerful evaluation methods is the experimental design, but because it is virtually impossible to utilize in field evaluation studies, the use of quasi-experimental and naturalistic (ethnographic) designs is the next best alternative. The advantages and techniques of qualitative evaluation methods is usefully described by Patton (1980). For each method, however, it is essential that it be appropriately utilized to deal with already specified evaluation and research questions.

Most studies investigating various links between education and development have been based on secondary analyses of already existing data, for example that found in OECD, UNESCO or World Bank sources,[3] or on research designs which have focused on various indicators related to outputs of schools or at a wider level, to the performance of educational systems (Johnstone, 1981).

(i) Linear Regression and the Educational Production Function

Survey studies of school effectiveness and other input-output studies have used ordinary least squares (OLS) regression strategies, sometimes referred to as the educational production function (EPF). The latter was first derived from studies of organizational effectiveness (the firm) and was later applied to analyses of schools. The educational production function, or the simple regression model, can be stated in the following form:

$$Y = f(F,I,P,S)$$

where the educational output Y is a function (f) of various inputs, including family background (F), pre-school ability (I), peer group influence (P), and school factors (S). The EPF model and its linear forms have been explained and critiqued at considerable length elsewhere and will not concern us here.[4] It is important to recognize that many of the evaluation studies which have had an impact on educational policy have used linear regression and the EPF in one form or another. In the developed societies the works by Coleman *et al.* (1966) and Jencks *et al.* (1972, 1979) are well-known examples, while the IEA studies and the review of EPF studies by Simmons and Alexander (1980) and Fuller (1987) include examples from developing countries. Therefore, as this general approach has been and no doubt will continue to be utilized in many future evaluation studies, a number of specific problems must be kept in mind when assessing past studies and designing future ones.

The first problem concerns the level at which the data are aggregated and analyzed; this can range from societies, regions, schools and to individual teachers and students, the latter two representing unaggregated data. However, the inferences which can be made from analyses of aggregate data are limited and caution must be exercised when inferences about individual-level effects are attempted. There has been considerable discussion about this "ecological effect" whereby relationships found between aggregated variables may or may not be extrapolated to individuals. Przeworski and Teune (1970), for example, recognize this difficulty in their distinction between variations between countries and variations within countries.

> ... countries differ with regard to their levels of education, class structure, and family socialization, but they do not differ *as systems* so long as their patterns of relationships are the same. *Systems differ not when the frequency of particular characteristics differ, but when the patterns of the relationships among variables differ* (Przeworski and Teune, 1970:45).

The importance of this distinction lies in the possibility that evaluations of education and development (as well as other development issues) based on aggregate data may present only a partial or even deceptive picture of the relationship. As an example, consider the question of teacher effects on student achievement. An important decision faced by many educationists and policy-makers in recent times has been whether an upgrading of teacher quality, in terms of costs and other investments, effectively improves the performance of students. The issue has been particularly relevant in less-developed countries where both the quality of teachers and the achievement of students is below that found in the developed countries. However, while many research studies have addressed this question in both developed and less-developed countries the cumulative results have not been conclusive (see, for example, Saha, 1978, 1983; Avalos and Haddad, 1981). One explanation for this lack of consistency pertains directly to problems of data aggregation.

In virtually all studies of teacher effects, school and teacher variables have been aggregated at the school level (for example, the proportion of teachers with university degrees, mean years of teaching service, etc.), while achievement scores have been collected and analyzed at the individual level. Thus while the unit of analysis has often been the individual student, measures of the effect variables have been the school. The assumptions implicit in this procedure are clear: all school facilities and teacher characteristics are assumed to have equal effects on all students, and that the distribution of resource inputs at the school level is independent of student characteristics.

There is evidence to indicate that this assumption is rarely met in real-life school processes: students do not receive equal benefits from school resources or their teachers. One way of getting around this difficulty through the research design would be to link the individual teacher and student in the analysis, or perhaps make individual teachers the unit of analysis. Ironically this latter strategy has almost never been utilized in school-effect research.

A second methodological difficulty often overlooked in research on educational processes is the extent to which characteristics of populations affect research findings. Not only are the results of procedures such as regression analyses contingent on the measurement and distribution of variables in the research model, but also on characteristics of the relationships between the variables. If we keep to the example already cited, one possible explanation for the differences in the effects of school and teacher variables in developed and less-developed countries is that the relative variation in school and teacher quality is greater in less-developed countries while variation in home background is greater in the developed countries. However, where there is little variance in the explanatory variable,

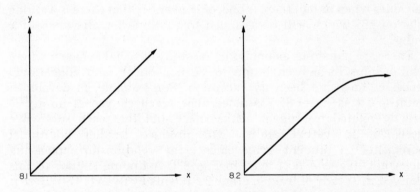

FIG. 8.1. Linear relationship between variables *x* and *y*.
FIG. 8.2 Non-linear relationship between variables *x* and *y*.

there will be little variance explained in the output variable. This may be one explanation why school and teacher quality have been found to have little "impact" on student academic achievement in developed countries, but considerable and consistent positive impact in less-developed countries (Saha, 1978, 1983; Avalos and Haddad, 1981; Heyneman and Loxley, 1983).

A third methodological problem is somewhat related to the above and concerns the nature of the relationships between the variables themselves. Most crucial is the case where these relationships are non-linear and interactive. The statistical consequences and means of resolution are not our concern here and should be sought elsewhere.[5] However, it is important that we recognize the difficulties and how they might distort the results and interpretations of evaluation research. In Figs 8.1 and 8.2 we can observe a linear and non-linear relationship between two variables *x* and *y*. In the first, for every increment in variable x there is a constant increase in variable y. The assumption of linearity assumes no threshold effects, such that the relationship is seen to hold for all values of x and y. On the other hand, in the non-linear example, we see that the strength of the relationship between x and y varies, depending on the particular values of x and y.

The difficulties produced by the latter case are in the main twofold. First, the failure to check for interactions in the data will result in a mis-specification of the model, such that the results may over- or under-estimate the true nature of the relationship, depending on the distribution of the variables themselves. Secondly, given the failure to take into account interaction or threshold effects may lead the researcher to conclude that there is no relationship between the variables when in fact there is one, or conversely that there is a strong relationship which will be assumed to continue for all values of x and y.

There are numerous examples in the study of social behavior where relationships have been found to be non-linear, and educational processes have not been an exception. For example, in developed countries it is generally assumed that teachers' verbal ability is directly related to student achievement, but that each successive increment in verbal ability will produce smaller additional increments in student achievement, the relationship appearing somewhat like that portrayed in Fig. 8.2. A finding similar to this emerged in a study of Iranian grade 2 students by Ryan (1974). Here it was found that the relationship between teacher ability and student achievement was strongest in rural areas and among the most disadvantaged children. On the other hand, when Thias and Carnoy (1972) estimated the marginal gains in earnings through schooling for each unit increase in teacher salary, they did not consider the possibility of diminishing marginal outputs, such that beyond a threshold of teacher salary increase, the gains in earnings become minimal or cease to exist at all.

In terms of system evaluation and policy decisions the problem of non-linearity is crucial. Clearly it would be erroneous to assume in any relationship between policy-related variables that constant marginal products or even of perfect substitutability among inputs (that is, that the same relationship would obtain with another input variable) would continue with unlimited increases of inputs. The policy decisions based on input–output analysis are particularly relevant for programs to prompt "small or *marginal changes* in resource allocation but should never suggest dramatic changes to points outside the existing (often quite narrow) range of observed data" (Bridge *et al.*, 1978:110). Carrying the implications further one should argue that the use of linear equations is never suitable for policy recommendations if the values are taken to extremes.

There are, of course, other limitations in the use of the educational production function (EPF) in evaluation and policy-related research. Simmons and Alexander (1980) identify five which can only be mentioned here: (1) multiple output interaction, (2) mis-specification of the regression model, (3) the conceptual and measurement limitations of the data, (4) multicollinearity, and (5) assumptions about appropriate levels of school efficiency. Each of these may bias the estimates of the effects of input variables on outputs, and in the case of evaluation studies of the impact of education on development, could be crucial for the formation of education policies or more extensive educational or societal reform.

These limitations of linear regression and EPF approaches should not be taken to mean that they represent useless strategies for evaluation research. Rosenholtz (1985), for example, argues that these studies cannot easily be dismissed because of the remarkable consistency in their findings. If the assumptions underlying linear equation models are carefully examined and research designs are constructed to overcome these limitations, then much can be gained in knowledge about educational processes which may be useful for policy, and for the improvement of the educational system with regard to the desired goals of development. However, alternative strategies for evaluation research must not be overlooked.

(ii) Alternative Evaluation Strategies

The increasing importance of evaluation research, as well as the recognition of the limitations of standard input–output research, has prompted a search for additional approaches which may serve to improve knowledge about education's possible role in the development process and to evaluate the impact of specific educational programs.

Not surprisingly, many attempts to overcome the limitations of input-output studies for evaluation research have focused on refinements to previous methodological procedures. Thus we find many authors concerned with the need to improve measurement of variables and to expand the number of variables in evaluation models. Although the concern with the inclusion and measurement of variables may appear, at first, to be relatively simple, the consequences are considerable. Already we have discussed problems of measuring not only the school outcome variables such as achievement, but also other demographic and system variables.

Greater sensitivity to the subtleties of variations in socio-economic status structures between societies, as well as the many school outputs other than academic achievements, are important examples.

Not less important than the above, but somewhat more innovatory, have been the concerns with units of analysis and the use of time-series (longitudinal) designs. We have previously noted the problems for standard analyses, but particularly with problems of inference and interpretation when the units of analysis are aggregated, or when they are mixed. For example, the use of school averages to measure teacher-quality impacts on individual achievement scores is based on a number of assumptions about the ways that school resources affect individual students, all of which are highly dubious. Ideally, evaluation research in education should focus on individual units of analysis. In like manner, research designed to evaluate the importance of schooling or the attainment of development-related objectives, such as work productivity, ultimately must focus on the individual as the unit of analysis.

The use of time-series or longitudinal data in input-output studies has been rare, and its inclusion in general evaluation research has been equally problematic. There have been some significant longitudinal studies, however, which merit mention. The Malmö study, which began with 1542 grade 3 schoolchildren in 1938, continues to provide important information on schooling and careers in Sweden, not only for the original sample but now for their children (Husén, 1969; Fägerlind, 1975; Tuijnman et al., 1988). The Wisconsin study began in 1957 with a survey of all high-school seniors in the State. Subsequent follow-up have not only produced important data on schooling and careers in the United States, but the study itself has been the center for the development and diffusion of important methodological procedures, particularly the use of path analysis in the social sciences (Sewell and Hauser, 1975, 1980). In 1976 a random sample of Form 5 students (N=321) in Botswana took part in an achievement study by the National Commission on Education. The students were studied again in 1979, and tracers on their achievement included data from 1974. The 5-year interval then provided information for the study of early career development in a less-developed and rapidly changing society (Kann, 1981). In 1970 Schiefelbein and Farrell (1982) surveyed a sample of ten students from each final year class of primary schools in Chile (approximately 3500 students). Seven years later they were re-surveyed in order to study inequalities in access and attainments in Chilean education and the labor market. In what they call the largest longitudinal study of an educational system in a developing nation, they found that schooling exercises an important effect in the transition from school to work. A study of transition from school to work in Australia will be discussed later in this chapter (Williams *et al.*, 1980, 1981).

In sharp contrast to the quantitative approaches thus far discussed, qualitative evaluation methods offer an alternative which directs more attention to in-depth analyses of process rather than structure. There has been considerable recent development in the use of qualitative methods, ranging from case studies to ethnographies, and including observational, documentary, and qualitative interview data. The contrast between the two kinds of approaches is found in Table 8.2. which also highlights the main features of each. Patton (1980), who has described at length the use of qualitative evaluation methods, is correct when he states that the challenge to the researcher is to select the methods most appropriate to the concerns of the policy-maker and to the specific evaluation situation. We take the view that any research design is as good as the questions it is expected to answer, and its usefulness hinges on the proper specification of the model, the conceptualization and measurement of the variables, and the use of appropriate data-gathering and analytic strategies.

TABLE 8.2. *Approaches to Evaluation Research*

Dominant approach	Alternative approach
Quantitative	Qualitative
Concerned about reliability	Concerned about validity
Objective	Subjective
Distant from data	Close to data
Focused on impact of components	Holistic analysis
Concerned about outcomes	Concerned about process
For scientists	For practitioners
Large samples	Case studies
Interested in generalizations	Interested in uniqueness
Tends to ignore interactions	Examines individual-treatment interactions

Source: Chinapah and Fägerlind, 1986: 34–35.

Ultimately, relevant evaluation research should address questions relating education with the three development dimensions already discussed, that is, economic growth and productivity, the improvement of social conditions, including changes in attitudes, values and aspirations, and finally the political mobilization of the population. Ultimately the link between education and development is contingent on the extent to which it contributes to each dimension. It may be that education exercises little or no effect on development, but as Dore (1980) observes, we are "children of the Enlightenment" in that we continue to believe that education "is the foundation of a good and economically productive society, and that the improvement of education is a means to a better society" (p. 69). Only well-designed and executed evaluation research can validate or at least test this belief.

Three Examples of Evaluation Research

In order to illustrate different approaches of evaluation research, three examples are presented here. These examples also represent attempts in different societies to evaluate educational processes in specific contexts and for the attainment of specific objectives. To this end we have chosen the evaluation of literacy campaigns in Mozambique using case studies, the macro-level evaluation of school effectiveness in less-developed countries, and finally an evaluation based on a national survey, the literacy and numeracy project in Australia. Taken together, it is our intention that these three examples demonstrate the range of design strategies used in evaluation research on the link between education and development.

(i) Evaluation of Literacy Campaigns
in Mozambique 1978–82:
A Case Study Approach[6]

At the time of national independence in June 1975 Mozambique had an illiteracy rate of 93 percent, which was one of the highest in the world. The expansion of the formal education system and mass literacy campaigns received top priority by the new government. The spread of literacy was regarded as one important factor to impove social, political and economic conditions, and to help develop human and material resources.

In a population that had been denied education during colonialism, the ground seemed fertile for a strong commitment to mass literacy campaigns. Literacy was looked upon as one of the most important means of promoting national unity by mobilizing the people politically and by spreading Portuguese as the national language to facilitate cross-national communication.

During the first five post-independence years, many of the local political committees which had been set up in residential areas and workplaces took the initiative for organizing literacy classes with local teachers and local economic resources. In this way literacy classes flourished all over the country (Marshall, 1988). At the same time a centrally organized and coordinated strategy was prepared by the State. The first National Literacy Campaign was launched in July

1978 and very soon it attracted more than two hundred thousand participants (Table 8.3).

TABLE 8.3. *Literacy Campaigns in Mozambique 1978–82: Targets, Enrolments, Outcomes.*

	1st NLC 1978/79	2nd NLC 1980	3rd NLC 1981	4th NLC 1982
Enrolment	>260 000	324 000	310 000	194 000
Target	110 000	200 000	300 000	300 000
Tested	320 000	199 000	117 000	55 000
Passed	140 000	119 000	61 000	37 000
Target	100 000	200 000	200 000	200 000

Source: Lind (1988). p. 69.

Teaching material had been prepared for the campaign, administrative structures had been set up in each province and district, and tutors had been given short duration training. However, to continue the National Literacy Campaigns information was needed both at central and provincial level. A statistical monitoring system was established to feed information to the organizers about initial enrolments, drop-out rates, number of persons tested and passed on the tests. As in other similar systems, many technical problems arose. Over and above statistical information different evaluation studies were performed which utilized both qualitative and quantitative methods. The case study approach was used to gather information from priority Literacy Centers. Methods involved in the case studies included: participant classroom observation, semi-structured interviews, achievement tests, lesson preparation meetings with tutors, interviews on variations in learning progress, observations of the learners' exercise books, and pretesting supplementary texts and exercises. The results and recommendations from these case studies were discussed and used at the National Directorate of Literacy and Adult Education when decisions were taken about pedagogical changes in class exercises and in providing teaching instructions in the Tutor's Guide.

From 1979 to 1983 five main case studies were performed. The first one was conducted in 1979 on the Maputo branch of a recently established state-owned fishing company. The second was performed in the Maputo harbour section of the Railway Company of Mozambique. The third case study in 1981 was directed towards a group of 79 Frelimo party members, which included 17 females, recruited for intensive literacy training in Nampula, the capital of the province with the same name. The fourth case study was completed in

1982 at an experimental literacy course when the final version of the new syllabus and some textbooks were tried out. The fifth case study was performed in 1983 within the framework of an integrated rural development project in the province of Maputo, where there was a total of 700 literacy students, the majority female, divided into 13 instruction classes.

The case studies provided valuable information about, and concrete examples of, the prevailing practices in the literacy program. The information was utilized by the planning units in their attempts to adjust and supplement the teaching material and in the provision of in-service pedagogical support and training. However, it was later found that written teaching instructions had very little influence on the actual teaching methods used in the classes. The previous schooling experience of the tutors and trainers determined the classroom methods more than any recommendations in the campaign materials. However, the textbooks did influence the content of the lessons, and because of this the National Literacy Service tried to adjust shortcomings in the texts. The third and the fourth National Literacy Campaigns were better equipped for the training and in-service support of the tutors than were the two first campaigns.

From the second campaign onwards the political/ideological preparation of the tutors was toned down in order to give more attention to the development of academic skills and of teaching methodology. All case studies confirmed that the motivation of the tutor was very important for the results of the students, and the need to sustain such motivation, though material and moral support, was shown to be important. The commitment for literacy manifested by political organizations and local leaders or production managers were also shown to be crucial for literacy participation and progress.

The first two campaigns showed growing participation, but from 1981 participation decreased gradually. The first two campaigns catered to strongly motivated persons and many semi-literates with some mastery of Portuguese. Once this group had been reached, the shortcomings of both an organizational and a pedagogical nature became apparent as factors influencing the subsequent decline of literacy programs. There was a tendency to bureaucratize the campaign management, to decrease mobilizing activities and to give more priority to academic objectives in line with class interests within the state bureaucracy to reproduce privileges based on academic qualifications.

The case studies used during the evaluation of the Literacy Campaigns in Mozambique played an important role in improving the quality of literacy teaching. These studies also might have been instrumental in stressing the importance of academic achievement. Ironically the attempts to improve the literacy learning among the enrolled adults at the same time might have contributed to decreasing political commitment and motivation. The internal efficiency of the campaigns played a minor role for their continuation. When political and economic constraints appeared the fall of the campaigns came very quickly.

The case studies made it possible to understand how important were the actions or lack of actions of local leaders and government agencies for literacy class attendance and results. Political commitment among the leaders was found to be more important than money spent. The case studies also showed that tutors were dependent upon the support they found in their environment. Through the information gathered it was possible to better understand the role of both the external and the internal factors related to difficulties in the campaign. This information did not make it possible to effectively change the negative directions of the fourth national literacy campaign in 1982. However, during a few years, such information had played a role in reducing illiteracy from 93 to 70 percent among adults in Mozambique.

(ii) Factors Related to School Effectiveness in Less-Developed Countries: A Meta-Analysis Approach

One difficulty in empirical research concerns the cumulative interpretation and synthesis of many independent research findings. Until recently attempts to utilize cumulative evidence from previous research have been limited to intuitive interpretations and sometimes strained attempts to explain inconsistent results. However, recent developments in the systematic analysis of many independent research results have opened new avenues not only to the expansion of our knowledge through cumulative evidence, but also have resulted in new approaches for the evaluation of educational processes at a macro-level across a wide range of topics.

Meta-analysis is a type ot secondary data analysis which focuses specifically on the results of other studies. In other words, meta-analysis is an analysis of analyses (Glass, 1976:3). The assumptions underlying meta-analysis is that there are hidden consistencies in the cumulative research findings, and systematic procedures which integrate these findings will uncover patterns which support conclusions which in turn can serve to guide future research and even contribute to the formation of policies. This contribution is even more explicit when meta-analysis is used to integrate the results of evaluation research. Clearly the prospect of tapping already existing research findings without great additional expense is appealing, but more importantly, the integration of these findings makes possible a kind of evaluation which hitherto has been extremely difficult.

Meta-analyses, at various levels of sophistication, have become a popular approach for the investigation of some central educational issues which have been extensively researched. One of these concerns the factors related to educational outputs and outcomes. Among the educational *outputs* are various kinds of academic achievement, the acquisition of manual skills, and changes in attitudes and behavior. Educational *outcomes* include eventual attainments in occupation, earnings and status, and associated changes in attitudes and behaviors (Windham, 1988). The factors which have attracted most research attention have been inputs such as the family, school, teachers and aspects of government policy toward schooling, for example funding and the effect of centralization and decentralization on outputs and outcomes. Although early research efforts into the determinants of outputs and outcomes were related to questions of inequality and were policy-oriented, recent activity has been framed in the context of the efficiency and effectiveness of schools.

The point of departure for the analysis of factors related to school efficiency and effectiveness was the Coleman Report (1966) and the work of Jencks and his colleagues (1972). The important implications of these two studies and the results they produced were policy relevant, and exerted considerable impact on those who believed that intervention strategies directed to the improvement of school performance would help alleviate the systematic disadvantages in school outputs and outcomes between the socially advantaged and disadvantaged students in American society. The findings of Coleman and Jencks were, in the main, negative, and suggested that schools and teachers exerted little independent effect on the academic performance of students; the key to explaining disparities in student achievement seemed to lie more on the original characteristics of students, in other words, their family backgrounds and the ways that these backgrounds formed them prior to, and during the school experience.

As might be expected, the reaction to these and other similar studies was immediate, and competing interpretations, explanations and criticisms of the findings were vigorously contested.[7] More importantly, this debate had considerable impact on the assessment of factors determining school outputs and outcomes, and on educational policies in less-developed countries. If the schools and teachers exercise little impact on student achievement, then the expensive efforts to upgrade schooling in poor countries becomes a poor investment for scarce funds which could better serve development interests if allocated to other sectors of national budgets.

Attempts to integrate the cumulative findings of research have not been uncommon in some of the developed countries (see Husén *et al.*, 1978), but probably the first such attempt for the less-developed countries was reported by Alexander and Simmons (1975). Their review located 17 EPF studies, of which they regarded nine as being acceptable for analysis. Alexander and Simmons concluded that the determinants of student achievement in less-developed countries were the same as in the developed countries, and thus policies directed to the improvement of school facilities and teacher training programs would have limited impact on raising student achievement. The findings of Alexander and Simmons generated enough discussion and concern among international organizations and other interested parties that a series of meta-analysis type studies followed in quick succession.

The World Bank commissioned a focused study to be conducted by the Institute of International Education at the University of Stockholm "on the current knowledge about the correlation between teacher training, the instruction given by teachers and the students' learning" (Husén *et al.*, 1978:1). Empirical investigations using legitimate and accepted survey or experimental designs were included, while exhortative, impressionistic or other poorly designed or executed studies were excluded from the analysis. The variables were grouped into four categories: (1) demographic and background variables, (2) teacher qualification and training variables, (3) teacher behavior and attitudes, and (4) block variables, which included general school and teacher characteristics. In the end, 16 precisely defined and operationally defined teacher variables were included in the study (Saha, 1978).

A thorough research of the literature identified 37 studies from 21 countries resulting in 230 independent research findings.[8] Each of these findings were then independently assessed to ascertain the strength and direction of the relationship between teacher and student achievement variable, and was subsequently classified as a positive (+), null (0), or negative (−) relationship. The distribution of research results alone indicated that there was a positive relationship between teacher characteristics and student achievement, and the pattern was therefore inconsistent with the findings from developed countries which suggested that the determinants of student achievement were largely outside the school.

When the teacher-effect estimates were broken down into more specific categories, for example studies relating only to teacher qualifications or those which used sophisticated multiple-regression techniques, the distribution of the results remained virtually the same. The data showing these patterns are found in Table 8.4.

TABLE 8.4. *Teacher Training and Student Achievement in Less-developed Countries, Summary of Empirical Results (Number in Brackets)*

		Positive +	Null 0	Negative –	Total
I	All teacher variables	58.3 (134)	38.2 (88)	3.5 (8)	100.0 (230)
II	Teacher qualification variables only	53.1 (43)	38.3 (31)	8.6 (7)	100.0 (81)
III	Fourteen selected EPF studies	57.1 (8)	28.6 (4)	14.3 (2)	100.0 (14)

Source: Saha (1983), Table 2.

On the basis of this form of meta-analysis of research findings, the conclusion of the evaluation was that in less-developed countries teacher characteristics do make a difference in the academic achievement of students. As part of the same project, Noonan (1978) found that when other variables were held constant, verbal IQ of 14-year-olds in Chile and India exerted the highest impact on science performance, followed by teaching methods and teacher training. These effects were higher than those for home background.[9]

Other studies confirmed these findings. In a review of reviews of teacher-effect studies written by researchers in less-developed countries, Avalos and Haddad (1981) concluded that the evidence for independent teacher impacts on student achievement in less-developed countries is apparent, although "...such research is still very much coloured by the use of imported designs and methods and by a selection of problems that do not necessarily represent the real issues that lie behind educational ineffectiveness" (p. 60). In perhaps the most critical and stringent meta-analysis conducted thus far, Fuller (1987) found in his analysis of 60 multivariate studies that a wide range of school characteristics exercise a significant impact on student achievement.

The differences between developed and less-developed countries in the determinants of school effectiveness have given rise to several explanations. Apart from methodological explanations (as discussed earlier in this chapter) some have suggested structural factors, and in particular those which may be unique to less-developed countries (Saha, 1983). Heyneman (1976) was able to document the importance of school and teacher variables for school effectiveness in less-developed countries. He argued that "the more industrialized a society, the more achievement in school is apt to be affected by a pupil's socioeconomic environment and other out-of-school influences" (1976:205). Subsequently Heyneman and Loxley (1983) suggested a range of explanations, including the possibility of competition for schooling across rich and poor families alike, with the effect that the social background of students is less important than school factors in explaining achievement results. According to Fuller (1987 it is no longer a question of whether school and teacher quality have an impact on school effectiveness in less-developed countries, but rather why and under what conditions this impact occurs.

Meta-analysis is an emerging and increasingly important strategy for evaluation research. If properly executed, the systematic study of cumulative research findings can be used to evaluate a wide range of questions relating to educational processes, and to evaluate the results of evaluations, particularly those concerning education and development. Furthermore, these can be directed to studies of a single society or across many societies. Already there is evidence that meta-analysis is increasing in importance for the analysis of specific educational processes;[10] it remains for the approach to be utilized for more large-scale enquiries which have importance for theoretical understanding and policy formation.

(iii) Literacy and Numeracy in Australia

Perhaps the most obvious strategy for evaluation research is the national survey. While the use of national testing to evaluate the quality of schooling or the levels of achievement of pupils is expensive, nevertheless it is probably the most potentially useful and accurate method of understanding and improving the performance of a national educational system. Furthermore, while most efforts directed at the evaluation of schooling have focused on student achievement, it is not unlikely that suitable instruments could also measure the relationship between schooling and other aspects of the social structure, for example the economic productivity of the workforce, value and attitude change, political participation, and other criteria related to social and economic development.

Australia is an example of a country which has extensively utilized national surveys as a means for evaluating the performance of its school system, in particular the level of achievement of its school students in basic skills of literacy, writing and numeracy. The national survey executed by the Australian Council for Educational

Research in 1975 represents an excellent illustration of this evaluation strategy.

The Australian national survey began as a political concern about special learning difficulties among children. In order to better understand the nature and extent of such difficulties the Commonwealth Government, through its various educational agencies, funded a national enquiry into literacy and numeracy, which was to be executed during 1975 and the report made available in 1976.

The concern for the attainment of basic skills was overtly humanitarian, but implicitly acknowledged the importance of these skills for society as a whole. For example, the concern for literacy was said to be a "basic value, underlying the programs of primary and secondary schools in Australia, that all children should attain minimum standards of competence for life in a modern, democratic, industrial society" (Keeves and Bourke, 1976:4). Furthermore, the possession of these skills was felt to be "important for all Australian citizens".

Although the Australian census had regularly sought information on literacy, the utilization of this information for precise estimates among the population were deemed inadequate for all but the most general impression of the distribution of these skills; test conditions are clearly superior mechanisms for accurate determination of reading and writing ability. Having decided on this latter strategy, the design of such a study was clearly a difficult and complex task, for not only was knowledge about the extent of the basic skills sought, and also the relationships between the possession of these skills and other factors, but estimates of the actual numbers of those deficient in these skills were desired in order that suitable programs might be launched to remedy their underattainment. In the end, the decision was made to test two groups of students in normal schools, those aged 10:00 to 10:11 years, and those between 14:00 and 14:11 years. A two-stage stratified sampling procedure was adopted, first sampling by schools, and then by students within schools. The sampling of schools followed the probability proportional to the number of students within the target population. All states and territories were included in the study, and adjustment procedures were utilized in order to accurately represent students from small schools. Ultimately the samples were designed such that 7000 students were to be tested at each of the two age levels, which would provide for minimum errors of estimates lying somewhere between 3 and 6 percent (Keeves and Bourke, 1976:16–17). While these sampling details may appear unduly complicated (and we have given only a summary in this brief description) it should be apparent that careful design can make evaluation research possible with relatively small samples and reduced costs. (The total cost per student in March 1976 was estimated to be A $ 5.95 (p. 112).)

The general results of the survey were striking. From the questionnaires administered to the teachers of the students, it was found that between 15 and 20 percent of the students in normal schools, at both the 10- and 14-year-old levels, were considered to be in need of remedial instruction in reading and numeracy. Approximately one-half of the 10-year-olds in this category were already being given some form of remedial help during 1975, the year of the study. In practical terms, then, teachers estimated that about three students out of an average class of thirty, who were in need of help, were not receiving it.

Turning to student performance on reading tests, it was found that 3 percent, or approximately 7500 students in the age-10 normal school cohort, had not reached the minimum level of reading proficiency. In the age-14 group this elementary level had not been reached by 0.8 percent of the sample. This proportion represents 2000 students in that age cohort. The results on the writing ability tests were even more disturbing. Approximately one-quarter of the 10-year-olds, and 10 percent of the 14-year-olds were unable to adequately record the contents of a simple phone message, and an even larger proportion could not correctly write a letter to a friend. Even more striking was the fact that one-half of the 14-year-old students were unable to meet the requirements to write a letter of application for employment. It is difficult to summarize the results of the numeracy tests because there were a large number of separate items which tapped ability on a variety of numeracy skills. In general, however, it was found that more than 90 percent of the 10-year-olds were able to perform simple calculations which are considered necessary and useful for everyday life. Performance on more complicated tasks was less consistent. The 14-year-olds did not perform consistently on any one skill item, although they performed these tasks better than 10-year-olds. Overall, the researchers concluded that there was much room for improvement in numeracy achievement of Australian school students.

Survey data of the type and quality described here makes possible extensive analyses of school outcomes. Once collected, far more than levels of performance or achievement can be examined in order to provide important insights into more sophisticated aspects of educational processes. The Australian national evaluation of literacy and numeracy represents an excellent example. In the final report of the study (Bourke and Keeves, 1977), not only was more precise information about reading, writing and numeracy abilities available, but performance in these skills by various subgroups of the Australian population were also presented. For example, it was found that 10 percent of the migrant students were, in the eyes of their teachers, incapable of understanding English sufficiently well to cope with normal classroom lessons, and that 35 percent needed remedial assistance in both reading and number skills. Apparently only half of those in need were actually receiving attention, suggesting directions for policy decisions concerning the provision of additional remedial programs. According to Bourke and Keeves, most of the difficulties of migrant children were due to their poor command of English, and further, to their limited exposure to and opportunities to use the English language (p. 177).

Other interesting findings of the evaluation concerned the importance of demographic variation in the mastery levels of literacy and numeracy. For example, it was found that numeracy ability was more evenly spread across schools than reading ability, suggesting that numeracy is more a school-related skill, while other factors affect literacy skills. There was likewise considerable variation between States which again pointed to specific policy areas where improvements might be attempted.

An additional bonus for evaluation research of this design is the subsequent use of the base for future studies. A well-designed and executed study makes possible follow-ups in later years, providing valuable (and indispensable) longitudinal information of the long-term trends and effects of schooling. Thus in Australia these follow-ups in 1979 have provided information of subsequent achievements, not only in later schooling, but also for work and career. By 1979 the 10-year-olds had become 14- or 15-year-olds, and the 14-year-olds were 17 to 18. As a rule, the analyses of the original 10-year-olds indicated that those who were experiencing learning difficulties at the early age were still experiencing those same difficulties 4 years later, in spite of various remedial programs in which they participated. Williams *et al.* (1981) predict that 20 percent of the sample in this category will be at high risk concerning future unemployment. The findings were not much different for those in the original 14-year-old group. In effect, the follow-up studies of the original 14-year-old sample clearly indicated the enduring effects of family background and early school deficiencies for both educational and occupational destinations in later years (Williams *et al.*, 1980; Williams, 1987). A national survey of the kind reported here clearly identifies national education problems and directs attention to aspects whereby these deficiencies might be remedied* and where policy innovations should be directed.

The Politics of Educational Policy and Reform

The execution of useful and viable evaluation studies of educational processes does not guarantee that relevant policy and reform which might remedy deficiencies automatically follow. Yet decisions are made each day throughout the world which have effects on schools and schooling, and ultimately the development destinies of nations. The contribution of evaluation research to these decisions is of considerable importance, for it is far better that decisions be made on the basis of factual information rather than no information at all.

Coleman (1972) has made some useful observations about the ways that evaluation research can assist in the formation of policy. Firstly, one must not confuse the kind of research which leads to policy. "Disciplinary research" is that which is derived from within academic disciplines designed in the main to advance knowledge. "Policy research", on the other hand, originates outside the discipline in the world of action, and is mainly concerned with action. Oftentimes disciplinary pursuits decry the use of research for practical ends, arguing that theoretical and methodological quality invariably suffer. This need not be the case. The prescriptions governing the design and execution of evaluation and policy research are the same as those governing scientific research generally. To have it otherwise would make a mockery of presumed informed decisions required for reform.

There are differences, however. Policy research does not require parsimony and elegance, and redundancy can sometimes be valuable. Of greater importance is the correctness of the estimates derived from the research regarding some educational or social condition in the general population. Furthermore, the selection of variables for inclusion must be subject to policy manipulation such that policy measures designed to intervene or remedy a social condition do not raise ethical or obtrusive issues. It does little good for policy formation to demonstrate that home background or innate ability contribute to academic achievement, as these two variables are not easily incorporated into school or development reform decisions. At least they would not be considered manipulable in the context of current political and ethical values in most countries of the world today.

In spite of these clear guidelines about the use of evaluation research for generating policy, there is no guarantee that viable policy will emerge. Coleman himself takes a pessimistic stance regarding the link between policy research and policy formation, the reason being the existence of conflicts between political interests and values regarding national goals, and how best to attain them. Even in the best of circumstances, the formation of policy is an inherently political process.

Nevertheless the accumulation of empirical findings from research involving several disciplines makes it increasingly difficult for those in responsible positions to initiate uninformed or irresponsible programs. The fundamental requirement for translating research into policy is that the right questions be asked and the underlying values be recognized. House (1978), for example, has argued that evaluation and policy cannot be based solely on the principles of scientific management. The efficiency of an educational system may not be the best criterion to use in the formulation of policy. He argues that a systems approach, in which a wider variety of issues are taken into account, may in the long run be more viable. Thus evaluation research and policy take values into account as well. In fact, House states that "the systems analysis approach to evaluation promises to substitute specific techniques derived from 'science' for the knowledge of craft in teaching, which is derived from experience and apprenticeship" (p. 400). He goes on to point out that the challenge for evaluation is to identify policies or approaches which are complementary to "professional craft" rather than to "replace" it. Evaluation and reform do not necessarily require scientific efficiency. "While efficiency may be relevant as a goal, it is certainly a distortion of the educational processes to take it as the overriding consideration" (p. 400).

We thus come to our final comment on evaluation and reform. Policies and reforms depend, in large part, on the values of a society. A society will invest in education, and place emphasis on particular reform strategies to the extent that there is consensus concerning its objectives and priorities (Emmerij, 1974). Where there is less consensus, or where a society can be said to be pluralistic, the execution of evaluation research and the formulation of policy becomes more problematic. Thus, for example, House (1978) argues that large-scale reforms in the United States have not been highly successful because of the pluralism of its society. On the other hand, Sweden, as we have seen in chapter 6, has apparently been more successful in its educational reforms. But compared to the United States, Sweden is a relatively homogeneous and consensus-oriented society. Thus the nature of evaluation and policy will depend, to some extent, on the degree of pluralism in a society. "A monolithic evaluation", contends House, "is not appropriate for a pluralistic society"(p. 401).

Given the problematic nature of education evaluation and reform in the pursuit of development objectives, it becomes even more apparent that there is no one path to follow in the integration of an educational system into a larger development strategy. Our analysis of the dimensions of development and of the "scientific" and political aspects of policy suggest that there are not one but many possible models of education and development, each incorporating unique relationships between education, the State and society generally. In Part 4 we proceed to the investigation of these various permutations, and attempt to derive models which are both theoretically and empirically sound, which link forms of education with types of societies in the pursuit of varying development objectives.

Notes

1. We do not wish to give the impression that the evaluation of education is only of recent origin. In 17th-century Sweden, for example, the extent to which the elite schools achieved their goals fell to the responsibility of the local bishop who then reported to the State educational commission. The bishops carried out their task of evaluation by school visitations. In this respect, the school inspector system, wherever it has or still exists, represents a form of evaluation.

   Our view, however, is that many aspects of education have often gone unevaluated, and that only recently has the process of evaluation itself begun to reach a respectable level of conceptualization and rigor.

2. The International Association for the Evaluation of Educational Achievement (IEA) is a cooperative research organization which was founded in 1959. Its purpose is to investigate the factors of school achievement at an international level both to advance knowledge and inform policy in matters related to schooling. Since its founding, IEA has conducted an international study of mathematics in 12 countries in the mid-1960s (Husén, 1967), and a second mathematics study in 24 countries currently in progress. In 1970–71 IEA conducted a six-subject survey of achievement in science (19 countries), reading comprehension (15), literature (10), French as a foreign language (8), English as a foreign language (10), and civic education (10). (See Walker, 1976, for an overview.) A second study of science achievement in 17 countries is currently in progress (IEA, 1988), as is a 14-country study of written composition (Gorman *et al.*, 1988).

3. One example of this kind of approach is found in the work of a group of researchers centered at Stanford University. An early example of their use of aggregate statistics to investigate society-level variables in the study of education expansion is found in Meyer *et al.*, 1977. Subsequent studies from this group have included a focus on vocational education (Benevot, 1983), educational ideology (Fiala and Lanford, 1987), and a general theory of educational expansion (Boli *et al.*, 1985).

4. For a thorough discussion of EPF and linear regression strategies see Simmons and Alexander (1980) and Cohn and Rossmiller (1987).

5. The use of transformation practices with non-linear data is well known and documented. These may include the use of standard scores, log-linear

transformations, or interaction terms. Practical treatments of these techniques can be found, for example, in Bridge *et al.* (1978) or Pedhazur (1982).

6. This description of the Literacy Campaigns in Mozambique is based on Lind (1988).

7. For example, even Jencks has somewhat modified his original position. His recent work, *Who Gets Ahead?* (1979), takes a perspective quite different from *Inequality*. In the United Kingdom, the work by Rutter *et al.* (1979), *Fifteen Thousand Hours*, likewise concludes that school effects may be more important than has been indicated in previous research.

8. In the original review there were 32 studies representing 19 countries and 194 individual findings. Although the number of original findings was smaller, the distribution of these findings in terms of positive, null, or negative effects was the same as in the revised figures.

9. Noonan carried his analysis further and attempted to calculate the actual increments in standardized test scores if teacher quality were improved. According to Noonan, "... if the mean level of formal teacher training in the respective countries were raised to the level of the most highly trained 50 percent of teachers today, mean student science achievement, as measured by the IEA test score, would rise from 9.6 to 10.3 in Chile and from 8.3 to 8.7 in India" (1978:67).

10. Recent volumes of the *American Educational Research Journal* and the *Review of Educational Research* contain examples of meta-analysis applied to specific research questions. See, for example, the articles by Smith and Glass (1980) on class size, and by Kulik *et al.* (1980) on computer-based teaching.

PART 4

Towards a Typology for Education
and Development

9

Education and Development under Capitalism and Socialism

IN the preceding chapters we have traced the origins of theories of development and examined in detail the link between education and what we consider the three most important dimensions of the development process: the economic, social and political. We have also discussed various strategies of educational reform and critically examined approaches for evaluation and policy-making.

Our goal in this chapter is to organize and systematize the various kinds of relationships between education and development. In other words, we want to answer the question as to how education functions in different kinds of societies, in particular capitalist and socialist, developed and less developed, and industrial and non-industrial. Ultimately we show the direction and content which educational reform should take if it is to contribute to the attainment of specific development goals. In saying this we acknowledge the fact that education is determined by the same economic, social and political forces to which it contributes. However, we take the position that all educational systems are immersed in a dialectical process whereby education and the changes in a society are reciprocally related in a causal system.

Education and Dialectics

Dialectics as a logical principle assumes that contradictions and their resolutions in either systems of knowledge or in history are necessary if progress is to be achieved. In order to unravel the complexity which seems to surround the education-development debate, one must view the relationship between education and society as a dialectical one. The contradiction lies in the fact that education is both an agent of change and in turn is changed by society. For example, it acts both as a producer of social mobility and as an agent for the reproduction of the social order. Furthermore, the manner in which this dialectical process occurs and is resolved, is contingent on

225

other characteristics of the social system itself. We have argued that the most important of these characteristics are the economic, the social and the political. Each of these three dimensions interacts dialectically with the other, and all three interact dialectically with education.

There are two levels at which the dialectical process occurs. The first and most general level concerns the relationship between education and society as a whole. In Fig. 9.1 this process is illustrated, showing that education is both a change agent and is changed by society. As indicated in the figure, education in the first instance is a product of society (1), but then acts on society bringing about change (2), which acts again on education (3). The process is a continual one and operates differently in different kinds of societies. Thus the manner in which the dialectical process operates appears to be different for different types of society, for example, the capitalist and socialist and it is our purpose later in this chapter to explore the nature of these differences.

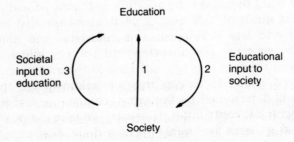

Education

Societal
input to   3
education

1

2

Educational
input to
society

Society

FIG. 9.1 The interrelationship
between education and society.

The second level at which the dialectical process occurs is more complex. Each of the major development dimensions both affects and is affected by the others and by the educational system. As such, education in any society is part of a dialectical process with the economic, social and political dimensions of society. Its contribution to the development process is therefore contingent on the configuration of these dimensions in any given society at any point in time.

At this stage, our discussion is necessarily complex and abstract. The process which we are describing will perhaps be more clear from the illustration in Fig. 9.2. In the figure, the three sides of the triangle represent each of the three dimensions of society. The dialectical relationships are indicated by the pairs of arrows connecting them. In the center, the educational system is indicated by a circle and its dialectical connection with the three dimensions is indicated

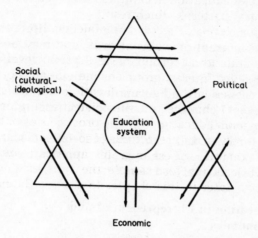

Fig. 9.2 Dialectical model of
education and development
dimensions

by pairs of arrows to each side. These relationships are in a constant state of change, and thus not only the educational system, but the features of the larger societal system are also constantly changing. Since the dialectical process occurs over time, elements of the old and new can exist simultaneously. Thus societies in transition from traditional to modern may contain elements of both in their educational systems, at least for a time. Finally, the dialectical process may or may not involve struggle or conflict as a result of these contradictions. In other words, the dialectical process produces changes ranging from the gradual to the revolutionary.

In effect, what we are describing in our model are the dynamics of societal systems with respect to education and development. Insofar as the notion of system is generally understood in the social sciences as the set of interdependencies of parts of a whole, our entire model depicts the components of the societal system which are of interest to us, namely the educational, the political, and so on. However, each of these components also may be described as a system, with its own set of interdependent parts. Hence, we have been speaking about the educational system, the economic system and the like. The pattern of relationships within and between systems are normally referred to as structures such that our model in Fig. 9.2 can be described as the dialectic structure formed by the relationship between the educational and other systems in society. Thus, we can speak of the particular place of education in capitalist and socialist social systems, and the structural patterns which result.

The forces for or obstacles to change which affect the dialectical system may be internal or external to it, and may be the result of actions at the individual, group or the system level. Thus global economic recessions, interest groups or individuals working through democratic processes are all examples of forces which may bring about or prevent changes in the dialectical interrelationships depicted in the model[1].

In order to further clarify our conceptualization of this dialectical process, the examples of change in American and Indonesian education are briefly analyzed here.

American Education in Entrepreneurial and Corporate Economies

One of the distinctive features of economic change in the United States has been the transition from an entrepreneurial to a corporate economy. The economic base of the colonies, and later, the young republic, consisted of a large proportion of self-employed workers. Shopkeepers, craftsmen, small-businessmen and farmers dominated economic life during the early and middle part of 19th-century America. During the colonial period, the family constituted the basic productive unit to which all members were expected to contribute. Schooling was limited to only a few, as the skills required for cottage industries and farming could be learned in the home. After the War of Independence, economic forces were gradually unleashed which resulted in the rapid expansion of commerce and foreign trade. The numbers of self-employed diminished with the increase of wage earners. Between 1795 and 1855 there was a fourfold increase in wage workers while, during the same period, there was a reduction by two-thirds in the number of independent merchants and proprietors. This trend continued into the 20th century, and for the United States as a whole the ratio of self-employed to wage workers decreased from one-third to one-fifth between 1890 and 1930 (Bowles and Gintis, 1976:157).

During the 19th and 20th centuries, the gradual increase in corporate enterprises and the growth of the factory system changed the role of the family both in terms of child-rearing and economic production. The role of the school was also affected, and according to

Bowles and Gintis (1976) the changes in the economic structure, in particular the composition of the labor force, brought about the rapid increase in public schooling. "Where manufacturing did employ any significant numbers of people, public schools followed" (p. 176).

In the face of a changing social structure, and in particular the emergence of a large wage-labor force, the school was seen as a means of easing the tensions and disruptive conflicts resulting from the transition to a capitalist industrial economy. In short, it was seen as an institution which would provide "moral guidance and control" to replace the family and church whose influence during this period had declined. "Schooling was seen by reformers and industrialists alike as promoting their common vision of an ordered, purposeful, and progressive society" (Carnoy, 1974:236).

There was no general agreement regarding the advantages and desirability of the introduction of the common public school during the 19th century. For the self-employed, schooling represented only a cost both in terms of taxes and the removal of their children from the family as productive economic units. On the other hand, for the professionals and factory owners, schools served their interests as a means. of improving skilled labor and as a means of imposing the ideology of democratic liberalism on the total population during this period of social and industrial change. Michael Katz (1968) cites an illustrative example of the conflict arising from the introduction of the common school. In 1860 the people of Beverly, Massachusetts, voted to close the new high school in the town. The professional and business people supported the school while the small craftsmen and entrepreneurs for the most part opposed it. "The underlying cause of both the establishment and abolition of Beverly High School was the shifting economic base and the consequent social division in both the town and the state" (Katz, 1968:85).

This analysis of the emergence of public schooling in 19th-and 20th-century America is basically an economic one whereby the educational system is seen as a product of the economic interests and forces of the society. In terms of our model in Fig. 9.2 this represents only one of the three dimensions we feel are important. However, the factors influencing education are much more complex.

A different perspective is presented in a study by Meyer *et al.* (1979) which challenges the economic interpretation of the public-school movement. Meyer and his colleagues are not convinced that the emerging industrial power of the Northeastern States and the rise of a wage labor force were solely responsible for rapidly increasing school enrolments. In particular, they argue that the expansion of schooling occurred too quickly in both rural and urban areas and during a time when state power over education was weak (pp. 595–598). The main stimulus to the growth of public schooling, Meyer *et al.* (1979) argue, was the ideology of nation-building combined with evangelical Protestantism. It was not the decision of a narrow elite or a powerful state which created the increase of schooling but "...hundreds of thousands of people who shared a common ideology" based upon a conception of the "nation" as composed of people free from ignorance, sin, aristocracy and old-world customs (p. 601). Schooling was seen throughout the country as the means of creating this kind of policy.

Whereas Bowles and Gintis (1976) stress the economic dimension in their analysis of the emerging educational system, Meyer and his colleagues stress both the political and the cultural–ideological dimensions. As we see it, no one of these explanations fully accounts for the unique characteristic of the American education system, for that system is the result of the convergence of influences from and to all three dimensions, as we argue in our model. In order to further illustrate our position in a completely different context, we now turn our attention to Indonesia and an examination of the factors playing a part in its education reform during the 1970s.

Indonesian Education and Cultural–Ideological Pluralism

In choosing Indonesia as our second case study to illustrate the dialectical process of the educational system we choose an example which contrasts sharply with the United States. Indonesia represents a developing country with all the problems faced by other developing countries throughout the world. Secondly, instead of analyzing an example from the historical emergence of an educational system, we are here examining an event which has occurred quickly, dramatically and recently. For much of the factual information underlying our analysis, we rely heavily on the work of C. E. Beeby, *Assessment of Indonesian Education: A Guide in Planning* (1979).

The problems experienced by Indonesia which are similar to other less-developed countries are those related to low general educational attainment, rapid increases in the demand for education, and until recently, a strained economy. Between 1960 and 1975 the literacy rate rose from 39 percent to 62 percent, a significant increase by any standard. During virtually the same period, the proportions of the relevant age groups enrolled in primary school increased from 71 percent to 86 percent, and for secondary school from 6 to 21 percent (World Bank, 1980b). In a small household survey in 1972 from the six major provinces, it was found that 40 percent of the fathers had no schooling, 39 percent had primary school without completing, 16 percent had completed primary school, and only 5 percent had gone beyond primary school (Pearse, 1977). In this context, the expansion of the demand for schooling and high-level occupations has been dramatic. In a survey reported by Beeby (1979:166–167), it was found that among secondary students, expectations for going to higher studies ranged from 91 percent in academic schools to 76 percent in teacher training schools. These expectations persisted in spite of the fact that only about 50 percent of academic school graduates, and a lower percentage of the others, could reasonably expect acceptance to higher studies. These patterns, however, are not that unusual from the situation found in other developing countries.

There are some unique characteristics which aggravate the Indonesian situation. Communication and contact is made difficult by the fact that the country is comprised of 3000 islands covering an area roughly equivalent to that bounded between London and Siberia from West to East and between Stockholm and Rome from North to South. In mid-1978 the population was reported to be 136 million with a complex ethnic structure and up to 250 different languages, most of which belong to the same linguistic family. The cultural development of this population ranges from almost Stone Age tribes in Irian Jaya to modern Westernized businessmen and professionals in Djakarta.

A further unique characteristic of the Indonesian educational system is the legacy of colonial domination. For almost 350 years, from around 1600 to 1941, Indonesia was under continual Dutch domination. In 1942 until 1945, the islands were under Japanese occupation, to be followed at the end of World War II by a short period during which the Dutch and Indonesian nationalists struggled with each other for sovereignty. Indonesia became independent in 1949 and ushered in a period of frequent political change as the country attempted to rid itself of colonial vestiges and embark upon a long-term "social revolution" (Thomas, 1970:329). Under the Dutch, the government was committed to traditional colonial goals: to make money and conserve Dutch superior positions. The society could only be described as a plural one, whereby the people lived among each other as interacting but separate sub-societies, rather than a closely integrated one. The schools were highly stratified, with the European schools on top of the status scale. Apart from the Dutch, the children of Chinese merchants and some Indonesian aristocracy attained high levels of schooling. On the whole, schooling except for the elite was neglected and in 1930 the literacy rate was around 10 percent

(Thomas, 1970:303). Under Japanese occupation there was serious initial disruption to education and for a period schools were even closed. However, the Japanese did initiate a program which attempted to eradicate the stratified system under the Dutch and downgrade the favored pre-war ethnic groups. Although the purpose of the Japanese reforms was to "Nipponize" Indonesia as a part of the "Greater East Asia Co-prosperity Sphere", their actions also paved the way to wider educational reforms after independence.

During what has been called the "Decade of Parliamentary Democracy", from 1950 to 1959, the significant advances in educational attainment represent the brightest spot on what was otherwise a politically troubled period. The government policy was to whole-heartedly endorse educational expansion and eradicate the remnants of the colonial stratified system, in particular the Dutch and Chinese schools. However, in spite of strong political support, the delicate economy placed limits on available funds. Throughout the fifties, in spite of the fact that the number of children in elementary schools nearly doubled (almost 5 million to more than 8 million), education received only 5 to 7 percent of the national budget, and in 1960, 45 percent of the children between 6 and 11 were still not in school.

During the first half of the 1960s, in what has been called the period of "guided Democracy" or "socialism à la Indonesia", the president assumed greater powers over political, social and economic affairs, but at the same time the economy declined and both growth and the quality of education deteriorated markedly. Even with the new regime from 1966, the depressed condition of education continued. The salaries of teachers were so low that "moonlighting", or the holding of multiple jobs, became quite common. School buildings were allowed to deteriorate and the building of new ones virtually ceased. The first Five-Year Plan, initiated during this period, resulted in an increase in funds for education (13 percent of the national budget in 1971), but most of this was directed to vocational and technical training without much regard for the needs of industry (Beeby, 1979:7).

Against this background, a most significant event occurred in 1974. The price of Indonesian oil rose dramatically, from $2.93 a barrel in April 1973 to $10.80 in January 1974. Almost overnight, the revenue available to the government multiplied many times. Beeby, who was a consultant to the Department of Education and Culture from 1970 to 1973, recounts that while there, the Department was, even by the humble standards of Asia and Africa, very poor. Yet by 1974, "...the same Department, if not yet rich, was at least temporarily embarrassed by the amount of money put at its disposal" (1979:1).

To be sure, the rags-to-riches transition should not be exaggerated, as the demands on these revenues were great. Nevertheless, money for education quickly increased in availability. However, what impact did this increase have on an educational system which had been previously chronically starved for funds? A purely economic determinist model would suggest that overnight the educational system would develop both in quality and quantity. In fact this did not occur. The reason, of course, is that the economy is only one of three important dimensions in the dialectical process relating to education. As indicated in our model, other dimensions continued to impose serious constraints. Beeby implicitly supports this interpretation in his cautious warning about the limits of money:

> This raises the question of what you *can* buy with money in education, and what there is that you cannot get with money alone. The Indonesians have been the first to admit that a major problem in education is to raise the quality and the relevance of the work in most of their schools and in their institutions of higher learning. Up till now they have met two main obstacles in their efforts to improve education. The first has been the grievous shortage of money and of the material things that it will buy; the second is a more subtle group of constraints that do not seem to be immediately responsive to rapid injections of finance. The increased revenues from oil promise to remove, at least for the present, the first of these obstacles, but, in so doing, they will intensify the need for sweeping and rapid changes in the second and more intractable set of constraints (1979:3–4).

These intractable obstacles, of which Beeby speaks, include both the political and social dimensions of our model.

Since 1969, Indonesia has initiated three 5-year plans for development, Repelita I (1969–1973), Repelita II (1974–1978) and Repelita III (1979–1983). Education played a particularly important part in the second five-year plan, in which the goals and aims were stated as follows:

1. Education is to produce the "ideal" Indonesian adult, referred to as the "*Panca-Sila*-minded man". Such a person is described as having "a high degree of dedication to the future of Indonesia", "knowledge and skills ...that correspond to development needs", and in general all the qualities which would promote the advancement of the society.
2. Education should promote development in the broad sense, for example, through both economic growth and the transition to a more rational and democratic society.

3.   The equality of opportunity.
4.   The improvement of the quality of education, for example, by raising standards and the promotion of creative thinking and problem-solving.
5.   The expansion of the school system.
6.   Curricula development in line with regional and local needs.
7.   The development of informal and other adult education programs.
8.   Setting up the mechanisms, namely administrative, organizational, and so forth, necessary to implement the other stated goals (Beeby, 1979:265–266).

According to Beeby, none of these goals can be achieved without conflict and tension. For example, there is disagreement regarding the choices of goals, of priorities among them, and of the methods used to achieve them. What, then, are the obstacles imposed by the political and social dimensions? The educational goals stated in Repelita II, for the most part, are contained within more general political objectives. However, the political elites in Indonesia, as in many other countries, hold unrealistic beliefs about the relationship between the educational goals and the educational system itself. Furthermore, even some of the goals contain in themselves the seeds of tension and conflict. The notion of *Panca Sila* is a case worth examining.

Panca Sila is a general philosophy having antecedents in Indonesian and Indian history, and is based on the principles of one God, humanity, unity of Indonesia, democracy and social justice (Fischer, 1965:110; Beeby, 1979:267). The ideology of *Panca Sila* forms an important part of political education in both high schools and universities, and is based on a wide variety of sources, such as Koranic dictums, extracts from Marx and Dewey, the speeches of political leaders and current ideological slogans. However, it has generally been conceded that *Panca Sila* has not been effectively imparted in the classroom. As a political ideology, *Panca Sila* is too amorphous a concept to be effectively transmitted, and furthermore, often conflicts with other realities of not only the classroom but also of society.

> The *Panca Sila* are essentially moral principles; so, in addition to having to discern the tensions between them in any practical situation he [i.e. the teacher] is discussing, he has the even harder problem of knowing how to deal in class with lapses from them in an imperfect society (Beeby, 1979:268–269).

According to our model, the effect of the political dimension on the educational system is problematic because of the dialectical relationship between it and the other dimensions. Ideally, political goals inform the educational system such that the products of the educational system conform to them. The principle of *Panca Sila,* if effectively transmitted, should produce Indonesian citizens supportive of the general objectives of a unified Indonesian nation-state. The evidence suggests that the policy has been achieved only to a minimal extent, that of keeping Indonesia intact. We argue that a major reason for the ineffectiveness of *Panca Sila* has been its tension or conflict with other dimensions in our model, in particular the social dimension.

The fragmentation and pluralism of Indonesian society, as we have already described, is part of the dialectical process which is in conflict with the political goals of education. The result is an educational system quite different from that intended, and which cannot be effectively bought with money alone. In order to facilitate our argument, we present in Fig. 9.3 a dialectical model of the Indonesian educational system. It is the same model as that presented in Fig. 9.2, except that we have included those aspects of the three dimensions which, through conflict and tension, produce the structure of the present educational system. Thus we can see in the Figure the potential contradiction between, for example, the egalitarian political goals of Repelita II, including *Panca Sila,* and the reality of the economic and social divisions persisting in the society.

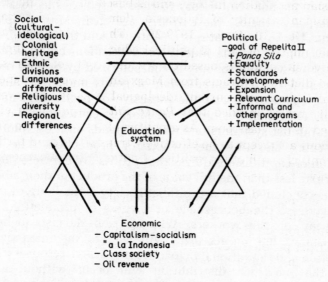

FIG. 9.3 Dialectical model of Indonesian education.

In the two brief case studies presented here, the historical interpretation of the American common school, and the dialectics of Indonesian education, we have shown some of the complexities of the relationship between education and development. In this section we have argued that the form which any educational system takes is the result of a dialectical process between the three basic dimensions of development. We now turn our attention to the full model of education and development in which we examine this process for capitalist and socialist, developed and less developed, and to a lesser extent, the industrialized and non-industrialized societies.

A Typology of Education and Development

Our basic contention is that the dialectical process which we have just analyzed operates in a unique fashion in different kinds of societies. Education can contribute to the development process in various societal contexts. Our goal is to develop a typology which classifies and explains these links between education and development. In doing so, we also argue that there are important policy guidelines which suggest the kind of education which is most appropriate for a given development strategy.

The most important distinction we make in our typology (see Table 9.1) is that between capitalist and socialist countries. Although we agree that it is not always easy to classify societies as totally one or the other, nevertheless the extremes are clear. Most people would agree that the United States is a capitalist and the Soviet Union is a socialist country. At the most basic level of meaning, a capitalist society is one whose economy is characterized by private ownership and investment in the production of goods under the auspices of economic competition and the incentive of profit. The notion has taken an additional meaning from Marxist critics who have argued that a capitalist system is one which depends on the exploitation of the working class by the owners of production. The effective operation of capitalism requires that profits are extracted by paying the workers less than the full value of the product of their labor. From this it is concluded that a capitalist society is made up of two main social classes: the bourgeoisie or owners of production, and the proletariat, or the workers. Whereas non-Marxists believe that capitalism, if left on its own, will lead to the maximization of production and the rational distribution of scarce resources, Marxists argue that no such distribution will occur without a central production plan which includes the planned distribution of material and social goods. There are variations in capitalist systems, especially as societies and technology have become more complex, and the influence of labor unions and the spread of worker participation in decision-making have dulled the sharp edges of the pure capitalist model. However, for our purposes we are concerned with capitalist societies as a type of economic and social structure which prevails in spite of these variations.

Socialist countries, by contrast, are those with economic systems where ownership of the means of production and the distribution of goods is theoretically controlled by the State. There are many variations in the forms that socialism can take, and the debates about the manner by which socialism is to be instituted, or its place in the stages of evolution towards communism, have become highly complex and sometimes heated. These do not concern us here. Our task, as stated above, is to identify and explain the unique form that education takes in a socialist country. Although there have also been disagreements as to which countries should be labelled as socialist, we use the term in its broad sense and include, for example, the Soviet Union, the Eastern European countries, the People's Republic of China, Cuba and Ethiopia.

In Table 9.1, we next make the distinction between developed and less-developed countries for both the capitalist and socialist categories. Thus we speak of developed capitalist countries and developed socialist countries. Likewise we can do the same with less-developed countries.[2] The importance of this distinction is that the forms of education which are appropriate for developed societies may not be appropriate for less-developed ones, and it is this kind of generalization that we wish to investigate. These four categories or types of societies provide the broad framework for our discussion. For each of these categories, we will now examine the appropriate development strategy, assuming that the societies continue on the same paths of development. We then examine the type of education system appropriate for the development strategies for a given category of society.

Development in the Capitalist State

Starting with developed capitalist societies, we contend that the crucial variable for a development strategy designed to further capitalist development is the maximization of economic surplus. For ultimately, it is the transformation of economic surplus through the accumulation of capital into productive capacity which determines the growth of the capitalist system. Thus the mobilization of resources, both human and material, the actual production of goods

TABLE 9.1. *Types of Education and Development*

Type of society	Type of development history	Relationship between education and development
A. Developed capitalist (United States, United Kingdom, Federal Republic of Germany, etc.)	1. Free market accumulation of capital 2. Historically developed industrialization 3. Capital intensive technology 4. Priority of growth over equity 5. Export-market oriented	1. High participation in education 2. Education for individual achievement 3. Emphasis on high intrinsic value of education 4. Hidden ideology in education (the "hidden curriculum") 5. Open recruitment and selection system
B. Less-developed capitalist (Brazil, Nigeria, Kenya, etc.)	1. Integrated with world capitalist system; free-market economy 2. Dual economy; small industrial base 3. Intermediate technology; oriented to capital-intensive technology 4. Priority of growth over equity 5. Export-market oriented	1. Expansion of educational system at all levels 2. Education for individual achievement 3. High value on academic curriculum; high orientation to public service sector 4. Hidden ideology in education ("hidden curriculum") 5. Elite (less open) recruitment and selection system
C. Developed socialist (Soviet Union, Poland, Czechoslovakia, German Democratic Republic, etc.)	1. Planned accumulation of capital 2. Planned rapid industrialization 3. Moderate labor-intensive technology 4. Priority of equity over growth 5. Domestic-market oriented	1. High participation in education 2. Education for collective achievement 3. Emphasis on high instrumental value of education 4. Overt ideology of education (the "new socialist man") 5. Planned recruitment and selection system
D. Less-developed socialist (People's Republic of China, Cuba, Angola, Ethiopia etc.)	1. Break with world capitalist system; planned economy 2. Dual economy; small industrial base 3. Intermediate technology; oriented to labor-intensive technology 4. Priority of equity over growth 5. Domestic-market oriented	1. Expansion of educational system with literacy and universal primary high priority 2. Education for collective achievement; education for self-reliance 3. High value on vocational curriculum; high agricultural orientation 4. Overt ideology of education (the "new socialist man"); formation of new state identity 5. Planned recruitment and selection system

and services, and the distribution of the national product are all an essential part of the economic system designed to accumulate economic surplus (Hoogvelt, 1976:155). Furthermore, it is argued that only in a free-market system with open competition will the profits go to the most efficient and productive of the entrepreneurs. Thus, part of a capitalist development strategy requires the most effective and efficient mobilization of human resources, as well as the exploitation of material resources.

Efficiency of production is a second essential part of capitalist development. This requires that the capital-output ratio is improved, meaning that the returns to investment in terms of production output are increased. This relates to both human and material resources. With regard to the first, education, health care, wage incentives, environmental improvement and similar measures are seen as means to improve human productivity. Likewise, the introduction of more efficient technology both in terms of machinery and science, as well as production techniques like assembly lines or self-steering groups, are seen to improve the latter. The balance between capital-intensive and labor-intensive techniques are allowed to reach their own levels on the open market. Hence, in a capitalist system the existence of some unemployment generally is not regarded as detrimental to the system, for it is seen as a necessary by-product of competition.

The third factor in the capitalist system, the distribution of the national product, involves a constant tension between policies of economic growth and economic equity. In the early days of the current developed societies, the problem of equity was not as crucial as the problem of growth. Foreign markets meant that the products could be sold even though there were considerable inequities in the domestic distribution system. Low wages meant greater economic surplus and thus greater accumulation of capital for re-investment into the productive process. In contemporary developed capitalist societies the tension between growth and equity has become more pronounced. Wage increases have not only become necessary for improved production, but also to generate a larger domestic market as competition in the foreign market increases. Thus today, more than in past years, the problem of equity has become more acute, and it is doubtful whether a capitalist model of development in developed societies can completely ignore it.

The entire structure of the capitalist system presumes that each person is the best judge of his or her own interests, and thus the free and unhindered pursuit of self-interest theoretically should result in higher productivity and in greater economic benefits to the entire population. Therefore a capitalist development strategy will tend to promote individual competition and will promote the ideology that social and economic differentiation is not only necessary for the system, but that at any given time it is justified by merit. The British economist, Adam Smith, observed in 1793: "Every man's interest would prompt him to seek the advantageous..." (Smith, 1961:518).

The principles of a capitalist development strategy are not always entirely applicable to developing societies and therefore must be appropriately adjusted if a capitalist model is to be pursued. Developing societies today find themselves in international and domestic contexts which are much different when compared to the situation which existed a century or more ago when the present advanced societies of the world were emerging as capitalist industrial powers. There is no way that the developing countries can copy or imitate the development process experienced by the advanced countries. Therefore, what is essential for those developing societies which are committed to a capitalist system, such as Kenya, Brazil or the Republic of Korea is that an appropriate development strategy be followed which takes their unique situations into account.

This is not an easy task, and indeed many would argue that it is virtually impossible. To begin with, most developing countries today have remnants of colonial legacies throughout their structures. Thus we find in them economic, political and social institutions which are not indigenous in form, but transplanted by colonial or neo-colonial powers. Examples of these are the foreign-owned companies which exercise economic dominance over some less-developed economies, but which serve the interests of previous colonizing powers. Often the main purpose of these companies was to extract raw materials from the colony for exportation to the mother country. At the political level, we frequently find the imposition of Western-styled parliamentary procedures upon societies where tribal customs have often been in conflict with them. Socially, a segment of the populations of developing countries, usually the elite, adopted life-styles, tastes and interests which were more in tune with the colonizing society than their own.

The implication of these intrusions into local social structures is that capitalist strategies of development based upon Western models often encounter seemingly insurmountable difficulties. The effective mobilization of manpower and material resources is caught between the dual needs of maintaining ties, at least on a short-term basis, with industrialized countries, as well as of striving for a level of economic independence. In order that dependent capitalist development be replaced by indigenous capitalist development, it is imperative that the interests of the ruling elites be oriented to the development of their own countries rather than to the satisfaction of their own need for power and material goods. In other words, the comprador elite must be transformed in some way into a domestic-oriented one.

The effectiveness and efficiency of capitalist production in less-developed countries are often hindered by the lack of competition both on the foreign and local markets for domestically produced goods. The dominance of multinationals and the problems of technological expertise hinder the growth of a national capitalist economic base. Furthermore, the permanent oversupply of labor, a by-product of contact with the West, requires that labor-intensive and capital-saving technologies should be preferred, at least in early stages of development. The utilization of "alternative", "intermediate" or "appropriate" technologies means the deliberate scaling down of investment-to-output ratios, and running the risk of labor disputes. However, it would appear that an adjusted capitalist model such as this, in the long run, would best serve the interests of many less-developed societies.

The distribution system in capitalist-oriented developing countries is equally problematic but crucial. The tension between growth and equity must be resolved in such a way that a domestic market can be produced for domestic products. The unrestrained growth commitment of the classical capitalist model appears inappropriate in this context. Thus , whether through taxation or more generous wage and welfare policies, it is necessary that there be greater commitment to equity if a capitalist strategy is to succeed at all. Obviously such a system represents something of an attenuation of the classical capitalist model, but as we pointed out earlier, it is doubtful whether the classical model is appropriate, or indeed possible, for developing countries in the context of the present economic world order.

Education and Capitalist Development

The dilemma in the relationship between education and capitalist development has already been foreshadowed in Chapter 2, where we have presented theories of education and development generally. There are two ways of viewing this relationship, the first from the point of view of those who espouse and are optimistic about the capitalist system, and the second of those, primarily from the Marxist and neo-Marxist schools, who take a deterministic view of capitalism as merely a stage on the road to socialism and communism. For the first, the problem is how education can be an effective instrument for furthering the development of the capitalist system. In this context, the human capital and modernization theorists have been most vocal.

In contrast, the Marxist and neo-Marxist theorists see education in terms of its contribution to the decline of capitalism and its eventual transition to socialism.

A preoccupation with the future of the capitalist industrial society characterizes the work of many who are committed to the capitalist system. This preoccupation is best reflected in the assortment of labels used to designate the perceived direction of the evolution of capitalist industrialism, for example "the post-modern era", "the post-bourgeois society", "the knowledge society", "the service class society", and perhaps the most well known, Daniel Bell's "the post-industrial society".

Common to all of these is the notion that with increasing technology and the automation of industry, the working-class or blue-collar sector of the workforce will decrease in size while the white-collar or those employed in the service sector will increase. Daniel Bell (1974), in particular, argues that the post-industrial society will be dominated by the importance of knowledge, both systematic and theoretical, and by those people who have mastered this knowledge. Thus professionals, scientists and other technological experts will comprise the crucial base for the economic structure. Along with this shift from manufacturing and industry is an anticipated decrease in working time or working hours, and also the prospect for lifetime careers.

Available statistics support the emerging importance of the service sector. Among the industrialized countries as a whole, between the years 1960 and 1983, the contribution of industry to the gross domestic product declined from 40 to 35 percent. At the same time the contribution of the service sector increased from 54 to 62 percent. These figures, however, mask even more extreme examples. During this period, for Sweden, industry declined from 40 to 31 percent while the service sector increased from 53 to 61 percent. Even in Japan, industry declined from 45 to 42 percent whereas services increased from 42 to 55 percent. These figures are even more striking when compared with many less-developed countries where sharp declines in the proportion of agricultural contribution to GDP is taken up by increases in the other two sectors: industry *and* services. For example, in what the World Bank calls the low-income countries, agriculture declined from 50 to 37 percent while industry increased from 17 to 34, and services declined from 33 to 29 percent (World Bank, 1980b:114 – 115, 1985:178 – 179). These and figures from other select countries are found in Table 9.2.

While there are numerous critics of the theory of the post-industrial society, the fact remains that capitalist development cannot continue at its present pace in its present form for the

TABLE 9.2. *Contribution to Gross Domestic Product (in percent)*

	Agriculture		Industry		Service	
	1960	1983	1960	1983	1960	1983
A. Low-income countries	50	37	17	34	33	29
B. Middle-income countries	22	15	31	36	47	49
C. Industrialized Countries	6	3	40	35	54	62
Selected countries from each category						
A. Tanzania	57	52	11	15	32	33
Kenya	38	33	18	20	44	46
Pakistan	46	27	16	27	38	46
B. Indonesia	54	26	14	39	32	35
Nigeria	63	26	11	34	26	40
Brazil	16	12	35	35	49	53
C. United Kingdom	4	2	43	32	53	66
Japan	13	4	45	42	42	55
Australia	12	5*	37	32*	51	63
FRG (West Germany)	6	2	53	46	41	52
USA	4	2	38	32	58	66
Sweden	7	3	40	31	53	66
Centrally planned economies						
Poland	26	16*	57	64*	17	20
USSR	21	17*	62	62*	17	21

Source: World Bank, *World Development Report,* 1980b, Table 3: "Structure of Production", Washington D.C., August 1980, pp. 114–115; 1985, pp. 178–179.
* *Figures* from 1978.

advanced societies of today.[3] Some aspects of capitalist evolution cannot be denied, as we have already mentioned, and these have profound implications for education. While the human capital and modernization theorists were probably correct in their understanding of education and development during the height of industrial expansion, it would be incorrect to assume that the same educational model would be equally relevant in these later stages of capitalist industrial transition. It is not true, at least for the future, that more money spent on education and research, with larger numbers of people remaining in the current educational systems for longer periods of time, will create a better-educated, more self-conscious, more productive and more "knowledgeable" society. Therefore, the educational model for continuing capitalist advancement must take a different form from that which previously prevailed. Is it possible to describe the kind of educational reform which will be necessary for an educational system to be compatible with the needs of a continually changing post-industrial capitalist society?

In a study of the future of schooling in Western societies, the

Swedish educationist Torsten Husén (1979) has identified a number of directions possible for schooling if it is to be viable in post-industrialism. One of the first is that the amount of formal, full-time schooling, in terms of numbers of years and classroom instruction, will be reduced to some extent. This is partly the result of the increasing costs of schooling coupled with stabilizing or even diminishing returns. Furthermore, as the shift to post-compulsory education tends to increase, funds for formal compulsory education will decrease. Advocates of recurrent or lifelong education recognize that the disillusionment with traditional schooling and the relevance of continuing education in a postindustrial society have justified their competition for limited educational funds.

Yet confidence in the efficacy of education and in the value of educational reform has plummeted over the last few years, provoking a marked reluctance to maintain a continually rising investment, as research increasingly exposes education's apparent impotence in the face of prevailing social conditions. Hence the claim of education to a growing share of limited resources is likely to find fewer and fewer supporters unless the resources allocated to it are more effectively deployed (Schuller and Bengtsson, 1977:636).

Along with the above, Husén also contends that as the emphasis on formal schooling declines and that on lifelong education increases, there will be a decrease in credentialism and a greater stress on the inclusion of work programs in the school curricula. Furthermore, the rising level of general education, which includes formal schooling and lifelong education, is likely to increase the demand for participation in decision-making in all sectors of the economic production process. Finally, with the emphasis on knowledge in the post-industrial society, and the increased importance on the mastery of highly specialized skills, there will be a need for the "generalist" who is able to deal with social and technological problems which cut across the disciplines.

An educational policy which promotes the further development of a capitalist post-industrial society must accomplish many difficult tasks. It must, in the first instance, provide the opportunity for the learning of specialized skills necessary for the few who will become the "professional elite". Assuming that the selection of these elite occurs within the educational system, then competition and the meritocracy must prevail in the classroom. Yet for many people, formal schooling will represent only a first stage in a lifetime of learning and an occupational history involving many different jobs.

The expressive function of schooling may be more important than instrumental functions, for example the need to learn for flexibility and change. Furthermore, a higher level of general education will also alter aspects of the production process, as the demand for participation in decision-making increases. It is here that the dialectic between the school and the three dimensions of society, about which we spoke earlier, becomes apparent: the demands of a post-industrial production system affects changes in the school (the expressive function system affects changes in the school (the expressive function and flexibility) which in turn feed back into the production system (participation in decision-making) which again affects the school through the introduction of more co-operative decision-making regarding the content and methods of learning. Finally, because the post-industrial society requires a larger domestic market than was the case during industrial expansion, the inherently elitist tendencies of the school must be counteracted by measures to promote equity in society.[4] It is questionable to what extent the school can teach equity principles, or participate in the equity process in society. It appears, however, that in the post-industrial era, credentials earned in schools cannot alone be the basis for economic rewards in society.

The place of education in capitalist-oriented less-developed countries is equally problematic, but in a different way (see Table 9.1.B). One cannot doubt the advances in schooling which have been made in many of these countries. In Kenya, for example, primary-school enrolment virtually reached 100 percent of the age group by 1978, whereas only 47 percent were attending in 1960. In the Republic of Korea participation in secondary schooling increased from 27 to 91 percent from 1960 to 1984. By 1976 many less-developed countries, particularly Thailand, the Philippines and most Latin American countries, had achieved adult literacy rates of 80 to 90 percent (World Bank, 1981:178 – 179). Irrespective of these gains it is clear that discontinuities exist between the educational systems of capitalist-oriented less-developed countries and their development needs. It is not merely a question of scale, that is, more of the same that is the problem, but rather a question of appropriateness. The school model which has been introduced to many Third World countries by colonial governments, missionary societies, and recently by the independent governments themselves, is one which was appropriate to an urban capitalist industrializing society: the city school of the early 20th century in the West. We have already seen that this model is inappropriate for capitalist post-industrial development; it is even more inappropriate for capitalist development in the less-developed world.

Less-developed countries are also poor countries. Stated bluntly, this means that there is much less money available both to the State as well as to individuals to finance the range of works and services that is found in developed industrial societies. As we have already noted in Chapter 2, education is only one aspect of a development strategy, and one that is increasingly expensive. Therefore, even if it were desirable, it is highly unlikely that any less-developed country could support an educational structure for all students at all levels. Given financial restraints, the question then becomes: what levels of education should receive the most emphasis in public expenditures, and what educational profile for the nation as a whole should be the goal of educational planning?

In a developing capitalist industrial economy, it is essential that there be a literate adult population; it is not necessary that there be a large tertiary educated and trained manpower. Insofar as the technology of the economy will be more labor-intensive rather than capital-intensive, large numbers of experts are not necessary, and thus neither is there a need for a large number of educational institutions to train them. Universal primary education with competitive and meritocratic entry to upper educational levels appears to be a viable and suitable educational strategy. While primary schooling should be free, secondary and higher education, because of the benefits accruing to the individual, should require some form of fee payment either from the students' families who can afford it, or through the students' later contribution to recognized public services (Edwards, 1980; World Bank, 1986).

Equitable distribution of resources is essential if a domestic market for domestic products is to exist. Furthermore, some form of equity is likely to reduce, at least to some extent, unrealistic aspirations among youth for high educational and occupational attainment (Saha, 1988). It is not easy for a system committed to free-market capitalism to introduce controls on wages, income, or access to other kinds of social rewards such as education. However, either through progressive taxation or other distributive mechanisms, the wage and income differentials in developing capitalist societies are seen by some as desirable, if not necessary, to promote motivation and work productivity.

Credentialism, although present in most societies today, has become even more troublesome in less-developed societies (Dore, 1976; Little, 1984). Educational attainment and the mastery of skills, where these are scarce, have led inevitably to high occupational and financial rewards, and have tended to exaggerate the value of diplomas, degrees and other credentials, both in terms of student aspirations and also of selection criteria by employers. If equity is to be achievable in a less-developed country, some reduction of credentialism is essential and consistent with the other measures we have already discussed.

The financial restraints, problems of equity, and credentialism are related to another aspect of education in less-developed societies, namely the inefficiency of the educational system. In some countries as many as 15 to 20 percent of those in primary grades are repeaters, and as such prevent others from having a place in the system. In addition, the high dropout rate suggests that many are not receiving the education which they are capable, or are being exposed to a kind of education of which is irrelevant or ill-suited for their needs. A UNESCO study of fifty-four developing countries from around the world produced the striking observation that of the 100 students entering grade 1, only sixty reached the third grade, and in the lowest income countries, only thirty-seven reached the fifth grade. It was estimated that in terms of grade completion, dropouts, and grade repetition, about one-half of the expenditures on education in these countries was "wasted" (Habte, 1980). In addition to system-level inefficiency, the lower levels of educational attainment by students in less developed countries suggests that inefficiency in the classroom also exists. There is considerable evidence that policy measures related to the improvement of educational facilities, in particular the upgrading of teacher quality through teacher training, will raise the level of student achievement and therefore improve the quality of human resources in these countries (Husén *et al.*, 1978; Dove, 1986).

Although education in developing capitalist societies to some extent must mirror those in the developed capitalist world, there is still considerable room for adaptation to the social and cultural context of the specific society. The formal structure of the school, especially if directly imported from Western societies, presumes a particularly Western mode of authority and social behavior. Often these assumptions and the resultant behavior conflicts with cultural patterns of the developing society. The use of initiation rites, kin or other social groupings and the less formal contexts for learning, such as social experiences, rituals and family-centered instruction, should be encouraged. Emphasis on the learning of the history and culture of the young person's own society is not necessarily contradictory to the more instrumental aims of capitalist-oriented education. Furthermore, the integration of instrumental aims with a foundation in culturally-relevant curricula will likely reduce the alienation and feelings of irrelevance of schooling which many young people feel in Third World countries. This irrelevance has contributed to drop-outs and other forms of wastage which are part of the inefficiency of Third World schooling. There should be: "The realization that education is an expression of one's own cultural identity and being, and that in the last analysis it should encourage being oneself, being different within the broader universal fraternity of man" (Habte, 1980:93).

We further argue that the curricula in less-developed countries should strike a balance between schooling for jobs in both the modern industrial sector and in the more traditional agricultural sector. As we have stated earlier, capitalist industrial development in these societies is of a modified form and therefore could not possibly absorb all school graduates. Agricultural production has been, and will continue to be, of considerable importance in most developing countries, and it is only logical that educational curricula should reflect this fact. Much has been written about education for rural development and we do not wish to add to the discussion except to note its significance for education in a developing capitalist society (Coombs and Ahmed, 1974).

If we look back over our discussion of education in capitalist developed and developing societies, some important similarities and contrasts can be highlighted. The needs for the future changes in the developed capitalist societies can be framed within the context of the anticipated post-industrial order. The continuing requirement of experts as well as generalists, the growth of the service sector, the need for job flexibility and the emerging importance of lifelong learning are aspects which we feel are most characteristic of these societies. On the other hand, the developing societies with capitalist-oriented development strategies must address educational policy with a quite different set of restraints and needs. The existence of a limited industrial sector and a sizeable agricultural one requires a curriculum program which is balanced between the learning of skills appropriate for the two sectors. Universal primary education, with competitive and meritocratic access to secondary and higher-level institutions, must be adjusted to suit financial resources. Measures to improve the efficiency and quality of learning, including input from indigenous cultures, are essential. It should be clear that although education in both types of societies is oriented to a capitalist model of development, the shape and form of the education systems required to promote that development are quite different.[5]

Development in the Socialist State

We now turn our attention to the second half of our typology, to the developed and less-developed socialist countries (See Table 9.2, C and D.). Without becoming immersed in debates about the classification of socialism, we take the Soviet Union as a prototype of the developed industrial socialist country, and Cuba or China as prototypes of less-developed ones. At the most general level, a socialist State is one where Marxist-Leninist doctrine is regarded as the only true science of society. Paramount in this doctrine is a commitment to the principle that ownership and control of the production process, including the distribution of goods, is in the hands of the workers themselves. Insofar as socialism is regarded as an evolutionary stage to communism, the State is seen as a temporary institution which, on behalf of the workers, not only exercises ownership and control over the means of production, but also holds the authority to mobilize human resources to achieve officially endorsed goals. The State consists of the government and the Communist Party, which, as the only political party is designed to formulate and express the unitary will of the working class, and is the official interpreter of Marxist-Leninist doctrine. Therefore, as there are no classes produced by the conflict between the owners and workers in the production process (as in the capitalist system), it is held that there are no antagonistic class contradictions in a socialist society.

Development for a socialist State is any program which will assist in the evolution towards communism.[6] Lenin saw this development mainly in terms of a struggle of opposites, not between classes, but rather between different forms of property (for example State and collective), different types of labor (manual versus non-manual), and finally town and country. He saw the resolution of these struggles as leading to the communist stage.

The components of Lenin's development strategy were rapid industrialization, collectivization and the cultural revolution (Lane, 1974:25). The underlying force directing these components was a form of "modernization" which for all practical purposes is identical to the processes of Western modernization today. Industrialization, as Lenin saw it, should take place in a society dominated by public participation in political matters, an adherence to norms based on secularism, rationality and science, and in which there occurs "transformation of the modal personality" towards one characterized by the achievement motive. The difficulties in Lenin's program in pursuing this kind of development lie in the apparent contradictions between the desired industrialization and a hostility toward the capitalist system which developed that industrialization, and between political participation and the centralization of authority. There is no question, however, that the original development plan of Lenin was to take the industrial character from advanced capitalism and combine it with the Marxist ideology of the classless society. In this process the role of the State, which comprises the government and the Communist party, is crucial. For it is the State which allocates high levels of investment from "forced savings" in order to stimulate economic growth. In addition the State is responsible for the diffusion of secular and rational norms, mainly through schools, youth organizations and the media. Finally, through similar means, the State takes active responsibility for changing the modal personality system of the traditional society, and for creating the new collective achievement-oriented "communist man" (Lane, 1976:73).

The development strategy in the Soviet Union has not always followed guidelines advocated by Lenin. To be sure, under Stalin "industrialization without capitalism" in the construction of socialism became almost synonymous with pure, large-scale industrialization with an emphasis on heavy industry. However, during the process of most rapid development, the principle of equity, officially endorsed in the socialist–communist ideology, gave way to known and tolerated income differentials in order to promote production.

Because of the ideological commitment to centralized authority and a belief in the collectivity over the individual, not only industrial but also agricultural production was removed from private ownership, sometimes against the will of the people. Therefore, for all sectors of Soviet society, cooperativeness and collective discipline were from the beginning essential for socialist development.

Even though the principles of socialism are followed generally in many societies, the specific form of socialist development differs between societies. The Eastern European countries all officially pursue socialist aims, but the economic, social and political structure of each is the result of unique historical events and cultural backgrounds which give each a unique character. In the Soviet Union, the level of industrialization and technology was relatively low at the time of the Bolshevik revolution in 1917 and the beginning of socialist-guided development. Consistent with a small industrial sector, there was a large, almost illiterate, peasantry following a rather primitive agricultural technology. However, in the Eastern European countries the level of industrial development differed between countries, with the result that the level of human mobilization, including literacy, required different socialist development strategies. For example, in Poland and the German Democratic Republic there was a small, almost non-existent Communist Party at the beginning of socialist rule, while in Yugoslavia the Party was of significant size from the beginning of the socialist State. Likewise the industrial infrastructure was already well developed in Czechoslovakia when the socialist government attained power, while in Poland and the German Democratic Republic it was either never well developed or had been destroyed by World War II. These varying characteristics affected the nature of the political structure, in particular as class divisions were already well established in the Eastern European countries at the time of transformation to socialism. Other divisions in these societies, which sometimes coincided with class lines, added to the complexity of the structural context and made the adoption of a consistent socialist development policy more difficult. The Catholic Church in Poland, whose autonomy and opposition to the socialist political system is well known, is an example of a unique influence on socialist development strategy. Industrialization without capitalism, which formed the nucleus of Soviet socialist development, was more difficult in countries such as these. This, of course, is in direct contrast to orthodox Marxist theory, which asserted that the transition to socialism would more likely occur in those societies where capitalist industrialization is most advanced and class divisions most pronounced.[7] As we will observe shortly, these complications also have consequences for the relationship between education and socialist development in advanced socialist industrial societies.

In the discussion about the future development of advanced capitalist societies, we spoke extensively about the transition to post-industrial societies, and in particular the prominence of the service sector or the "knowledge industry" in those societies. The evidence seems to suggest that no similar development is taking place in socialist countries. In contrast to the advanced capitalist societies, the service sector in the "centrally planned economies" has remained quite small with only minor increases between 1960 and 1978. For the Soviet Union, the contribution of the service sector to GDP increased from 17 percent to 21 percent during this period; while Czechoslovakia increased from 11 to 19 percent (World Bank, 1980b:115). At the same time the contribution of industry remained high by capitalist country standards, the figures being around 60 to 70 percent.

In general, then, the development profile for advanced socialist societies contrasts markedly with that of the capitalist. Rapid industrialization is sought within the context of a centrally planned economy. Accumulation of surplus occurs not by extraction from the workers in an open-market competitive system, but rather through "forced savings" by means of the utilization of surplus product for reinvestment into the system. Wage and price controls counteract the inflationary tendencies of an open-market system, and full employment, coupled with a preference for labor-intensive technology in some industrial sectors, reduces the competitve nature of the labor market. In principle, social equity is stressed over economic growth, but as we have already mentioned, there is tolerance of inequality if such is seen as necessary to promote production and exists as a "non-antagonistic contradiction". These principles of socialist development strategy are not always easily applied nor are the goals always achieved; the phraseology is optimistic and democratic, but in practice there are frequent compromises. However, it is the set of principles which guides the educational system and the way it operates in a socialist society which is of interest to us.

Both capitalist and socialist societies, whether developed or less developed, seek to achieve a quality of life comparable to that in the most advanced societies of the world. To this end most of the less-developed societies which follow a socialist development strategy do so as a means of achieving the goals of modernization and economic growth. However, the appeal of the socialist development model for many less-developed countries rests upon the perception that the world capitalist system, with the exploitative activities of multinationals, colonial and neo-colonial ties, and the obligations linked to trade and aid, hinders their development possibilities. It has been the opinion of some development strategists that a less-developed country can hope to achieve economic growth and development *only* by breaking with the world capitalist system (Hoogvelt, 1976:158). Not all less-developed socialist-oriented societies can follow the path of industrialization espoused by the Soviet model. Tanzania, for example, is an important illustrative case of the utilization of socialist principles to pursue an economic strategy based on agricultural development.

In pursuing a socialist model of development, the first task for the less-developed countries is to effectively mobilize their human and material resources to support the growing productivity of either an industrial or agricultural economic base. The first step in this task is that of detachment from dependency on the world capitalist system (Wallerstein, 1979). The expropriation of foreign-owned holdings, either of industry or land, is considered essential. The utilization of production surplus must be reinvested in the production system, using manpower as a primary capital resource. Furthermore, not only full employment but also control over consumption prevents capital outflow from the economy through the importation of unnecessary foreign-produced goods. Additional economic autonomy and self-subsistence is maintained by restrictions on the flow of capital, either in the form of purchases, travel to, or investment in other countries.

The utilization of human resources forms an essential component in the production of goods and services. The Chinese saying, "The people are our capital", appropriately describes the importance of labor-intensive technologies for those operations which do not require heavy capital investment. Thus the construction of roads and dams as in China, or the use of urban dwellers to assist in the harvest of sugar cane as in Cuba, are examples of this labor-intensive strategy. Labor-intensive technologies, and in particular those which produce goods for the consumer market require both a protection from outside competition from goods produced with higher-level technologies and the assurance of a domestic market. These measures are consistent with socialist policies and the operations of a centrally planned economy.

The principle of equity is even more important for the less-developed socialist societies for two reasons. In the first place, the socialist ideology is committed to the equal participation of all members of society in the responsibilities and rewards of society, even though in practice this equity is not always achieved. The second is that in a society striving for autonomous development and self-sufficiency, a viable domestic market is necessary to sustain local productivity. However, there is no reason to believe that in a socialist-oriented less-developed society the principle of social and political equity is incompatible with the principle of economic growth. Unlike the capitalist model, which presumes a competitive market system whereby growth is most likely to occur with increasing inequity, a socialist development model presumes cooperation and collective effort whereby, at least in theory, equity makes growth possible. It is for this reason that Hoogvelt (1976) observes that the capitalist model "tries to make the best of human nature at its worst" (that is, competitive greed), while the socialist model "requires the presence of saints" (that is, total dedication, commitment and cooperation) (p. 163).

The optimism of socialist ideals and the difficulties of practical implementation are illustrated in the experience of Tanzania, which was faced from the beginning with cultural, religious and linguistic differences due to the formation of the country from two previously distinct societies. Although following a path slightly different from the orthodox socialist model, Tanzania, under the presidency of Julius Nyerere, (1961–85), followed a development strategy uniquely socialist and agrarian. Nyerere's program of self-reliance and *ujamaa* was devised precisely to overcome the social inequalities and other divisions of Tanzanian society, which he argued were not only morally unethical but also detrimental to social and economic development. The development policy was based on agrarian development rather than industrialization, and on a formula which was rooted in peasant society and understandable to them. It was, in effect, a policy of "modernization by traditionalization" (Hydén, 1980:98).

Ujamaa, as an ideology, was based on the traditional peasant practices in Tanzania of village cooperation in agricultural tasks during certain peak seasons. The practice originally known as *ujimaa* did not entail communal ownership, as those who assisted their neighbors did not receive a share of the products. However, Nyerere pressed the practice further to include the sharing of common property and basic necessities of life, and described it in terms of three principles: (1) respect, (2) common property and (3) obligation to work. To this end there were massive campaigns to implement *ujamaa* through the restructuring of the Tanzanian countryside, extensive school and adult educational programs, and above all, the work of the TANU Party, the ideological arm of the government.

Nevertheless, it appears that *ujamaa* was not without its difficulties. For example, there were apparent contradictions between the principles of *ujamaa* and the authoritarian methods both as used in Tanzanian schools as well as among the government bureaucrats. The persistent inequalities among individuals and regions, and the difficulties encountered in motivating people to embrace the principles of *ujamaa* in their daily activities, in spite of little personal reward or gain, hindered the effectiveness of the campaign. It would appear that the optimism of a socialist model of development, and its requirement to have "saints" in order that it succeed, posed difficulties for its implementation.

The requirements for the socialist development strategies of developed and less-developed societies appear somewhat different. The developed socialist societies, to be sure, require the continued cooperation of the "new socialist man". However, the more advanced stage of industrialization also implies the need for a skilled labor force, at least in part. The less-developed socialist societies also need the commitment of the "new socialist man" and it seems, to a lesser extent, a need for a large skilled labor force. The ideological component emerges in both as the basic underpinning of any socialist-oriented development policy. It is this need which most impinges on the link between education and socialist-oriented development.

Education and Socialist Development

Although Marx never spoke extensively about education, he nevertheless regarded it as important for building socialism and communism. A fundamental tenet of Marx's materialism was that human society and human consciousness are determined by material conditions. Thus the key to the revolution lay in changing these conditions, and for this Marx recognized the pervasive importance of education and re-education, even for the teachers.

> The materialist doctrine that men are products of circumstances and upbringing, and that, therefore, changed men are products of other circumstances and changed upbringing, forgets that it is men that change circumstances and the educator himself needs educating (Marx, 1968 (1888):28).

In the capitalist societies which Marx observed, he implicitly identified the educational system as part of the apparatus which served the interests of the privileged class. Furthermore, even though many from the working classes were receiving education, he saw this as part of the superstructure whereby the class system and its relationships were legitimated.

However, more important in Marx's theory about the proletarian revolution was the supremacy of practice . Consistent with Marx's view about consciousness being informed by experience rather than ideas, was his view that the revolution would be brought about by action more than by education. This did not mean, of course, that he considered knowledge and skills unimportant, but rather that he saw them as subservient to the effectiveness of active political involvement.

Whereas Marx carried out the task of articulating a theory of socialism, communism and the revolution of the workers, it was Lenin who was faced with putting the theory into practice. Like Marx, Lenin saw education as secondary to political action, and flatly denied that the revolution could come about through gradual reform and the education of the working classes. For Lenin, the political revolution must come first and the cultural revolution (including educational reform) must follow (Lilge, 1977:558). Lenin's unclear attitude toward schooling made it possible for many views about education to be voiced in the early Soviet socialist system. On one extreme there were the educators who were satisfied to see the system of education continue as before the Revolution. On the other hand, there were those who argued that the school had little place in socialist society and none whatsoever in communist society. As they saw it, schools were retrograde and pernicious institutions which only helped to prolong the class and other divisions of society. Nevertheless, the importance of education for building the new socialist society was evident immediately following the October Revolution, when school reforms and experimentation were initiated. Already in 1919 Lenin signed the Decree on the Elimination of Illiteracy whereby all illiterate citizens were instructed of their duty to learn to read and write, and the literates were told of their duty to teach them. Literacy was felt to be so important that workers who were illiterate were given 2 hours a day with pay to receive instruction. These measures were based upon the arguments of Marx and Engels that both in a capitalist and socialist society workers must be literate to become conscious of their exploited situation and to contribute to the building of a socialist society (Tomiak, 1972; Löfstedt, 1980).

The "clean sweep" which had taken place in the Soviet Union following the revolution affected the structure and content of schooling. Along with the drive to eradicate illiteracy was the attempt to form the "new socialist man" who would be fully developed and "fit for a variety of labors". This led to considerable experimentation at all levels of the education system, stressing the importance of collective learning and the minimization of class distinctions by the eradication of selective entrance procedures, examinations and marks. The ideas of the American educator John Dewey were influential during the 1920s and the early 1930s, and he, in turn, was not only favorably disposed to but even participated in Soviet school reforms through lectures and consultations. Lenin's wife, Nadezhda Krupskaya, was the person most responsible for educational progressivism in the Soviet Union at this time. But the main figure in Soviet education during this period was Paul Blonsky, whose book, *The Unified Labour School,* was published in 1919. Blonsky, often called the "Father of Pedology", was the Soviet Union's counterpart to Dewey, and like Dewey he placed stress on learning by doing, and further emphasized that the child should be prepared for participation in modern industrial culture (Löfstedt, 1980:53).

With respect to promoting socialist development, two underlying principles guided Soviet education: the notion of the "new socialist man" as a not-too-specialized person capable of many jobs, and the "collective" man who puts group interest before his own. The first of these principles was most evident in the notion of "polytechnic" education, which flourished prior to the Stalinist period. The notion of polytechnic education is based upon Marx's contention that theory and practice be combined and that undue specialization of skills be discouraged. During Lenin's period, the polytechnic became a means whereby the differentiating consequences of extreme specialization might be avoided. In practical terms it meant that fusion of the general and vocational schools whereby everyone was expected to learn the general knowledge and skills needed to serve the advancement of a socialist society (Price, 1977). With the "tightening up" of Soviet education during the Stalinist era, the polytechnic, as well as other forms of experimentation, gave way to a return to a more rigid, selective, science-oriented and unified educational system. In many respects the changes in the Soviet schools under Stalin represented a return to an educational format which resembled that under Tsarist rule. Thus, by the end of World War II Soviet education, although retaining its socialist-oriented and ideological character, had become highly committed to the learning of science and technology, perhaps even more so than education in many capitalist industrial systems. However, the second major characteristic of Soviet education considered essential for socialist development remained, namely the focus on the collective.

Consistent with the economic theory of socialism, which rejects individual gain and competitiveness among individuals, the school system, virtually from the beginning of the October Revolution, has stressed the importance of the collectivity in learning. The notion of the collectivity is more extensive than the subordination of individuals to the interests of society as a whole. In schools it is utilized as a means whereby the individual student is not in competition with other students for achievement rewards, but rather one group is in competition with other groups.[8] The group not only serves as an effective means of motivation and social control, but also serves to provide the individual student with a source of identity. Urie Bronfenbrenner, who researched the comparison between family up-bringing and schooling in the United States and the Soviet Union, has documented the unique organizational structures of the Soviet classroom and the important out-of-school settings such as found in Pioneer and other youth associations which promote collective identity. For example, Bronfenbrenner points out the impact of the Soviet tactic of organizing the classroom into "links", which typically correspond to the rows of desks. In classroom achievement, and in dealing with disciplinary problems, it is the link which is the significant reference unit rather than the individual. One consequence of this structural arrangement is that classroom deviance appears less prevalent than in United States' schools, and incidences of cheating are almost non-existent (Bronfenbrenner, 1974:37, 77).

In 1983–84 the implementation of new reforms to education in the Soviet Union suggests that the education system was not regarded as completely integrated into Soviet development priorities. The reforms consisted of three goals: (1) the enrolment of six-year-olds in primary school (instead of enrolling at seven years, the previous practice), (2) universal vocational training for secondary school students, and (3) changes in the curriculum both in terms of pedagogic materials and in content, the latter with a greater focus on polytechnic courses. At the same time, the reforms re-emphasized the virtues of the "socialist man", that is, the virtues of industry, patriotism, comradeship, useful labor and socialist responsibility (Szekely, 1986).

Socialist education in Eastern Europe is largely based on the Soviet model, but the implementation of this model varies considerably between countries. Even though different levels of commitment to industry exist between these countries, the role that education plays in furthering socialist development remains. The importance of science and technology is reflected in school curricula, and the ideological component of schooling, as well as that in youth and other political organizations, is considerable. In addition, the dominance of the Soviet Union is apparent in the fact that the study of Soviet political institutions plays a prominent part in school curricula.

> The dominance of the Soviet Union led to the adoption of many specifically Russian features too, hence the prominence of the study of Soviet political institutions in Czechoslovakia and elsewhere, of Russian revolutionary history in, for example, East Germany, or Russian language and literature in the school curricula practically everywhere, and so on (Grant, 1969:71).

In many respects, the role of education in the developed industrialized socialist societies resembles that found in the capitalist industrial societies of the 1950s and 1960s. A conviction about the importance of science and technology in the curriculum, and the importance of a highly specialized and trained labor force resembles that dictated by the human capital theory which prevailed in the capitalist societies several decades earlier. There is little evidence that development in advanced socialist societies is moving in the same direction as the capitalist. The service society and the post-industrial State do not seem to be emerging, at least to the same extent. Clearly this is one area where the educational differences between the two systems are most apparent. However, more importantly, the emphasis on ideology in the socialist system in bringing about the "new socialist man", with a commitment to collectivism, is much more explicit and central to the socialist system. It may be that the reason for this ideological component is the need to counteract the deeply ingrained traditions which existed prior to the transition to socialism. Nevertheless, this characteristic alone represents a unique aspect of the link between education and socialist development which is virtually absent from educational programs for capitalist development. Our discussion of the development models of these two strategies have shown why this is so.

Education for socialist development in less-developed societies represents a situation much different from the one we have been describing. As with the less-developed capitalist-oriented societies, not only is the level of industrial development in the socialist societies much less, but in many cases agricultural productivity must, out of necessity, receive greater priority in development objectives. This is certainly the case for socialist-oriented less-developed countries such as Cuba, Tanzania, Angola, Mozambique, Guinea-Bissau and Algeria. It may be less true, however, for a country like China, which, while placing considerable importance on the attainment of agricultural goals, has recently also committed itself to rapid industrialization.

However, the role of education in socialist less-developed countries is similar, in many respects, to that in the advanced socialist countries, for irrespective of level of industrial or technological development, the objectives of development are shared, namely to further build a socialist state.[9] This means, in the first instance, the achievement of clearly defined ideological goals – the creation of the "new socialist man" – who will place collective interests ahead of his own. Where these societies have emerged from colonial rule and capitalist economic systems, these ideological objectives have meant also the eradication of not only capitalist structures but also capitalist modes of thought. This has had profound implications for altering the underlying values formally transmitted in the pre-socialist school system. The aspirations and expectations for educational and occupational achievement in a colonial or post-colonial capitalist structure clearly conflict with the social–psychological and economic objectives of socialist development.

A second common objective which the less-developed socialist-oriented societies share with their advanced counterparts is the fusion of school and work. As in the more conventional socialist ideologies, not only is the closer link between school and work seen as ideologically desirable but also as being, in some cases, of practical necessity. For example, in the early 1970s, university students in Cuba were required to work 20 hours a week in productive labor as part of their studies (Carnoy and Werthein, 1977:574). Similar measures have also been introduced in less-developed countries with a focus on agricultural development, for example Tanzania, where there is also some effort directed to the use of a "national service" for school graduates in filling jobs such as teaching.

In 1981 the Zimbabwe Ministry of Education initiated eight experimental school-production programs whereby schools became agricultural production units to assist in their own finance, and for the benefit of local communities. Based upon Marxist-Leninist principles of polytechnic education, the Zimbabwe Government intends to replicate this work-study program at the national level (Gustafsson, 1987). Naturally in countries where there is a strong emphasis on agricultural production, the academic year and the curriculum are both adapted in such a way as to take into account the agricultural cycle, such as periods of sowing and harvesting. As noted previously, there is growing evidence to suggest that there is no "magic" number of school days per year required to instil a certain level of literate and numerate skills as was found in research in Norway and Sweden (Husén, 1972; Gerger and Hoppe, 1980). Given appropriate organization and curriculum, there is no reason why the requirements of a formal school setting need be incompatible with those of an agricultural economy and extensive school-work programs.

As we have already pointed out many times in previous chapters, literacy is one of the main needs, and in most cases, objectives of development in all less-developed countries. There have been striking achievements in the literacy programs of many countries, but the successes of the socialist-oriented countries have been even more remarkable.

A unique characteristic of literacy programs in the socialist-oriented less-developed countries has been the political component of literacy education. The emphasis on a national culture and identity, a non-Western and non-capitalist orientation to social behavior and consumption, and a lesser concern .with high technology are the dominating characteristics of educational systems in this group. We have already noted that the achievement of these goals is not always as intended due to colonial residues, such as the institutional, bureaucratic and linguistic remnants of outside domination. Therefore, in many respects the success of educational reforms are contingent on other structural changes which are essential if a strategy for independent socialist development is followed.

Education, and Development under Capitalism and Socialism 261

There are many similarities in the development and educational strategies of the socialist-oriented societies, irrespective of their levels of development. Yet there are also striking differences. Whereas most of the advanced socialist societies are committed to industrialization, the less-developed are not. Modified industrial programs often take second place to agricultural and rural programs, with the result that differences in the forms of education are important consequences. The immediacy of colonialism in many less-developed socialist countries, and its negative effects on independent economic and social development, require a greater focus on the political content of education in order that a break with the past is possible. Any development and educational program less than this is doomed to mixed success.

Education and Development in Changing Perspective

Our discussion of education and development models is now completed. The description of these models presented in Table 9.1 can be seen within the context of our analysis. Clearly, on the basis of our discussion, the link between education and development is complex, and contingent on the economic, social and political development goals.

However, we do not intend to give the impression that the relationships which we have described are static. Societies, as we made clear in Chapter 1, have always been in a process of change. Irrespective of the direction of this change, whether growth or decline, it is certain that the character of the education system, in particular its relationship to development strategies, also changes. For example, one type of change has been called "revitalization movements", which include any deliberate effort by a society to improve its quality of life. These movements may manifest themselves as revolutionary or reactionary, depending on whether the efforts are directed to *creating* a new structure or bolstering the old. Thus in the former, the educational system may place primary emphasis on political indoctrination or moral education with the learning of skills and technology being given lesser prominence. Likewise, in a reactionary society, political indoctrination receives higher priority but with the learning of skills remaining important. It is only in the conservative phase that societies have the opportunity to focus educational efforts on instrumental learning (Paulston, 1972:479).

In addition to societal transitions, it is important to also keep in mind the ever-changing nature of the power relations within a society. If education and its link with development is at least in part a product of the wishes of the dominant group, then as the position of this group changes, so too will the educational system. Such positional changes do not necessarily imply a fall from power, but do take into account the conflicts between groups within society. Hegemony is never total, and the unresolved conflict between classes or other social groups can have a considerable impact on education. Furthermore, it has been suggested that the expansion of facilities to make possible the education of the non-elites may represent a form of co-optation by those in power to ensure the acquiescence of a potentially vocal and perhaps threatening minority (Cohen, 1970; Bowles, 1980). Whatever the reason, then, educational systems, like development strategies and trends, are never static but always in process. As such, an historical analysis of educational systems, in particular their links with development, must complement other cross-sectional and static approaches to understand the relationship.[10] To this extent the typology which we have developed must be seen as an attempt to classify the relationship between education and development at particular points in time. Probably no society perfectly fits into any one category, and to this extent our efforts only partially describe reality. Nevertheless, we contend that the identification of important dimensions in the education and development process has implications both for the diagnosis of the condition of any given society in time, as well as for the generation of policy issues for a given set of development objectives. It is to this latter subject that we now turn in our final chapter.

Notes

1. We have been using the term "social dimension" broadly, to include the configuration of attitudes, values and beliefs which characterize particular types of societies (see Chapter 4). Thus, the social dimension in Figure 9.2 broadly includes the cultural and ideological aspects of societies as well as those aspects related to the modernization process. We use these terms interchangeably throughout this and the following chapter. Although our discussion of the dialectical model has focused on the educational system, there is no reason why it cannot be used to analyze other sectors in society. Therefore one could study the health, welfare, legal and other similar systems using the same model.
2. We have chosen the terms "developed" and "less developed" with deliberation, but not without some reservation. We could have followed the policy of The World Bank (1980 a, b) and used the terms "Low-Income", "Middle-Income", etc., but we felt that for our typology the meaning that we desired was not conveyed. We realize that the dichotomy we have chosen is not without difficulty, especially if one attempts to locate every country in one or the other category. Our intention is to discuss general principles and not specific cases
3. Critics have generally questioned the accuracy and relevance of the increase of the service sector of the economy and the knowledge industry. For a summary of these criticisms, see Kumar (1978:185–240).
4. The notion of the domestic takes on broader and more complex meanings in the post-industrial society. For example, the policies of the European Economic Community (EEC) can be interpreted as the expansion of the domestic market to a given set of countries who enjoy unrestricted trade.

5. Our discussion here represents the point of view that capitalism is a desired objective and will continue to evolve. It should be noted that capitalism can be viewed quite differently, especially from the Marxist and neo-Marxist perspectives. Strictly speaking, the neo-Marxists would regard development as any movement which would help bring about the demise of the capitalist State. Thus they would see education as possibly performing a subversive role in this process whereby it exposes the exploitative nature of the capitalist system and produces a proletariat committed to its inevitable downfall. For a further discussion see Chapter 2.
6. A communist society can best be defined as follows:

> In a full communist society, the State will 'wither away', differences between manual and intellectual labor, and between urban and rural life will disappear, there will be no limits to the development of individual human potentialities and of productive forces, and social relations will be regulated by the principle 'from each according to his ability, to each according to his needs' (Bullock and Stallybrass, 1977:177)

7. The problem of explaining why the transition to socialism should be more difficult in the more advanced capitalist industrialized countries has concerned writers on both sides of the Marxist fence. We do not intend to enter into this debate, as our main concern is in development strategies and the way education is linked with them.
8. This does not mean that competition is non-existent in Soviet education. The use of examinations and other selective entrance procedures, which were introduced after the 1920s, meant that there has been considerable competition for entry to tertiary institutions (Price, 1977).
9. We cannot say the building of the "communist" state, because it is not altogether clear to what extent these societies are committed to the achievement of full communism. Unlike the Eastern European countries, many of the socialist-leaning less-developed countries are not aligned with the Soviet Union, and do not form part of the Soviet block. Some of these countries, in particular Tanzania, have committed themselves to following their own brand of socialism, without any commitment, it seems, to the achievement of full communism in the Marxist sense.
10. There have been numerous recent attempts to demonstrate the importance of historical dimensions in the analysis of education and society. For a thorough discussion of this process from a more theoretical perspective, see Archer (1979).

10

Education, the State and Development

IN this chapter we focus our attention on three aspects of the relationship between education and development which, in effect, conclude our work. However, rather than see these aspects as a conclusion, we prefer to view them as opening the way to future theoretical and research efforts. Thus, the following sections point to issues which we feel have not yet been adequately explored in the study of education's role in national development. The first of these concerns the tendencies to regard education in a deterministic manner, thus exaggerating its potential for change. The second concerns the contradictions for society and for individuals inherent in rapid educational expansion, and the third focuses on the role of the State in affecting the relationship between education and development. Each of these aspects describes broad contexts which affect the way that the dialectical process operates.

The Determinate Effects of Education

One of the major fallacies of theories of education and development has been their overdeterministic nature. An important underlying assumption often dominating such theories has been the belief that formal education can both manipulate and be manipulated in order to attain specified educational goals. Thus the human capital theorists and modernizationists seemingly overlook or fail to take into account the possibility that the acquisition of literacy or of schooling provides individuals with the ability to reject the conditions of "productive" labor, or of modern attitudes, values and beliefs. The return to traditional values does not always occur among the uneducated, and often can be the result of rational and deliberate decisions by the educated.[1] For example, colonial schools may have been intended to provide middle-level public administrators for colonial governments, but they also made it possible for the colonized to deal more equally with the colonizer. In much the same way the structuralists and neo-Marxists equally assume that the hegemony of capitalist education is completely effective in creating a docile workforce subservient to the ruling class, without allowing for the possibility that an educated workforce in itself constitutes a potentially revolutionary element which can recognize its disadvantaged condition in society. Some writers, however, take the above into account by arguing that the differentiated system of knowledge distribution, at least in capitalist societies, excludes the dominated classes from full access to knowledge and thus prevents them from becoming fully conscious of their subordinate condition (Bourdieu, 1973). Furthermore, it has been suggested by some (for example, Touraine, 1973) that education has become the basis of the class struggle, and that the struggles for knowledge or access to it have become the new focal point of the class struggle. They argue that the school can be seen as the arena within which conflicts between various interest groups and more fundamental class and power groups are resolved.

The difficulty in much of the debate about education and development is that these kinds of questions have largely been ignored. While governments may adopt educational plans consistent with specific development goals and strategies, they can only be partially certain that the outcomes of those plans will correspond to original intentions: the more political the goals of education, the more problematic the outcomes. To this extent, the view of education as a form of liberation or "conscientization" as put forward by Freire takes on additional importance, and perhaps greater research attention should be directed to this question. As an example, research in Tanzania suggests that attempts to inculcate collective-oriented political attitudes and beliefs among peasants were unsuccessful because the peasants could recognize that the "top-down" flow of decision-making affecting their economy in the end would only serve the interests of bureaucrats, and not improve their own condition. Their "liberation" through adult education programs made it possible for them to be critical of the very "villagization" reforms which it was intended that they accept (Kweka, 1987).

Given the above considerations, the temptation to view education as a single panacea for the attainment of development objectives is risky, to say the least. Education in general, and schooling in particular, cannot of its own achieve the desired societal goals without additional structural supports. Research in both developed and developing countries has clearly documented the fact that educational goals (academic achievement, career orientations and attitudes and beliefs) are only partially determined by educational factors such as teacher quality or curricula. Considerable impact on these presumed school outcomes is actually exercised by both home background, peer groups and structural features of the society itself. Indeed, our main concern throughout this work has been to show the dialectical relationship between education and the economic, social and political dimensions of society. Although the differences between developed and less-developed societies in the relative importance of these factors is considerable, it remains that the school is hardly the single determining factor in the attainment of educational, much less development goals. To regard it as such, as do many researchers and policy-makers, is to take an overdeterminate view of education and its effect on society.

The Contradictions of Educational Expansion

We have previously indicated that one of the single most dramatic events to occur in education on a global scale has been the rapidity and universality of its expansion. In the industrial West, universal primary schooling was reached by 1960, and virtual universal secondary schooling had been attained in some countries like the United States by the mid-1970s. For all industrialized countries 90 percent of the relevant age groups were enrolled in secondary schooling in 1984, an increase of 22 percent over the 1960 figure. Higher education rates were equally dramatic in their increase during

TABLE 10.1. *Educational Expansion for Country Groups*

	Percent of age group in primary		Percent of age group in secondary		Percent of 20–24 age group in higher	
	1960	1984	1960	1984	1960	1984
Low-Income (a) countries	54	97	14	32	2	4
Middle-income(b) countries	81	104	17	47	4	13
Industrialized(c) countries	114	102	68	90	17	38
Capital-surplus(d) oil exporters	43	99	12	37	1	10
Centrally planned(e) economies	101	105	45	93	11	21

Source: Adapted from World Bank (1980b; 1987), Table 23 pp. 154–155, Table 31, pp. 292–293.
(a)Bangladesh, Ethiopia, Vietnam, Tanzania, Angola, etc.
(b)Egypt, Thailand, Nigeria, Malaysia, Turkey, Greece, Israel, etc.
(c)Italy, Japan, France, Australia, UK, Sweden, USA, etc.
(d)Libya, Saudi Arabia, Kuwait, etc.
(e)China, Cuba, Hungary, Poland, USSR, Czechoslovakia, GDR, etc.

the same period: the percentage for industrialized countries rose from 17 to 38 percent, the 1984 figures ranging from a high of 57 percent in the United States to a low of 20 percent for Great Britain. The overall comparisons in educational expansion are given in Table 10.1.

There have been many explanations for the origins and expansion of mass education. From the economic perspective, it has been argued that across all types of societies educational systems have expanded in response to emerging modern production systems, or at least where those systems have been planned (Ramirez and Meyer, 1980). Neo-Weberians and Marxists, on the other hand, have explained the expansion of education at all levels as a result of conflicts and rivalries between interest groups, or by the need to exercise ideological domination and hegemonic control by those in power over their subordinates. Somewhat related are those who explain the growth of education in terms of the increasing differentiation of society, in that it serves as an integrating mechanism which socializes individuals into a more complex system of roles and norms which the kin system or modern family are no longer able to do.

A newer perspective has focused on the political dimension of educational expansion. With the rise of a universalistic and rational ideology in the nineteenth century, it became necessary to incorporate the new individual into society as a citizen with rights and duties. This incorporation empowers the individual to act in a rational, purposive and competent manner in a universalistic system, and at the same time promotes State stability and survival (Boli *et al.*, 1985). Once institutionalized in Europe, the modern educational system became part of a worldwide ideology which was seen as essential for the building of a strong nation state (Fiala and Lanford, 1987; Ramirez and Boli, 1987).

Irrespective of the explanation given for global educational expansion, the consequences of this expansion for social systems can be problematic. The tensions and strains of educational expansion can impede and place obstacles to economic social and political development. To take the most simple example, the accelerating costs of expanding educational systems compete with other sectors of the respective societies for finite resources. As mass primary education is attained, expansion shifts to the second and tertiary levels as these too are gradually transformed into mass systems. At the same time, the increase in costs is not arithmetic but geometric (Husén, 1979:72).

Educational expansion produces tensions at the social level as well. Irrespective of type of society, whether developed or less developed, the social benefits which accrue to those who participate in educational systems change dramatically. The differential rewards to educational attainment are dependent upon the distribution of both education and benefit variables throughout the population. The phenomenon at work here is known as the Law of Zero Correlation, which becomes effective in any population where the educational attainment ratio level approaches 0 percent or 100 percent.

The importance of the Law of Zero Correlation for development, and in particular for understanding the tensions brought about by educational expansion, is that it points to the source of some of these tensions. In effect as levels of school attainment rise, the social values accruing to attainment will decline. Thus as participation rates at any level, for example secondary school, increase, the aggregate social benefits to those reaching that level will decrease. When 100 percent of a population or relevant subgroup have a secondary education, then that level loses its advantage. However, on the other side of the coin, if almost the entirety of a population increasingly attains certain levels, then for those who have not done so there is increasing liability.

> As zero correlation is approached, the aggregate social benefits once associated with high school attainment decline and the aggregate social liabilities of non-attainment increase. Where high school attainment was once a highly sought after good, it now becomes a necessity to be endured (Seidman, 1982:272).

There are at least three consequences of this process which have immediate relevance for both developed and less-developed societies. Firstly, as levels of school attainment increase, the disparity between the attainer and non-attainer in terms of social benefits (income, occupational status, etc.) will also increase. Secondly, as participation rates for any given educational level approach 100 percent, with the consequent decrease in social benefits, there will be pressure for expansion at the next higher level, resulting in a spiralling effect so commonly experienced in all countries. Finally, it has been argued that because of the intersect between the benefit and liability curves which tend to level off when 75 to 80 percent of any cohort have become attainers, there occurs a "systemic equilibrium" which tends to slow down the pressures for complete attainment. According to Seidman (1982), this explains the "levelling off" of high school attainment rates in the United States at about that figure. Presumably these system-level phenomena can be observed in all societies at any level of development.

The increasing demand for education, particularly in less-developed countries, seems a highly appropriate context where these systemic forces might be operating. As we observed in Chapter 5, the high level of aspirations, both for educational and occupational attainment, has been seen as a potentially destabilizing phenomenon, such that frustration and unrest might ensue. The provision of educational facilities able to meet demands at one level seems only to lead to increased demands at the next level, with consequent high expectations for that level of attainment. These pressures ultimately create dilemmas for governments who must realistically assess and determine spending priorities for scarce economic resources. Rather than planned educational expansion, many of these societies have experienced *forced* and *rapid* expansion.

The control of educational expansion, and especially the apparent exaggeration of educational demand, has received some attention by specialists from within both structural-functional and radical camps. Adopting a position based on the assumptions of the human capital and modernization theorists, Todaro (1977) has argued that in developing countries at least, educational demands must be tempered in order to bring costs and benefits to more realistic levels. Among his suggestions are that the costs of education should be borne by the beneficiary or recipient by means of family assistance or self-help schemes, rather than the State (the user-pays principle)[2]; the income differentials between the traditional and modern sectors should be reduced, which in effect lowers the benefits accruing to educational attainments; the educational requirements for particular jobs should not be exaggerated; and finally, the wage structure should be tied to occupational requirements rather than educational attainments. Todaro further suggests that funds might be diverted from educational expansion and directed to building up urban and rural infrastructures in order to increase the number of job opportunities.

This approach to tension reduction brought about by accelerated education expansion falls within the structural-functional paradigm, and neglects factors outside the society. These latter factors may have considerable effect on the nature of educational expansion, and in fact may be the main source of the difficulty. Ultimately the most unique feature of less-developed countries is the extent to which their economies and cultures have been penetrated by the interests of Western industrialized societies. One of the characteristics of this penetration and resulting dependency is that the modern sector is distorted such that economic growth does not necessarily result in the expansion of jobs (Irizzary, 1980).

The dependency cycle can be stated in fairly concise form. As we have noted in Chapters 3 and 9, most less-developed countries have had to or still do rely on a large agricultural base and a small modern industrial sector. To complicate matters, the proportion of the populations engaged in agriculture has been rapidly decreasing in the less-developed countries, partly because of the displacement of small landowners and peasants by larger, more technologically sophisticated estates and plantations, and partly by the voluntary migration from the countryside to the cities in search of more lucrative and higher status occupations in the modern sector.[3] (See Table 9.2 for examples of shifts between sectors.) In actual numbers, the population shifts in the less-developed countries are quite large, and they take place in contexts where the level of industrialization is relatively low.

We have also noted that the modern sectors of the less-developed countries tend to be highly penetrated by foreign capital, with the result that the industrial sector is typically small and capital intensive, and the service sector is relatively large and highly bureaucratic (Evans and Timberlake, 1980). This disarticulation in the modern sector thus produces a situation in which the skills required in the industrial sector are limited, the capital-intensive foreign-imported technology of the sector reduces the number of jobs, and the service sector, consisting of middle-range administrative positions, comes under considerable pressure from expansion (Evans and Timberlake, 1980). This uneven, restricted and distorted modern sector, typical of many if not most less-developed countries, is unable to absorb the migration from the countryside, with the result that unemployment increases rapidly and the avenues for entry into and upward mobility within the modern sector become restricted to highly skilled jobs in the industrial sector or the service sector, which generally means the government bureaucracy.

The implications of this structural context, both in terms of internal distortion as well as external dependency, has important consequences where the educational system is rapidly expanding. We know from previous chapters that education itself exerts considerable influence on values and beliefs, and as a result is of itself responsible for raising the ambitions of young people. Thus in a society where agricultural occupations are becoming fewer and less desirable because of income and status differentials, the expansion of schooling independently raises the aspiration levels of larger segments of the population. Where the modern sector, because of its distorted and disarticulated character due to the penetration and intrusion of foreign capital and other forms of dependency, the pressures and tensions will be extremely high and the economic and political structures may become unstable or at least under considerable strain and imbalance. Finally, of considerable importance are the system-level pressures for educational expansion which were discussed earlier: the law of zero-correlation, and the changing benefits and liabilities of increased participation under conditions of rapid expansion.

But what have these structural factors to do with the exaggerated demand for education and the tensions produced by it? Those who consider structural factors as central to problems of development, for example dependency and world systems theorists, as well as those espousing more specific neo-Marxist and radical perspectives, would argue that unless there are structural changes which alleviate the source of these distortions, the attempts to redress or resolve these tensions are likely to prove futile.

In essence, the structuralists argue that the tensions of educational expansion and the ensuing structural distortions represent interactive and mutually reinforcing mechanisms. The increasing demand for education, the ambitions produced by education as a modernizing experience, the highly restricted avenue for mobility, mainly focused on the public service, and finally the increasing use of credentials by employers combine to create an unhealthy and possibly detrimental condition for any strategy of development. Furthermore, to attempt to manipulate ambition by deliberately lowering aspirations or expectations, without any structural alterations, will in all likelihood not be successful. Similarly, to attempt to replace the content of education with more agricultural and vocational curricula will not likely reverse the trend of rural-urban migration as long as the structural conditions causing that migration are allowed to continue (Irizarry, 1980).

Thus a development strategy which includes education, and particularly educational expansion, must ensure that the latter be accompanied with structural adjustments which promote a consistency or balance between the educational outputs and the absorbing capacity of the economic structure, and particularly the modern sector.

Education, the State and Development

We have already discussed in Chapter 5 the relationship between education and political development. Of particular relevance for the discussion here is the relationship between education and the State, and the role of the State in educational planning.

In this section we focus on the question of how much control the State exercises in educational decisions, in whose favor or according to what set of priorities these decisions are made, and finally to what extent can the State coordinate both educational and development objectives. These questions relating to the State lie at the heart of much of what has been said throughout this book, particularly with respect to our dialectical model.

There have been two general views about the State. The first, which is often called the classical liberal view, holds that the State is created by its members and is dependent on consensus for its continued existence. The State is seen as representing the common good or common interests, and provides for social needs, for example education, welfare, defense and the legal system. In this context, the State is viewed as a democratic institution which regulates economic power and protects the people from economic exploitation in the interests of society as a whole. The State in pluralist societies becomes more complex whereby interest groups compete within limits for State control and benefits, on the assumption that the result is "the greatest good for the greatest number".

The second view regards the State, and in particular the capitalist State, also in a pluralist context, but argues that it emerges not from consensus, but from the relations of production, and represents the interests of only one social group in competition with others. This version of Marxist structuralist theory sees the State as an arena in which the conflicts between social classes with different relations to the means of production appear to be resolved in the interests of all, but in fact serve the interests of the dominant class. This resolution of conflict is not seen as democratic, but rather domination through the exercise of power. According to this radical perspective, the capitalist State is controlled by the bourgeoisie class which exercises dominance over the working class. In Marxist theory the capitalist State takes on a different form in the transition to socialism, and will disappear altogether with the transition to communism (Carnoy, 1983, 1984).

Of particular importance in these two views of the State is the manner in which the various State institutions (or in the language of Althusser's theory of the State, the State apparatuses), are organized and used to achieve the goals of the State. In the first view of the State, social institutions are benign and serve the interests of all, whereas in the second view social institutions serve the class which controls the State. Furthermore, in the latter view these institutions are used by the State to maintain the dominance of the ruling class, hence they repress the subordinate class and prevent it from gaining power and control. These two views of the State come to very different conclusions about the role of education in society generally, and in particular about the relationship between the State, education and development.

The general view which prevails among those who see the State as an instrument for the common good is that the educational system operates, at least in theory, on behalf of the society's interest as a whole. Thus as an instrument to promote equal opportunity, political consensus and integration, and the mobilization of human resources, the school is seen to serve the best interests of the entire society, and gives legitimation to the social order resulting from these processes. If the educational system has not, in fact, been functioning on behalf of the collective citizenry, then the problem is seen as an inefficiency of the system rather than a defect in the system itself. Thus programs of educational reform so characteristic of England from the 1940s, and Sweden even more recently, are seen as attempts to make the system work better for the common good. The concern that these systems operate meritocratically rather than by privilege reflects the underlying conviction that the State and its institutions exist to promote the welfare of all its citizens rather than a particular interest group or class.

The Marxist structuralist view of the State is more extensive in that it directly includes education and other social institutions. Thus education is seen not as an institution to promote the common good, but rather as an instrument of those in power to maintain control over those in subordinate positions. In the context of the capitalist system, the school becomes a means whereby the bourgeois maintain their dominant role over the proletariat first by ensuring that their own sons and daughters have greater access to the system, are more successful in achievement within it, and enjoy higher levels of occupational and other career rewards as a result of that participation and achievement. Everything from the use of presumed value-free criteria to assess innate cognitive ability (and therefore educational potential) – such as IQ – to the curriculum, the nature of classroom interaction, and language itself, are seen as a mechanism through which this control over the schools is maintained. [4] Thus the same educational outcomes which are considered "legitimate", or at the most "inefficiencies" by those espousing the liberal democratic view of the State, are regarded as manifestations of class dominance of the bourgeois over the proletariat. Furthermore, these manifestations cannot be alleviated by mere reform, but require a complete restructuring not only of the educational system, but of society itself.

The question central to both perspectives, then, concerns the nature of the State, and more specifically the link between the State and the educational system. For us the question is even more precise: to what extent can the State use education to promote social and economic development? Already we have touched upon aspects of this question in previous chapters. Insofar as education can be deliberately planned to maximize the attainment of development objectives, the State can attempt to control the organization of education itself: access, curriculum and criteria for achievement and attainment. But it is here that the problem occurs, for the State (by this we mean *any* State) has never completely controlled the agents of education.

The history of education and the State is itself illuminating in this regard. Apart from some unique examples, such as the education of the *literati* in ancient China or the scribes in Egypt and Mesopotamia, most education and schooling has occurred outside the control of the State. One must recall that in the Middle Ages in Europe education was almost entirely in the hands of the Church, and only in relatively recent times has the State assumed greater power and authority in this sphere of social activity. Of crucial importance in questions of State intervention is the extent to which matters related to schooling are centralized or decentralized. Even in advanced industrialized countries there is considerable variation in this regard. On the one hand, France might be seen as an example of a highly centralized system where every minute detail of what goes on in schools is specified by the government Ministry of Education. On the other hand, the United States has been regarded as a typical example of a decentralized system. In the United States, although some fundamental and minimal conditions about schooling are specified, compulsory schooling until about age 16, and in particular some rights are guaranteed (for example, no exclusion from school on the basis of race, creed or color), much of the organization and content of schooling is left for State-level decisions, and even here much is left to the discretion of local school districts. However, recent trends toward consolidation and rationalization have greatly reduced the number of independent school districts from 40,000 in 1960 to 19,000 in 1970, and by 1978 to 16,000 (Cantor, 1980). This trend has had the effect of concentrating authority at the State level, though still allowing for considerable variation within the United States as a whole. Under these conditions, it is difficult to argue that the State is totally in control over the educational system, much less over what goes on in individual classrooms, except at a very general level.

The question of decentralized or centralized control becomes even more complex in the less-developed societies, both capitalist and socialist. In many poor countries the State apparatus is weak and the control of State processes lie outside the national boundaries (Carnoy, 1984). These "dependent" States owe their condition to many factors: the absence of political consolidation and stability, a weak and dependent bourgeoisie or ruling class, financial constraints, and for some, a complex history of schooling which includes mixtures of mission schools of various denominations, elite private non-denominational schools, and government operated schools. Thus where the State does not exercise adequate control over schooling, it cannot exercise efficient impact over those aspects of education which promote development.

It is here in the less-developed societies, that we find the least documentation about the role of the State in education and development. There has been some analysis of the role and impact of mission schools in less developed countries, and to some extent also of colonial school systems. There seems to be general agreement that for the most part these systems promoted either the interests of the various religious bodies or of the colonial rulers. These schools produced much-needed manpower and indigenous elites at a time when colonial powers needed middle-level administrators and managers to assist in colonial management. But the overall impact of these schools was a form of "cultural imperialism" whereby interests outside of the country received highest priority (Carnoy, 1974). According to those espousing liberal democratic theories of the State, and structural-functional/evolutionary theories of development, these forms of education are seen as necessary prerequisites to the further economic and social development of less-developed societies. However, more radical perspectives see these forms of schooling as parallel to schools in capitalist industrial societies which operate in the interests and advantage of the dominating classes. Thus mission schools and other elite colonial schools, in the long run, are seen as detrimental to the full economic and social development of these societies. As long as the heritage of these schools continues to influence education in many less-developed societies, the control of the State is lessened, and thus the link between education, the State and development is prevented from becoming consistent and strong[5].

In any assessment of education and development, then, the autonomy and strength of the State, particularly with respect to education, must be taken into account. Furthermore, the extent to which the State acts independently of interest groups and classes, or operates on behalf of or to the advantage of any group or class, will greatly affect the institutions which come under its control. Thus the possibility of predicting the contribution of education to the attainment of development goals in any given context to a large extent depends on the homogeneity of the school system and the consensus between educational goals and the goals of the State. The latter is greatly enhanced to the extent that the centralization of control of education by the State is achieved.

Education, the State and Development in Capitalist and Socialist Societies

In the previous chapter we put forward models of education and development for societies pursuing capitalist and socialist strategies of development. Insofar as these two represent, at the most general level, the alternatives available in the present world context, we now return to this distinction and comment on the role of the State in coordinating the operations of the educational system in achieving development objectives.

At the outset it is important to recognize that many of the problems encountered by the State in capitalist and socialist societies are common to both types of societies. The structure of the present world system is such that no economy is completely immune from the world-wide fluctuations in trade, inflation and supply and demand brought about by droughts, bumper harvests, price controls by international cartels and the like. Nevertheless with regard to basic aspects of economic structure, particularly in terms of ownership and control over the production system and the distribution of surplus in the society, there are striking, even radical differences between the two systems. Having said this, however, it must also be recognized that not every country can be precisely and unambiguously classified as capitalist or socialist. This is true even in advanced industrial societies where the degree of mix sometimes leads to designations such as "social democracy" or "middle way". The problem is more acute among the less-developed societies where there is sometimes disagreement among the experts as to how societies are best classified.[6]

Insofar as the capitalist State assumes a free-market economy and protects the interests of those who control the means of production, its development goals include the mobilization of human resources such that productivity of the system is maximized. Tolerance of market supply and demand in the determination of wage levels, and ultimately the distribution of material goods (through wages and open consumption), means that few restrictions are imposed on the system. This does not mean that the State and the interests of the capitalist classes are completely in agreement about the goals of the society. Conflicts of interest can occur within the capitalist classes themselves, and between the capitalist classes and the State. Yet because the capitalist State espouses the common good view of society and the State, it sees itself as primarily concerned with representing the interests of the people and ensuring free access to the rewards which society has to offer. Thus the capitalist State is to some extent caught between a *laissez-faire* stance regarding the production system, and an *interventionist* position regarding the guarantee of freedoms. This is how the capitalist State justifies its subsidization of schools in an otherwise *laissez-faire* context. However, insofar as the capitalist State allows control over schools to be decentralized, to that extent can schools, at least theoretically, pursue diverse goals not entirely consistent with those of the dominant capitalist class or the State itself. This is why in many capitalist industrial societies the schools are often oriented to promote the well-being of segments of the population not part of the dominant class, for example working-class communities and minority groups (Shapiro, 1980).

Given these aspects of the relationship between the school and the capitalist State, the radical critics have difficulty in supporting the notion that schools in capitalist societies merely reproduce the social order and maintain the *status quo*. While it may be true that the school serves to *legitimate* the social order as it exists, it may not function only to *reproduce* that order, for by subsidizing and extending educational opportunity to the masses, it makes possible the mobilization of human resources and the further possibility that individuals or groups may improve their social position or even challenge the system itself.

The socialist State, insofar as it comprises the government and the ruling Party, at least in theory, operates quite differently. With both its control over the means of production and the mobilization of resources, the socialist State is able to prevent power from being concentrated in any group and functions in a manner which should benefit all segments of the population. Since the means of production are in the hands of the State, the question of schools serving specific interest groups or merely reproducing the social order becomes irrelevant.

However, there is considerable disagreement about the effectiveness of the socialist State to build a classless society, at least where it has been attempted. The Soviet Union, for example, has been criticized from all directions for having espoused a form of state capitalism rather than true socialism, and it has produced a society in which forms of inherited privilege continue to exist. Lane (1976), for example, observes that "state ownership of the means of production may give rise to a ruling class deriving its power from *control* of the means of production" (p. 36). In spite of its centralized control over the educational system, many studies in the Soviet Union have shown the advantage of the non-manual strata both in access to education, particularly institutions of higher education, and to the more professionally-oriented institutions. For example, in a 1968 study of the social origins of first-year students in various academic departments of higher-education institutions in Sverdlovsk, students of non-manual origin were more represented in the Teacher Training Institutes, Medical Institute and the Polytechnic Institute. Students of manual backgrounds were dominant in the Agricultural Institute, Railways Institute and the Mining Institute. It was also found that while students of non-manual origin tended to pursue their studies during the day, those of manual origin generally studied in the evening or by correspondence (Lane, 1976:187; Dobson, 1977:267). Similar patterns are found between students from urban and rural areas (Blumenthal and Benson, 1978).

Turning to socialist States other than the Soviet Union, similar results have been found. For example, in both Hungary and Poland it seems that students of non-manual social origins are much more likely to remain in school after the compulsory school age, and a much larger proportion of non-manuals enter institutions of higher education. The figures for Poland clearly illustrate this pattern: 48 percent of non-manual origins, compared to 32 percent manual and 16 percent peasant enter higher education. Furthermore, the attendance in these institutions tends to be stratified by type of course, for example full-time, evening and correspondence courses, in much the same way as in the Soviet Union (Lane, 1976:188–189).

What is remarkable in this evidence of "new" inherited privilege in socialist industrial societies is that it survives in spite of official attempts by the state to prevent it. In most socialist societies a point system or quotas favoring those from the more disadvantaged groups have been adopted in order to eliminate inequality. In the Soviet Union work experience can be used as a criterion for admission to higher education. Yet, in spite of these measures, educational inequalities continue to exist. Ironically the patterns which emerge from these studies do not drastically depart from those found in capitalist industrial societies. Furthermore, closer investigation into the mechanisms of school attainment and achievement have found that in spite of deliberate attempts to eradicate inequality, the determinants of the educational process lie outside the control of the State. As in capitalist societies, the success of children of non-manual origins in socialist schools is due in large part to their cultural advantage which they inherit from their home and family background. Studies in the Soviet Union and Hungary have shown, for example, that parental interest, often expressed in the form of private tuition for children, and the aspirations of both parents and children tend to be higher in non-manual families. Thus inequality persists not because the education system subsidized by the State promotes it, but because some aspects of the educational process are autonomous with respect to the State (Dobson, 1977). Thus, while the link between education and the State varies considerably between capitalist and socialist industrial societies, the power to control educational processes and outcomes is limited in both contexts. Likewise, insofar as development objectives may be explicitly articulated by the State, there are limits to which the State can harness the educational system in the attainment of these objectives.

Let us now turn our attention to the less-developed countries and ask to what extent the State, both capitalist and socialist, exercises a determining role in linking education and development. As we noted in the previous section of this chapter, the State in less-developed societies is often less consolidated than in advanced societies; it is generally poorer in resources, less secure in its hold on power, and must often contend with a more heterogeneous population than is usually the case in more developed societies. In many former colonial countries, the political boundaries of the State and the nature of the political bureaucracy and economic infrastructure are ill-suited to the needs of a new country trying to build upon indigenous strengths rather than on colonial residues. These conditions place serious disadvantages on the State in pursuing development goals, irrespective of whether the political and economic system is capitalist or socialist.

There have been few empirical studies which have compared capitalist and socialist governments in terms of their effectiveness in achieving development objectives, and more particularly in the utilization of education as an agent for achieving these goals. In the research comparing Kenya and Tanzania, in spite of the differences in political systems and development goals, the educational systems in both societies, were found to function in a similar manner: unequal access and attainment seemed to be a common characteristic of both countries, and in socialist Tanzania, political values and slogans endorsing egalitarian ideals were apparently not incompatible with high individual occupational aspirations and expectations. Furthermore, the empirical evidence suggests that in spite of an educational system designed to minimize regional inequalities, those inequalities have continued to persist (Court, 1976).

In general, the little evidence which does exist seems to suggest that socialist-oriented less-developed countries do not perform any better than their capitalist counterparts in development terms, and indeed may not perform as well. In a study of Burma, Cuba, Sri Lanka and Tanzania, Morawetz (1980) found that since the time that socialist-oriented policies were introduced, economic growth appears to have been slower than in many of the capitalist less-developed countries, and there has been virtually no eradication of unequal income distributions. On the other hand, Burma and Sri Lanka have done well with respect to basic human needs, particularly education. However, as Morawetz points out, in both countries the pre-socialist educational systems were virtually retained, and at the time when both countries adopted socialist policies there already existed relatively high literacy rates (58 percent or over). Taking into account all of the various dimensions analyzed by Morawetz, Cuba emerged as the country which made the greatest improvement in socio-economic development under socialism, while Tanzania and perhaps Sri Lanka seem to have made the least.

One important factor which seems to have emerged from the study is the extent to which mass mobilization may be related to the effective implementation of socialist development strategies. Cuba, for example, along with the charisma of Castro, carried out a widespread program whereby the population as a whole was incorporated into the revolutionary program, whereas in Tanzania success depended more on the charisma of one man, President Nyerere. Furthermore, the ability to transform the educational system to promote mass mobilization and to support more directly the development objectives of the State may constitute an additional factor. It is here that the utilization of education to support development goals may be the most important contribution of education to planned development. This possibility is clearly recognized by Morawetz, as is apparent in the following statement:

> The extent to which the mass of the people share the government's socialist ideals no doubt plays at least some role in the extent to which wide-ranging policy changes can be introduced. With the benefit of hindsight, it is no surprise that most Tanzanian villagers resisted attempts to collectivize production, since they do not ever seem to have declared themselves to be particularly socialist; their (apparently misunderstood) African traditions of mutual self-help tended to be family-based, and did not usually extend to communal ownership of land. Again with the benefit of hindsight, it was perhaps predictable that, of the four SDCs, Cuba and Sri Lanka should have had the greatest and least degree of success respectively in transforming their educational systems to serve national needs. The new Cuban educational system focuses on agriculture and public health in rural areas and on co-operation rather than competition, and encourages schools to pay their own way by growing their own food. In Sri Lanka, by contrast, the

ruling elite was unlikely to adopt a system that might deny to some of its children the chance of following in its footsteps: hence, more education in Sri Lanka has meant more of the same (p. 360).

The implication of the Morawetz study of four socialist developing countries is that socialism may be a viable development strategy for some less-developed countries, but that a socialist strategy is also subject to the same factors inhibiting development as in a capitalist development strategy. With regard to education, there seem to be further implications which cast additional light on the link between education and development. For socialist societies in particular, it appears that the mobilization of resources through education as well as through other social institutions is essential if development goals will be accepted and pursued cooperatively by the general population. While the capitalist strategy, and the role of education within it, has the advantage of a competitive open-market system whereby motivation can be generated by the ambitions of individuals to get ahead, the socialist system must motivate individuals for collective rather than individual rewards. In the capitalist educational system the inculcation of skills and knowledge has the advantage of being seen as advantageous both to the individual and society, even though on a subtle level the system itself, that is, the *status quo*, is reproduced by the school. The socialist educational system, on the other hand, must also inculcate skills and knowledge appropriate to the development needs of the society, but at the same time must deliberately foster the collective-oriented development values and objectives of the society as a whole, and minimize individual ambitions and pursuits.

It would appear that many of the characteristic and performance of educational systems in capitalist and socialist countries, both developed and less-developed, are similar. Fidel Castro has explained the dramatic success of the Cuban educational system in terms of the revolution: "What we have done would have been impossible without a revolution" (Richmond, 1987:191). Yet, although Cuban progress has been outstanding, so has the educational progress of some other non-socialist Latin American and Caribbean countries. In a study of national educational indicators for all available countries, Inkeles and Sirowy (1983) found evidence that national educational systems were becoming strikingly similar. This is also true in the use of standardized testing as a means of selection and quality maintenance in schools.

In recent years the use of standardized tests has spread to many less-developed countries, both capitalist and socialist, in spite of evidence that tests are biased in favor of those social groups who already enjoy privilege in society. It is ironic, therefore, that Castro, like many other leaders and governments, has expressed concern about low standards while praising the mass expansion of Cuban education. In 1986 he observed in the same speech:

> One of the most promising ideas in the field of education during these five years was to turn vocational schools – 6th through 12th grades – into vocational high schools – 10th to 12th grades – where students are admitted according to their academic records and scores on competitive exams. (cited in Richmond, 1987:193).

The need for filling many skilled and complex occupational positions has lead China to the use of tests as a means of selecting and also maintaining quality, both in the school and the workplace (Heyneman, 1987; Zhen, 1987). However, standardized testing is also political, for someone must decide what knowledge is to be tested and for what purpose. Through testing, education is more centrally controlled and standardized, but the possibility of selection being made on social, as well as scientific criteria, is likely. Thus the issue of equality versus quality seems to represent an inroad whereby the protection of privilege is maintained in both capitalist and socialist societies.

In the end, issues related to education and development cannot be resolved without taking into account the role of the State. Whether one views the State from the common good or the Marxist perspective, it seems inevitable that the State is never neutral, irrespective of type of economy or level of development. The goals of both education and development in any country are inherently political.

Education and development can be conceptualized in a way whereby all individuals and groups in a country are equally affected. However the adoption of educational and development programs, with specific aims and objectives, resides in the hands of the State, and these programs inevitably affect some individuals and groups more than others. Therefore educational and development programs are rarely neutral, and to understand the complexities of their origins, processes and outcomes, it is essential that the role of the State be examined and evaluated.

Education and Development: Concluding Comments

Although there is much which has been said about education and development, there is still much we do not know. In these chapters we have ranged widely, and we believe exhaustively, in our attempt to critically examine the problematic nature of the relationship between the two. We have focused our attention on the empirical evidence showing the contribution, or lack of it, which education has made in the attainment of development objectives. At the same time, we have attempted to examine the various theoretical perspectives which have been important in the evaluation of the role of education in the development of both industrialized and non-industrialized developed and less-developed societies, and both capitalist and socialist societies.

The task is not an easy one. The fact that views have ranged from extreme optimism to cynicism and skepticism should not detract from a more realistic view of what education can and cannot do in furthering the economic growth and improvement of social life in all societies. Yet insofar as there is much we still do not know about the different and complex ways that education is linked to society, there is room for improvement. As we have repeated often, it is not so much a question of whether one can be optimistic or pessimistic about education and development, but rather of knowing what kind of education is appropriate for what kind of development. We have tried to show that prescriptions are rarely "either-or" or "right-wrong", but rather "under what conditions" and "for what purpose" are the education and development strategies to be implemented. Finally, the decision as to what outcomes are to be desired is a political act. Of all the conclusions we have made in these chapters, these are the most important.

Yet underlying this complexity are empirical realities which require action, and to take an overly cynical view about the potential of education as an agent of change begs the response: "why bother with planning at all?" The fact is that educational strategies directed to the attainment of development objectives can be successful. However, the implementation of plans takes time, and the attainment of goals requires even longer. But clearly, there is much room for further research directed to the full range of conditions affecting the education-development relationship. As we look back to our first attempt to grapple with this issue, we are confident that our understanding has improved. Even in the failures of development programs, there is something to be learned. The first step has been made. What remains is to recognize that the journey is difficult. Nevertheless we remain optimistic about future possibilities for a better understanding of, and planning for, the relationship between educational processes and the attainment of national development objectives.

Notes

1. The rejection of aspects of modern society often occur among the educated. The rise of countercultures and the advocates of scaling down modern bureaucratic organizations are examples. Schumacher's *Small is Beautiful* (1974) is one economist's response to the bureaucratic growth of modern society, and he also espoused the notion of an intermediate technology for developing countries.
2. Todaro's argument is slightly different from that put forward by Edwards (1980), as discussed in Chapter 9. Whereas Todaro is primarily concerned with programs to reduce high levels of educational demand, Edwards is concerned with the financial burdens of expanding educational systems in less-developed countries.
3. Rural–urban migration has been regarded as both "a symptom of and contributing factor to Third World underdevelopment" (Todaro, 1977:187). One of the most consistent characteristics of those who migrate is their higher levels of educational attainment, with the result that education (and by implication the inculcation of modern attitudes) is often seen as a causal factor to migration. However, this interpretation should be made with caution: as the number of educated increases as a result of educational expansion, one would expect a higher proportion among the migrant population. However, in at least one study in Tanzania (cited by Todaro, p. 193), it was found that as requirements for urban employment became more fixed to secondary-school credentials, the numbers of rural to urban migrants with primary schooling only began to decrease.
4. The literature reflecting this radical point of view is considerable. Of particular interest, however, is the work of Bowles and Gintis (1976), critiquing the school in capitalist America, particularly what they call "IQism", and the first collection of papers reflecting the "new sociology of education", found in Young (1971).
5. An example of the problematic control of education by the State in less-developed societies can be found in the study of Swedish Protestant schools in Zaire by Chinapah and Daun (1981). The authors document the efforts of the Zaire government in 1974 to nationalize all schools. Prior to that date, 90 percent of primary and 70 percent of all secondary schools were owned and operated by Church organizations and other private bodies. However, by 1977 the government was forced to return these schools to their former owners, "because of lack of experience as well as lack of competent administrators" (p. 59). In effect, while the Zaire government continues to pay for most schooling costs, it has virtually no control over what goes on in the schools, or where they are located, with the result that there are considerable inequalities in the country in educational opportunities and quality.
6. A good illustration of this difficulty is found in Morawetz (1980), who chose Burma, Cuba, Sri Lanka and Tanzania as examples of Socialist Developing Countries (SDCs). He comments:
   > Not everyone would agree that all of the countries examined here are socialist, which is not surprising since 'there is... no agreement among the experts as to what socialism is supposed to mean'. Certainly the governments of these countries all *call* themselves socialist (p. 337).

Selected Bibliography

ABRAHAMSSON, KENNETH (ed) (1988) *Implementating Recurrent Education in Sweden: On Reform Strategies at Swedish Adult and Higher Education*, Stockholm: Swedish National Board of Education.

ABRAHAMSSON, KENNETH, MATS MYRBERG and KJELL RUBENSON (1988) "Recurrent Education in Sweden – obselete Policy Concept or Guideline for the Future?, in KENNETH ABRAHAMSSON (ed.) *Implementing Recurrent Education in Sweden: On Reform Strategies of Swedish Adult and Higher Education*, Stockholm: Swedish National Board of Education.

ACKER, SANDRA (1984) "Sociology, gender and education", in SANDRA ACKER et al. (eds.), *World Yearbook of Education*, New York: Nicholas Publishing Co.

ADAMS, DONALD K. (1977) "Deelopmental education", *Comparative Education Review*, 21 (2+3) (June/October): 296–310.

ALEXANDER, JEFFREY C. (ed.) *Neofunctionalism*, Beverly Hills: Sage

ALEXANDER, LEIGH and JOHN SIMMONS (1975) *The Determinants of School Achievement in Developing Countries: The Educational Production Function*, Staff waking paper 201, Washington, D.C.: The World Bank.

AL–HARRI, RAFEDA (1987) "Islam's Point of View on Women's Education in Saudi Arabia", *Comparative Education*; 23 (1): 51–57.

ALMOND, GABRIEL A. and SIDNEY VERBA (1965) *The Civic Culture: Political Attitudes and Democracy in Five Nations*, Boston: Little, Brown & Company.

AMSDEN, ALICE H. (ed.) (1980) *The Economics of Women and Work*, Harmondsworth: Penguin Books.

ANDERSON, C. ARNOLD (1961) "A skeptical note on education and mobility", in A. H. HALSEY et al. (eds.) *Education, Economy and Society*, New York: The Free Press of Glencoe.

ANDERSON, C. ARNOLD and MARY JEAN BOWMAN (eds.) (1965) *Education and Economic Development*, Chicago: Aldine Publishing Company.

ANOSIKE, BENJI J. O. (1977) "Education and economic development in Nigeria: The need for a new paradigm", *African Studies Review*, XX, No. 2 (September): 27–51.

APPLE MICHAEL W. (1978) "Ideology, reproduction and educational reform", *Comparative Education Review*, **22** (3) (October): 367–387.

APTER, DAVID E. (1965) *The Politics of Modernization*, Chicago: University of Chicago Press.

ARCHER, MARGARET (1979) *Social Origins of Educational Systems*, London: Sage Publications.

ARMER, MICHAEL and ROBERT YOUTZ (1971) "Formal education and individual modernity in an African society", *American Journal of Sociology*, **76** (4): 604–626.

ARMER, MICHAEL (1977) "Education and social change: An examination of the modernity thesis", *Studies in Comparative International Development*, **XII** (Fall): 86–99.

ASPEN INSTITUTE FOR HUMANISTIC STUDIES (1975) *The Planetary Bargain. Proposals for a New International Economic Order to meet Human Needs*, Report of an International Workshop, Princeton N.J.: Aspen Institute for Humanistic Studies, Program in International Affairs.

AUSTRALIA, SCHOOLS COMMISSION (1975) *Girls, Schools and Society*, Canberra: Australian Government Printing Service.

AVALOS, BEATRICE and WADI HADDAD (1981) *A Review of Teacher Effectiveness Research in Africa, India, Latin America, Middle East, Malaysia, Philippines and Thailand: Synthesis of Results,* Ottawa: International Development Research Centre.

BARAN, PAUL A. (1957) *The Political Economy of Growth,* New York: Monthly Review Press.

BARBAGLI, MARZIO and MARCELLO DEI (1977). "Socialization into apathy and political subordination", in JEROME KARABEL and A. H. HALSEY (eds.) *Power and Ideology in Education,* New York: Oxford University Press.

BECKER, G. S. (1964) *Human Capital: A Theoretical and Empirical Analysis, with Special Reference to Education,* New York: Columbia University Press.

BECKER, HOWARD and HARRY ELMER BARNES (1961) *Social Thought from Lore to Science* (third edition), New York: Dover Publications (Vols. I, II, III).

BEEBY, C. E. (1979) *Assessment of Indonesian Education,* London: Oxford University Press.

BELL, DANIEL (1974) *The Comming of Post-Industrial Society,* London: Heinemann Publishing Co.

BENAVOT, AARON (1983) "The Rise and Decline of Vocational Education", *Sociology of Education,* **56**: 63–76.

BENERIA, LOURDES and GITA SEN (1981) "Accumulation, Reproduction, and Women's Role in Economic Development: Boserup Revisited", *Journal of Women in Cultura and Society,* **7** (2): 279–298.

BENSON, JERI and WILLIAM B. MICHAEL (1987) "Developing Evaluation Studies: a Twenty-Year Perspective", *International Journal of Evaluation Research,* **11** (1): 43–56.

BEREDAY, GEORGE Z. F. (1983) "Types of Student Unrest in Comparative Perspective – Buenos Aires, Tokyo, Paris, Barcelona", *Compare,* **13** (2); 167–183.

BEREDAY, GEORGE Z. F. and BONNIE B. STRETCH (1963) "Political education in the U.S.A. and the U.S.S.R.", *Comparative Education Review,* 7:9–16.

BEREITER, CARL (1973) *Must We Educate?,* Englewood Cliffs, N.J.: Prentice-Hall.

BERG, IVAR (1971) *Education and Jobs: The Great Training Robbery,* Boston: Beacon Press.

BERNSTEIN, HENRY (1979) "Sociology of underdevelopment vs sociology of development?", in DAVID LEHMANN (ed.) *Development Theory,* London: Frank Cass.

BEST, EDWARD E. JR. (1969) "Cicero, Livy and educated Roman women", *The Classical Journal,* **65** (October): 199–204.

BIRAIMAH, KAREN L. (1987) "Class, Gender, and Life Chances: A Nigerian University Case Study", *Comparative Education Review,* **31** (4):570–582.

BIZOT, JUDITHE (1975) *Educational Reform in Peru,* Paris: The Unesco Press, Experiments and Innovations in Education. No. 16.

BLACK, C. E. (1966) *The Dynamics of Modernization,* New York: Harper & Row.

BLAKEMORE, KENNETH P. (1975) "Resistance to formal education in Ghana: Its implications for the status of school leavers", *Comparative Education Review,* **19**: 237–251.

BLAUG, MARK (1970) *Economics of Education,* Harmondsworth: Penguin Press.

BLAUG, MARK (1976) "The empirical status of human capital theory: A slightly jaundiced survey", *Journal of Economic Literature,* **14** (September): 827–855.

BLAUG, MARK (1980) "Common assumptions about education and employment", in JOHN SIMMONS (ed.) *The Education Dilemma,* New York: Pergamon Press.

BLAUG, MARK (1985) "Where are we now in the economics of education?", *Economics of Education Review,* **4** (1): 17–28.

BLUMENTHAL, IRENE and CHARLES BENSON (1978) *Educational Reform in the Soviet Union: Implications for Developing Countries,* Washington D.C.: The World Bank.

BOLI, JOHN (1989) *New Citizens for a New Society. The Institutional Origins of Mass Schooling in Sweden.* Oxford: Pergamon Press.

BOLI, JOHN, FRANCISCO O. RAMIREZ, and JOHN W. MEYER (1985) "Explaining the Origins and Expansion of Mass Education", *Comparative Education Review,* **29** (2): 145–170.

BOOTH, DAVID (1975) "Andre Gunder Frank: An introduction and appreciation", in IVAR OXAAL, TONY BARNETT and DAVID BOOTH (eds.) *Beyond the Sociology of Development,* London: Routledge & Kegan Paul.

BORNSCHIER, VOLKER, CHRISTOPHER CHASE–DUNN and RICHARD RUBINSON (1978) "Cross-national evidence of the effects of foreign investment on aid and economic growth and inequality: A survey of findings and reanalysis", *American Journal of Sociology,* **84**(3):651–683.

BOSERUP, ESTER (1970) *Women's Role in Economic Development,* London: Allen and Unwin.
BOSERUP, ESTER and CHRISTINA LILJENCRANTZ (1975) *Integration of Women in Development,* United Nations Development Programme.
BOUDON, R. (1974) *Education, Opportunity, and Social Inequality. Changing Prospects in Western Society,* New York: John Wiley & Sons.
BOURDIEU, PIERRE (1973) "Cultural reproduction and social reproduction", in RICHARD BROWN (ed.) *Knowledge, Education and Cultural Change,* London: Tavistock.
BOURKE, S. F. and J. P. KEEVES (1977) *Australian Studies in School Performance,* Volume **III**. *The Mastery of Literacy and Numeracy: Final Report,* Canberra: Australian Government Publishing Service.
BOURKE, S. F., J. M. MILLS, J. STANYON, and F. HOLZER (1981) *Performance in Literacy and Numeracy: 1980,* Canberra: Australian Government Printing Service.
BOWEN, JAMES (1972) *A History of Western Education,* Vols. I and II, London: Methuen & Co. Ltd.
BOWLES, SAMUEL, (1971) "Cuban education and the revolutionary ideology", *Harvard Educational Review,* **41** (4): 472–500.
BOWLES, SAMUEL (1980) "Education, class conflict, and uneven development" in JOHN SIMMONS (ed.) *The Education Dilemma,* New York: Pergamon Press.
BOWLES, SAMUEL and HERBERT GINTIS (1972) "IQ in the U.S. class structure", *Social Policy,* **3** (November–December), 65–96.
BOWLES, SAMUEL and HERBERT GINTIS (1976) *Schooling in Capitalist America: Educational Reform and the Contradictions of Economic Life,* New York, Basic Books.
BOWMAN, MARY JEAN (no date) *The Participation of Women in Education in the Third World,* Chicago: Comparative Education Center.
BOWMAN, MARY JEAN and C. ARNOLD ANDERSON (1973) "Human capital and economic modernization in historical perspective", in F. C. LANE (ed.) *Fourth International Conference of Economic History,* Paris: Mouton Press.
BRAND, EUGENE (1987) "Functional illiteracy in industrialized countries", *Prospects,* **XVII** (2): 201–211.
BRANDELL, GEORG (1931) *Svenska undervisvgsnäsendets och uppfostrans historia,* Del I, II. Lund: Gleerup.
BRIDGE, R. GARY, CHARLES M. JUDD and PETER R. MOOCK (1978) *The Determinants of Educational Outcomes: The Impact of Families, Peers, Teachers and Schools,* Cambridge, Mass: Ballinger Publishing Co.
BRONFENBRENNER, URIE (1974) *Two Worlds of Childhood,* Harmondsworth: Penguin.
BULLOCK, ALAN and OLIVER STALLYBRASS (ed.) (1977) *The Fontana Dictionary of Modern Thought,* London: Fontana–Collins.
BYRNE, EILEEN (1982) *Women's Vocational Choices and Career Paths – a Research Overview of Some Principal Issues,* Canberra: Bureau of Labour Market Research
CAIN, C. G. (1976) "The challenge of segmented labor theories to orthodox theory: A survey", *Journal of Economic Literature,* **14**: 1215–1257.
CAMPBELL, ANGUS *et al.* (1965) *The American Voter,* New York: John Wiley & Sons.
CANTOR, LEONARD M. (1980) "The growing role of the States in American education", *Comparative Education,* **16** (1) (March): 25–31.
CARDOSO F. H. (1972) "Dependency and development in Latin America", *New Left Review,* **74** (July–August): 83–95.
CARNOY, MARTIN (1974) *Education as Cultural Imperialism,* New York: David McKay.
CARNOY, MARTIN (1975a) "Educational change: Past and present", in MARTIN CARNOY (ed.) *Schooling in a Corporate Society,* 2nd ed., New York: David McKay.
CARNOY, MARTIN (1975b) "The role of education in a strategy for social change", *Comparative Education Review,* **19**: 393–402.

CARNOY, MARTIN (1977) *Education and Employment: A Critical Appraisal*, Paris: UNESCO: International Institute for Educational Planning:

CARNOY MARTIN (1980) "Can education alone solve the problem of unemployment?", in JOHN SIMMONS (ed.) *The Education Dilemma*, New York: Pergamon Press.

CARNOY, MARTIN (1983) "Education and Theories of the State", *Education and Society*, **1** (2): 3–25.

CARNOY, MARTIN (1984) *The State and Political Theory*, Princeton, N.J.: Princeton University Press.

CARNOY, MARTIN and JORGE WERTHEIN (1977) "Socialist ideology and the transformation of Cuban education", in JEROME KARABEL and A. H. HALSEY (eds.) *Power and Ideology in Education*, New York: Oxford University Press.

CARNOY, MARTIN, HENRY M. LEVIN and KENNETH KING (1980) *Education, Work and Employment – II*, Paris: UNESCO, International Institute for Educational Planning.

CARNOY, MARTIN and HENRY LEVIN (1985) *Schooling and Work in the Democratic State*, Stanford, California: Stanford University Press.

CARRON, G. and A. BORDUA (eds.) (1985) *Issues in Planning and Implementing National Literacy Programmes*, Paris: Unesco, IIEP.

CARY, CHARLES D. (1976) "Patterns of emphasis upon Marxist–Leninist ideology: A computer content analysis of Soviet school history, geography and social science textbooks", *Comparative Education Review*, **20:** 11–29.

CASTLE, E. B. (1961) *Ancient Education and Today*, Harmondsworth: Penguin Books.

CHINAPAH, VINAYAGUM and INGEMAR FÄGERLIND (1979) *The Role of Education in the Basic Human Needs Strategy*, Report No. 39, Stockholm: Institute of International Education, University of Stockholm.

CHINAPAH, VINAYAGUM AND INGEMAR FÄGERLIND (1986) *The Design and Elaboration of the Evaluation/Monitoring Techniques for the Implementation of Educational Policies*. Research Studies, S. 123, Division of Educational Policy and Planning, Paris: UNESCO.

CHINAPAH, VINAYAGUM and HOLGER DAUN (1981) *Swedish Missions and Education in the Republic of Zaire*, Report No. 53, Stockholm: Institute of International Education, University of Stockholm.

CHODAK, SZYMON (1973) *Societal Development*, New York: Oxford University Press.

CHUKUNTA, N. K. ONUOHA (1978) "Education and national integration in Africa: A case study of Nigeria", *African Studies Review*, **XXI** (2):67–76.

CIPOLLA, CARLO M. (1969) *Literacy and Development in the West*, London: Penguin.

COCCO, IGNAZIO and JERALDO NASCIMENTO (1986) "Trends in Public Expenditure on Education 1975–1983", Prospects, **XVI** (2):??

COCHRANE, SUSAN H. (1982) "Education and Fertility: An Expanded Examination of the Evidence" in GAIL KELLY and CAROLYN ELLIOTT (eds), *Women's Education in the Third World*, Albany: State University of New York Press.

COHEN, YEHUDI, A. (1979) "Schools and Civilizational States", in JOSEPH FISCHER (ed.) *The Social Sciences and the Comparative Study of Educational Systems*, Scranton: International Textbook Company.

COHN, E. and R. A. ROSSMILLER (1987) "Research on Effective Schools – Implications for Less-Developed Countries", *Comparative Education Review*, **31** (3): 377–399.

COLEMAN, JAMES S. (ed.) (1965) *Education and Political Development*, Princeton, N.J.: Princeton University Press.

COLEMAN, JAMES S. *et. al.* (1966) *Equality of Educational Opportunity*, Washington, D.C.: U.S. Government Printing Office.

COLEMAN, JAMES S. (1972) "Methodological principles governing policy research in the social sciences", paper presented to the American Association for the Advancement of Science, Washington D.C.

COLLINS, RANDALL (1979) *The Credential Society*, New York: Academic Press.

COMBER, L. C. and JOHN P. KEEVES (1973) *Science Education in Nineteen Countries*, Stockholm: Almqvist & Wiksell.
CONVERGENCE (1986) "The State of the World's Women", *Convergence: The International Journal of Adult Education*, **XIX** (2): 9–12.
COOLEY, WILLIAM W. and PAUL R. LOHNES (1976) *Evaluation Research in Education*, New York: Irvington Publishers.
COOMBS, P. H. (1968) *The World Crisis in Education: A Systems Analysis*, London: Oxford University Press.
COOMBS, PHILIP H. (1985) *The World Crisis in Education: The View from the Eighties*, New York: Oxford University Press.
COOMBS, P. H. and M. AHMED (1974) *Attacking Rural Poverty*, London: The Johns Hopkins University Press.
COURT, DAVID (1976) "The education system as a response to inequality in Tanzania and Kenya", *The Journal of Modern African Studies*, **14** (4): 661–690.
COURT, D. and K. PREWITT (1974) "Nation versus region in Kenya: A note on political learning", *British Journal of Political Science*, **4**: 109–120.
CUNNINGHAM, INEKE (1974) "The relationship between modernity of students in a Puerto Rican high school and their academic performance, peers and parents", *International Journal of Comparative Sociology*, **24** (3–4):203–220.
CURLE, ADAM (1973) *Education for Liberation*, New York: John Wiley.
DAHLLÖF, URBAN (1960) *Kursplaneundersökningar i matematik och modersmalet* (Report No. 15), Stockholm: Statens Offentliga Utredning.
DELACROIX, JACQUES and CHARLES RAGIN (1978) "Modernizing institutions, mobilization, and Third World development: A cross-national study", *American Journal of Sociology*, **84** (1) (July):123–150.
DENISON, EDWARD F. (1962) "Education, economic growth and gaps in information", *Journal of Political Economy*, Vol. LXX (October).
DEWEY, JOHN (1966 (1916)) *Democracy and Education*, New York: The Free Press, Macmillan.
DOBSON, RICHARD B. (1977) "Social status and inequality of access to higher education in the USSR", in JEROME KARABEL and A. H. HALSEY (eds.) *Power and Ideology in Education*, New York: Oxford University Press.
DODGE, NORTON Y. (1966) *Women in the Soviet Economy*, Baltimore: The Johns Hopkins Press.
DORE, R. P. (1965) *Education in Tokugawa Japan*, Berkeley: University of California Press.
DORE, RONALD (1976) *The Diploma Disease*, London: Allen & Unwin.
DORE, RONALD (1980) "The future of formal education in developing countries", in JOHN SIMMONS (ed.) *The Education Dilemma*, New York: Pergamon Press.
DOVE, LINDA A. (1986) *Teachers and Teacher Education in Developing Countries*, London; Croom Helm.
DREEBEN, ROBERT (1968) *On What Is Learned in School*, Reading, Mass.: Addison-Wesley Publishing Co.
DURKHEIM, EMILE (1977) *The Evolution of Educational Thought*, London: Routledge & Kegan Paul.
EDWARDS, EDGAR O. (1980) "Investment in education in developing nations: Policy responses when private and social signals conflict", in JOHN SIMMONS (ed.) *The Education Dilemma*, New York: Pergamon Press.
EDWARDS, EDGAR O. and MICHEL P. TODARO (1972) "Education demand and supply in the context of growing unemployment in less developed countries", *World Development*, **1** (3&4):107–117.
EISENSTADT, S. N. (1970) "Breakdowns of modernization", in S. N EISENSTADT (ed.) *Readings in Social Evolution and Development*, Oxford: Pergamon Press.
ELKAN, WALTER (1976) *An Introduction to Development Economics*, Harmondsworth: Penguin Books (Revised Edition).
ELZINGA, AANT (1981) *Evaluating the Evaluation Game*, Stockholm: Swedish Agency for Research Cooperation with Developing Countries (SAREC).
EMMERIJ, LOUIS (1974) *Can the School Build a New Social Order?*, Amsterdam: Elsevier Scientific Publishing Company.

EVANS, EMMIT B., JR. (1975) "Secondary education, unemployment, and crime in Kenya", *The Journal of Modern African Studies*, 13 (1):55–66.

EVANS, EMMIT B. JR. (1977) "Sources of socio-political instability in an African state: The case of Kenya's educated unemployed", *African Studies Review*, XX (1): 37–52.

EVANS, PETER B. and MICHAEL TIMBERLAKE (1980) "Dependency, inequality and growth in less developed countries", *American Sociological Review*, 45 (4) (August):531–552.

FÄGERLIND, INGEMAR (1975) *Formal Education and Adult Earnings*, Stockholm: Almqvist & Wiksell International.

FAHRMEIER, EDWARD D. (1975) "The effect of school attendance on intellectual development in Northern Nigeria", *Child Development*, 46 (1): 281–285.

FIALA, ROBERT and AUDI GORDON LANFORD (1987) "Educataional Ideology and the World Educational Revolution, 1950–1970", *Comparative Education Review*, 31 (3) (1987): 315–332.

FINN, J. D., L. DULBERG and J. REIS (1979) "Sex Differences in Educational Attainment: a Cross-national Perspective", *Harvard Educational Review*, 49: 477–503.

FISCHER, JOSEPH (1965) "Indonesia", in JAMES S. COLEMAN (ed.) *Education and Political Development*, Princeton, N.J.: Princeton University Press.

FLETCHER, RONALD (1974) "Evolutionary and developmental sociology", in JOHN REX (ed.) *Approaches to Sociology*, London: Routledge & Kegan Paul, pp. 39–69.

FOSTER, PHILIP (1965) "The vocational school fallacy in development planning", in C. ARNOLD ANDERSON and MARY JEAN BOWMAN (eds.) *Education and Economic Development*, Chicago: Aldine Publishing Co.

FOSTER, PHILIP (1975) "Dilemmas of educational development: What we might learn from the past", *Comparative Education Review*, 19: 375–392.

FOSTER-CARTER, AIDAN (1976) "From Rostow to Gunder Frank: Conflicting paradigms in the analysis of underdevelopment", *World Development*, 4 (3): 167–180

FRANK, ANDRE GUNDER (1967) *Capitalism and Underdevelopment in Latin America*, New York: Monthly Review Press.

FRANK, ANDRE GUNDER (1969) "Sociology of development and underdevelopment of sociology", in *Latin America: Underdevelopment or Revolution*, New York and London: Monthly Review Press.

FRANK, ANDRE GUNDER (1972) *Lumpenbourgeoisie and Lumpendevelopment*, New York: Monthly Review Press.

FREDRIKSSON, VIKTOR (1942) *Svenska folkskolans historia*, Stockholm: Bonnier.

FREIRE, PAULO (1972) *Pedagogy of the Oppressed*, New York: Herder & Herder.

FREIRE, PAULO (1985) *The Politics of Education*, London: Macmillan.

FREY, FREDERICK W. (1965) *The Turkish Political Elite*, Cambridge: MIT Press.

FREY, FREDERICK W. (1970) "Political science, education, and development", in JOSEPH FISCHER (ed.) *The Social Sciences and the Comparative Study of Educational Systems*, Scranton: International Textbook Company.

FULLER, BRUCE (1987) "What School Factors Raise Achievement in the Third World?" *Review of Educational Research* 57 (3): 255–292.

FULLER, BRUCE, JOHN H. Y. EDWARDS., and KATHLEEN GORMAN (1987) "Does Rising Literacy Spark Economic Growth? Commercial Expansion in Mexico, In DANIEL WAGNER (ed.), *The Future of Literacy in a Changing World*, Oxford: Pergamon Press.

FURTADO, CELSO (1977) "Development", *International Social Science Journal*, XXIX (4): 628–650.

GALTUNG, JOHAN (1971) "A structural theory of imperialism", *Journal of Peace Research*, 8 (2): 81–117.

GALTUNG, JOHAN (1976) "Towards new indicators of development", FUTURES, (June): 261–265.

GAY, JOHN and MICHAEL COLE (1967) *The New Mathematics and an Old Culture: A Study of Learning Among the Kepelle of Liberia,* New York: Holt, Rinehart & Winston Inc.

GERGER, TORVALD and GÖRAN HOPPE (1980) *Education and Society: The Geographer's View,* Stockholm: Almqvist & Wiksell International.

GHAI, D.P. (1978) "What is a basic needs approach to development all about?", in D. P. GHAI *et al.* (eds.) *The Basic-Needs Approach to Development,* Geneva: ILO.

GLADWIN, THOMAS (1970) *East is a Big Bird: Navigation and Logic on Puluwat Atoll,* Cambridge: Harvard University Press.

GLASS, GENE V. (1976) "Primary, secondary and meta-analysis of research", *Educational Researcher,* **5** (1) November: 3–8.

GOODY, JACK and IAN WATT (1977) "The consequences of literacy", in JEROME KARABEL and A. H. HALSEY (eds.) *Power and Ideology in Education,* New York: Oxford University Press.

GORHAM, ALEX (1980) *Education and social change in a pastoral society,* Stockholm: Institute of International Education, University of Stockholm

GORMAN, TOM P., ALAN C. PURVES and R. ELAINE DEGENHART (eds) (1988) *The IEA Study of Written Composition I: The International Writing Tasks and Scoring Scales.* Oxford: Pergamon Press.

GRANT, NIGEL (1964) *Soviet Education,* Harmondsworth: Penguin Books.

GRANT, NIGEL (1969) *Society, School and Progress in Eastern Europe,* London: Pergamon Press.

GUSFIELD, JOSEPH R. (1967) "Tradition and modernity: Misplaced polarities in the study of social change", *American Journal of Sociology,* **72** (4) 351–362.

GUSTAFSSON, STET (1987) *Schools and the Transformation of Work,* Stockholm: Institute of International Education.

HABTE, AKLILU (1980) "Notes on the appropriateness of the formal schooling model for non-industrial societies", in TORSTEN HUSÉN (ed.) *The Future of Formal Education,* Stockholm: Almqvist & Wiksell International.

HADAS, MOSES (1971) *Imperial Rome,* Nederland: Time-Life International.

HALLAK, JACQUES and FRANÇOISE CAILLODS (1980) *Education, Work and Employment – I,* Paris: UNESCO, International Institute for Educational Planning.

HANCOCK, M. DONALD (1972) *Sweden: The Politics of Postindustrial Change,* Hinsdale Ill.: The Dryden Press.

HANF, THEODOR, KARL AMMANN, PATRICK V. DIAS, MICHAEL FREMERY and HERBERT WEILAND (1975) "Education: An obstacle to development? Some remarks about the political functions of education in Asia and Africa", *Comparative Education Review,* **19** (February): 68–87.

HANNA, WILLIAM JOHN (1975) "Students, universities and political outcomes", in WILLIAM JOHN HANNA and JUDITH LYNN HANNA (eds.) *University Students and African Politics,* New York: Africana Publishing Company.

HARBER, C.R. (1984) "Development and Political Attitudes: the Role of Schooling in Northern Nigeria", *Comparative Education,* **20** (3): 387–403.

HARBISON, FREDERICK H. (1973) *Human Resources as the Wealth of Nations,* London: Oxford University Press.

HÄRNQVIST, KJELL and ALLAN SVENSSON (1980) *Den sociala selektionen till gymnasiestadiet* (Report No. 30), Stockholm: Statens Offentliga Utredningar.

HARVEY, F. D. (1966) "Literacy in the Athenian democracy", *REG,* LXXIX (2): 585–635.

HAVIGHURST, R. J. (1968) "Education in Hopi society", in R. J. HAVIGHURST (ed.) *Comparative Perspectives on Education,* Boston: Little, Brown & Co.

HEIDENHEIMER, ARNOLD J. (1978) *Major Reforms in the Swedish Education Systems,* Washington, D.C.: World Bank Staff Working Paper No. 290.

HEYNEMAN, STEPHEN P. and INGEMAR FÄGERLIND (eds.) (1988) *University Examinations and Standardized Testing,* Washington, D.C.: The World Bank.

HESS, ROBERT D. and JUDITH V. TORNEY (1967) *The Development of Political Attitudes in Children*, Chicago: Aldine Publishing Co.

HEYNEMAN, STEPHEN P. (1976) "Influences on academic achievement: A comparison of results from Uganda and more industrialized societies", *Sociology of Education*, **49** (July): 200–211.

HEYNEMAN, STEPHEN P. (1987) "Uses of examinations in developing countries: selection, research, and education sector management", *International Journal of Educational Development*, **7** (4): 251–264.

HEYNEMAN, STEPHEN P. and INGEMAR FÄGERLIND (1988) *University Examinations and Standardized Testing*, Washington, D.C.: World Bank Technical Paper No. 78.

HEYNEMAN, STEPHEN P. and WILLIAM A. LOXLEY (1983) "The Effect of Primary-School Quality on Academic Achievement Across Twenty-Nine Nigh- and Low-Income Countries", *American Journal of Sociology*, **88** (6): 1162–1194.

HIGLEY, JOHN, DESLEY DEACON and DON SMART (1979) *Elites in Australia*, London: Routledge & Kegan Paul.

HOBSBAWM, E. J. (1977) *The Age of Revolution: Europe 1789–1848*, London: Abacus Edition.

HOLSINGER, DONALD B. (1974) "The elementary school as modernizer: A Brazilian study", *International Journal of Comparative Sociology*, **24**: 24–46.

HOOGVELT, ANKIE M. M. (1976) *The Sociology of Developing Societies*, London: Macmillan Press.

HORTON, ROBIN (1967) "African traditional thought and Western science", *Africa*, **37**: 50–71, 155–187.

HOUSE, ERNEST R. (1978) "Evaluation as scientific management in U.S. school reform", *Comparative Education Review*, **22** (3) (October): 388–401.

HOUSE, ERNEST R. (1980) *Evaluating with Validity*, London: Sage Publications.

HUNTINGTON, SAMUEL P. (1976) "The change to change: modernization, development and politics", in CYRIL E. BLACK (ed.) *Comparative Modernization*, New York: The Free Press.

HURN, CHRISTOPHER J. (1978) *The Limits and Possibilities of Schooling*, Boston: Allyn & Bacon, Inc.

HUSAIN, S. S. and S. A. ASHRAF (1979) *Crisis in Muslim Education*, HODDER AND STOUGHTON, Jeddah: King Abdulaziz University.

HUSÉN, TORSTEN (1969) *Talent, Opportunity and Career*, Stockholm: Almqvist & Wiksell.

HUSÉN, TORSTEN (1972) "Does more time in school make a difference?", *Saturday Review* (April 29): 32–35.

HUSÉN, TORSTEN (1976) "Swedish University research at the crossroads", *Minerva*, Vol. XIV, No. 4: 419–446.

HUSÉN, TORSTEN (1977) "Pupils, teachers and schools in Botswana: Primary and secondary education", in *Education for Kagisano: Report of the National Commission on Education*, Vol. 2 Annexes, Gaborone, Botswana.

HUSÉN, TORSTEN (1978) "Educational research and educational reform. A case study of Sweden", in PATRICK SUPPES (ed.) *Impact of Research on Education: Some Case Studies*, Washington, D.C.: National Academy of Education.

HUSÉN, TORSTEN (1979) *The School in Question*, Oxford: Oxford University Press.

HUSÉN, TORSTEN et al. (1973) *Svensk skola i internationell belysning I. Naturorienterande amnen*, Stockholm: Almqvist & Wiksell.

HUSÉN, TORSTEN (1984) "Issues and their Background" In TORSTEN HUSÉN, and MAURICE KOGAN (eds.), *Educational Research and Policy: How Do they Relate?* Oxford: Pergamon Press.

HUSÉN, TORSTEN (1986) "Why Did Sweden Go Comprehensive?", *Oxford Review of Education*, **12** (2): 153–163.

HUSÉN, TORSTEN, LAWRENCE J. SAHA and RICHARD NOONAN (1978) *Teacher Training and Student Achievement in Less Developed Countries*, Washington, D.C.: The World Bank.

HUTTON, CAROLINE and ROBIN COHEN (1975) "African peasants and resistance to change: a reconsideration of sociological approaches", in IVAR OXAAL, TONY BARNETT and DAVID BOOTH (eds.) *Beyond the Sociology of Development,* London: Routledge & Kegan Paul.

HYDÉN, GÖRAN (1980) *Beyond Ujamaa in Tanzania,* Berkeley: University of California Press.

ILO (1971) *Matching Employment Opportunities and Expectations. A Programme of Action for Ceylon: Report,* Geneva: International Labour Office.

INKELES, ALEX (1979) "National differences in scholastic performance", *Comparative Education Review,* 23 (3) (October): 386–407.

INKELES, ALEX and DAVID H. SMITH (1974) *Becoming Modern,* London: Heinemann Education Books.

INKELES, ALEX and LARRY SIROWY (1983) "Convergent and Divergent Trends in National Educational Systems", *Social Forces* 62 (2): 137–165.

INTERNATIONAL ASSOCIATION FOR THE EVALUATION OF EDUCATIONAL ACHIEVEMENT (1988) *Science Achievement in Seventeen Countries: A Preliminary Report,* Oxford: Pergamon Press.

INTERNATIONAL LABOUR OFFICE (1984) *World Labour Report,* Vol. 1, Geneva: International Labour Office.

INTERNATIONAL LABOUR OFFICE (1985) *World Labour Report,* Vol. 2, Geneva: International Labour Office.

INTERNATIONAL LABOUR OFFICE (1987) *World Labour Report,* Vol. 3 Geneva: International Labour Office.

IRIZARRY, RAFAEL (1980) "Overeducation and unemployment in the Third World: The paradoxes of dependent industrialization", *Comparative Education Review,* 24 (3) (October 1980): 388–352.

ISLING, ÅKE (1974) *Vägen till en demokratisk skola,* Stockholm: Prisma.

ISLING, ÅKE (1980) *Kampen för och mot en demokratisk skola,* Stocholm: Sober.

JAMISON, DEAN T. and PETER R. MOOCK (1984) "Farmer Education and Farm Efficiency in Nepal: The Role of Schooling, Extension Services and Cognitive Skills", *World Development,* 12 (1): 67–86.

JAMISON, DEAN T. and MARLAINE E. LOCKHEED (1987) "Participation in Schooling: Determinants and Learning Outcomes in Nepal", *Economic Development and Cultural Change,* 35 (2): 279–306.

JANSEN, M. B. (ed.) (1965) *Changing Japanese Attitudes toward Modernization,* Princeton N.J.: Princeton University Press.

JENCKS, CHRISTOPHER *et al.* (1972) *Inequality: A Reassessment of the Effect of Family and Schooling in America,* New York: Basic Books.

JENCKS, CHRISTOPHER *et al.* (1979) *Who Gets Ahead? The Determinants of Economic Success in America,* New York: Basic Books.

JOHANSSON, EGIL (1977) *The History of Literacy in Sweden in Comparison with Some Other Countries,* Umeå: Department of Education, Report No. 12, University of Umeå.

JOHNSTONE, JAMES E. (1981) *Indicators of Education Systems,* London: Kogan Page.

KAHL, JOSEPH A. (1968) *The Measurement of Modernism: A Study of Values in Brazil and Mexico,* Austin: University of Texas Press.

KANN, ULLA (1981) *Career Development in a Changing Society,* Stockholm: Institute of International Education, University of Stockholm.

KARABEL, JEROME and A. H. HALSEY (eds.) (1977) *Power and Ideology in Education,* New York: Oxford University Press.

KARIER, CLARENCE J. (1967) *Man, Society and Education,* Glenview, Ill.: Scott, Foresman & Company.

KASDAN, ALAN RICHARD (1973) *The Third World: A New Focus for Development,* Cambridge, Mass: Schenkman Publishing Company.

KATZ, MICHAEL B. (1968) *The Irony of Early School Reform*, Cambridge, Mass.: Harvard University Press.

KEEVES, J. P. and S. F. BOURKE (1976) *Australian Studies in School Performance.* Vol. 1 *Literacy and Numeracy in Australian Schools:* A First Report, Canberra: Australian Government Printing Service.

KELLY, ALISON (1978) *Girls and Science*, Stockholm: Almqvist & Wiksell International.

KELLY, GAIL P. (1987a) "Conflict in the Classroom: a Case Study from Vietnam, 1918–38", *British Journal of Sociology of Education*, 8 (2): 191–212.

KELLY, GAIL P. (1987b) "Setting State Policy on Women's Education in the Third World: perspectives from comparative research", *Comparative Education*, 23 (1): 95–102.

KENYON, FREDERIC G. (1951) *Books and Readers in Ancient Greece and Rome (2nd edition)* Oxford: Clarendon Press.

KHALDUN, IBN (1980 (1394)) The *Muqaddimah*, Princeton, New Jersey: Princeton University Press (Vols. I, II, III).

KIROS, FASSIL G., SELMA J. MUSKIN and BRADLEY B. BILLINGS (1975) *Educational Outcome Measurement in Developing Countries*, Washington, D.C., Public Services Laboratory, Georgetown University.

KNELLER, GEORGE F. (1965) *Educational Anthropology*, New York: John Wiley & Sons.

KULIK, JAMES A., CHEN-LIN C. KULIK and PETER A. COHEN (1980) "Effectiveness of computer-based college teaching: A meta-analysis of findings", *Review of Educational Research*, 50 (4) (Winter): 525–544.

KUMAR, KRISHAN (1978) *Prophecy and Progress*, Harmondsworth: Penguin Books.

KWEKA, AIKAEL N. (1987) *Adult Education in a Village in Tanzania*, Stockholm: Education Division Documents No. 36, Swedish International Development Authority.

LALL, SANJAYA (1975) "Is "dependence" a useful concept in analysing underdevelopment?", *World Development*, 3: 799–810.

LANE, DAVID (1974) "Leninism as an ideology of Soviet development", in EMANUAL DE KADT and GAVIN WILLIAMS (eds.) *Sociology and Development*, London: Tavistock.

LANE, DAVID (1976) *The Socialist Industrial State*, London: Allen & Unwin.

LAPIDUS, GAIL WARSHOFSKY (1978) *Women in Soviet Society: Equality, Development and Social Change*, Berkley: University of California Press.

LAPIDUS, GAIL WARSHOFSKY (1982) "Sexual Equality Through Educational Reform: The Case of the USSR", in PHILIP ALTBACH, ROBERT ARNOVE, and GAIL P. KELLY (eds.) *Comparative Education*, New York: Macmillian.

LATUKEFU, SIONE (1988) "The Modern Elite in Papua New Guinea" in MARK BRAY and PETER SMITH (eds), *Education and Social Stratification in Papua New Guinea*, Melbourne: Longman Cheshire.

LA PIERE, RICHARD T. (1965) *Social Change*, New York: McGraw-Hill.

LERNER, DANIEL (1964) *The Passing of Traditional Society: Modernizing the Middle East*, New York: The Free Press.

LEVINE, ROBERT (1963) "Political socialization and culture change", in CLIFFORD GEERTZ (ed.) *Old Societies and New States*, New York: Free Press.

LEVY, MARION J. Jr. (1966) *Modernization and the Structure of Societies*, Princeton: Princeton University Press.

LEWIN, KEITH M. (1984) "Qualification, selection and curriculum reform", in J. OXENHAM (ed) *Education versus Qualification*, London: Allen and Unwin.

LILGE, FREDERIC (1977)"Lenin and the politics of education", in JEROME KARABEL and A. H. HALSEY (eds.) *Power and Ideology in Education*, New York: Oxford University Press.

LIMAGE, LESLIE J. (1980) "Illiteracy in industrialized countries: a sociological commentary", *Prospects*, **X** (2): 141–155.

LIMAGE, LESLIE J. (1986) "Adult Literacy Policies in Industrialized Countries", *Comparative Education Review*, 30 (1) (Feb.): 50–72.

LIND, AGNETA and ANTON JOHNSTON (1986) *Adult Literacy in the Third World: a Review of Objectives and Strategies,* Stockholm: Swedish International Development Authority.

LIND, AGNETA (1988) *Adult Literacy: Lessons and Promises. Mozambican Literacy Campaigns 1978–1982,* Stockholm: Institute of International Education, University of Stockholm.

LINDBECK, ASSAR (1974) *Swedish Economic Policy,* Berkeley: University of California Press.

LITTLE, ANGELA (1978) *The Occupational and Educational Expectations of Students in Developed and Less-Developed Countries,* Education Report 3, Sussex University: Institute of Development Studies.

LITTLE, ANGELA (1984) "Combatting the Diploma Disease" in JOHN OXENHAM (ed) *Education Versus Qualifications?,* London: George Allen and Unwin.

LOCKHEED, MARLAINE, DEAN JAMISON, and LAWRENCE LAU (1980) "Farmer Education and Farm Efficiency: a Survey", *Economic Development and Cultural Change,* **29** (October): 37–76.

LÖFSTEDT, JAN-INGVAR (1980) *Chinese Educational Policy,* Stockholm: Almqvist & Wiksell International.

LUNGU, G. F. (1986) "Attacking the Elephant: Reforming Educational Administration in Zambia", *Studies in Educational Administration No. 40,* Commonwealth Council for Educational Administration, Armidale, N.S.W., Australia.

McCLELLAND, DAVID C. (1961) *The Achieving Society,* New York: The Free Press.

McHALE, JOHN and MAGDA CORDEL McHALE (1975) *Human Requirements. Supply Levels and Outer Bounds. A Framework for thinking about the Planetary Bargain.* A Policy Paper for Aspen Institute for Humanistic Studies, Program in International Affairs, Princeton, N.J.: Aspen Institute for Humanistic Studies.

McKAY, R. M. (1977) *Internationalization of Human Rights. Comments on an Aspen Institute Workshop,* Princeton, N.J.: Aspen Institute for Humanistic Studies.

MAKINO, TATSUMI (1966) "Some notes on literacy and education in Japan", *The Sociological Review, Monograph 10,* PAUL HALMOS (ed.), (September): 83–93.

MAO ZEDONG (1967) "Analyses of the Classes in Chinese Society", (March, 1926) in *Selected Readings from the Works of Mao Tse-tung.* Peking: Foreign Language Press.

MARKLUND, SIXTEN (1980a) *The Democratization of Education in Sweden. A Unesco Case Study,* Stockholm: Institute of International Education.

MARKLUND, SIXTEN (1980b) *Skolsverige 1950–1975,* Stockholm: Liber,

MARKLUND, SIXTEN (1984) "Sweden", in J.R. HOUGH (ed) *Educational Policy. An International Survey,* London: Croom Helm.

MARKLUND, SIXTEN and GUNNAR BERGENDAL (1979) *Trends in Swedish Educational Policy,* Stockholm: The Swedish Institute.

MARROU, H. I. (1956) *A History of Education in Antiquity,* London: Sheed and Ward.

MARSHALL, JAMES (1976) *A School in Uganda,* London: Victor Gollancz Ltd.

MARSHALL, JUDITH M. (1988) *Literacy, State Formation and People's Power: Education in a Mozambican Factory,* Totonto: Ontario Institute for Studies in Education.

MARX, KARL (1968 (1888)) "Theses on Feuerbach: III", in *Karl Marx and Frederick Engels: Selected Works,* London: Lawrence & Wishart.

MASSIALAS, BYRON G. (1969) *Education and the Political System,* Boston: Addison-Wesley.

MBILINYI, M. J. (1985) "Women in Education", In TORSTEN HUSÉN and T. NEVILLE POSTLETHWAITE (eds.), *International Encyclopedia of Education,* Oxford: Pergamon Press.

MEAD, MARGARET (1966) "Our education emphases in primitive perspective", in DON ADAMS (ed.) *Introduction to Education: A Comparative Analysis,* Belmont, Calif: Wadsworth Publishing Co.

MEIER, GERALD M. and ROBERT E. BALDWIN (1957) *Economic Development: Theory, History, Policy, New York:* Wiley & Sons.

MELOTTI, UMBERTO (1977) *Marx and the Third World,* London: The Macmillan Press Ltd.

MERNISSI, FATIMA (1975) *Beyond the Veil: Male-Female Dynamics in a Modern Muslim Society,* New York: John Wiley and Sons.

MEYER, JOHN and RICHARD RUBINSON (1975) "Education and political development" in F. KERLINGER (ed.) *Review of Research in Education* (vol. 3), Itasca, III.: Peacock Publishers.

MEYER, JOHN W., FRANCISCO O. RAMIREZ, RICHARD RUBINSON and JOHN BOLI-BENNETT (1977) "The World Educational Revolution, 1950–1970", *Sociology of Education,* **50** (4): 242–258.

MEYER, JOHN, DAVID TYACK, JOANE NAGEL and AUDRI GORDON (1979) "Public education as nation-building in America: Enrolments and bureaucratization in the American States 1870–1930", *American Journal of Sociology,* **85** (3) (November). 591–613.

MILKIAS, PAULOS (1976) "Traditional institutions and traditional elites: The role of education in the Ethiopian body-politic", *African Studies Review,* **XIX** (3): 79–93.

MICKELWAIT, DONALD R., MARY ANN RIEGELMAN and CHARLES F. SWEET (1976) *Women in Rural Development,* Boulder, Colorado: Westview Press.

MOOCK, P. R. (July 1981) "Education and Technical Efficiency in Small-farm Production", *Economic Development and Cultural Change,* **29:** 723–739.

MOORE, WILBERT E. (1979) *World Modernization: The Limits of Convergence,* New York: Elsevier Press.

MORAWETZ, DAVID (1980) "Economic lessons from some small socialist developing countries", *World Development,* **8:** 337–369.

MUSGRAVE, P. W. (1970) "Middle-class families and schools, 1780–1880: Interaction and exchange of function between institutions", in P. W. MUSGRAVE (ed.), *Sociology, History and Education,* London: Methuen.

MYRDAL, GUNNAR (1972) *Asian Drama,* Harmondsworth: The Penguin Press.

MYRDAL, GUNNAR (no date) "What is development", paper for the volume in honor of the later Professor Ayres, Stockholm.

NARUMIYA, CHIE (1986) "Opportunities for Girls and Women in Japanese Education", *Comparative Education,* **22** (1): 47–52.

NASH, MANNING (1973) "Industrialization: The ecumenical and parochial aspects of the process", in NANCY HAMMOND (ed.) *Social Science and the New Societies: Problems in Cross-Cultural Research and Theory Building,* East Lansing: Social Science Research Bureau.

NATIONAL CENTRAL BUREAU OF STATISTICS (1979) *Yearbook of Labour Statistics 1978,* Stockholm: Liber/Allmänna Forlaget.

NELSON, NICI (1979) *Why has Development Neglected Rural Woman?,* Oxford: Pergamon Press.

NISBET, ROBERT A. (1969) *Social Change and History,* London: Oxford University Press.

NOONAN, RICHARD (1978) "An empirical study of two countries: Chile and India", in TORSTEN HUSÉN, LAWRENCE J. SAHA and RICHARD NOONAN, *Teacher Training and Student Achievement in Less Developed Countries,* Washington, D.C.: The World Bank.

OECD (1968) *Social Objectives in Educational Planning,* Paris: OECD.

OECD (1978) *From Marshall Plan to Global Interdependence,* Paris: OECD.

OECD (1981a) *Educational Reforms in Sweden,* Paris: OECD.

OECD (1981b) *The OECD Observer,* No. 113, November: 12–13.

OECD (1982) *The OECD Observer,* No. 115, March: 23–30.

OECD (1987) *The OECD Observer,* No. 145 April/May: 17–24.

OBBO, CHRISTINE (1980) *African Women,* London: Zed Press.

PAPANEK, HANNA (1985) "Class and Gender in Education-Employment Linkages", *Comparative Education Review,* 29 (3): 317–346.

PARNES, HERBERT (ed.) (1962) *Planning Education for Economic and Social Development,* Paris: OECD.

PARSONS, TALCOTT (1966) *Societies: Evolutionary and Comparative Perspectives,* Englewood Cliffs, N.J.: Prentice-Hall, Inc.

PASSIN, H. (1965) *Society and Education in Japan,* New York: University of Columbia Press.

PASSOW, A. HARRY, HAROLD J. NOAH, MAX A. ECKSTEIN and JOHN R. MALLEA (1976) *The National Case Study: An empirical comparative study of Twenty-one Educational Systems,* Stockholm: Almqvist & Wiksell.

PASTNER, CARROLL McC, (1974) "Accommodations to Purdah: The Female Perspective". *Journal of Marrlnun and the Family.* 30 (7): 193–414.

PATTON, MICHAEL QUINN (1980) *Qualitative Evaluation Methods,* Beverly Hills: Sage Publications.

PAULSTON, ROLLAND (1968) *Educational Change in Sweden,* New York: Teachers College Press, Columbia University.

PAULSTON, ROLLAND (1971) *Society, Schools and Progress in Peru,* Oxford: Pergamon Press.

PAULSTON, ROLLAND (1972) "Cultural revitalization and Educational change in Cuba", *Comparative Education Review,* 16: 474–485.

PAULSTON, ROLLAND (1976) *Conflicting Theories of Social and Educational Change: A Typological Review,* Pittsburgh: University Center for International Studies.

PAULSTON, ROLLAND (1977a) "Social and educational change: Conceptual frameworks", *Comparative Education Review,* 21 (June/October): 370–395.

PAULSTON, ROLLAND (1977b) "Educational Stratification and Cultural Hegemony in Peru", in JEROME KARABEL AND A. H. HALSEY (eds.), *Power and Ideology in Education,* New York: Oxford University Press.

PEARSE, R. (1977) "The prediction of private demand for education: Indonesian case study", *International Review of Education,* XXIII (3): 265–285.

PEDHAZUR, ELAZAR J. (1982) *Multiple Regression in Behavioral Research.* Second Edition, New York: Holt, Rinehart and Winston.

PLATT, WILLIAM J. (1975) "Policy making and international studies in educational evaluation", in ALAN C. PURVES and DANIEL U. LEVINE (eds.) *Educational Policy and International Assessment,* California: McCutchan Publishing Co.

PLEIJEL, HILDING (1935) *Svenska kyrkans historia,* Stockholm: Svenska kyrkans diakonistyrelses bokförlag.

PLEIJEL, HILDING (1970) *Hustavlans värld,* Stockholm: Verbum.

POLYDORIDES, GEORGIA (1985) "Women's Participation in the Greek Educational System", *Comparative Education,* 21 (3): 229–240.

POPHAM, W. JAMES (1987) "Two-plus Decades of Educational Objectives", *International Journal of Educational Research,* 11 (1): 31–41.

PORTES, ALEJANDRO (1973)"Modernity and development: A critique", *Studies in Comparative International Development,* VIII (3): 247–279.

PORTES, ALEJANDRO and ADREAIN A. ROSS (1976) "Modernization for emigration: The medical brain drain from Argentina", *Journal of Inter-American Studies and World Affairs,* 18 (4): 395–422.

POSTLETHWAITE, T. NEVILLE (1987) "Comparative Educational Achievement Research: Can it Be Improved?", *Comparative Educational Review,* 31 (1): 150–158.

PRICE, RONALD F. (1977) *Marx and Education in Russia and China,* London: Croom Helm.

PRZEWORSKI, ADAM and HENRY TEUNE (1970) *The Logic of Comparative Social Inquiry,* New York: Wiley-Interscience.

PSACHAROPOULOS, GEORGE (1972) "Measuring the marginal contribution of education to economic growth", *Economic Development and Cultural Change*, **20** (4): 641–658.

PSACHAROPOULOS, GEORGE (1973) *Returns to Education: An International Comparison*, Amsterdam: Elsevier Scientific Publishing Company.

PSACHAROPOULOS, GEORGE (1985) "Returns to Education: a Further International Update and Implications, *Journal of Human Resources*, **XX**: 583–604.

PSACHAROPOULOS, G. and MAUREEN WOODHALL (1985) *Education for Development: an Analysis of Investment Choices*, Baltimore: John Hopkins University Press.

RAM, RATI and RAM D. SINGH (1988) "Farm Households in Rural Burkino Faso: Some Evidence on Allocation and Direct Returns to Schooling, and Male-Female Labour Productivity Differentials", *World Development*, **16** (3): 419–424.

RADO, EMIL R. (1972) "The relevance of education for employment", *The Journal of Modern African Studies*, **10** (3): 459–475.

RAMIREZ, FRANCISCO and JOHN W. MEYER (1980) "Comparative education: The social construction of the modern world system", *Annual Review of Sociology*, **6**: 369–399.

RAMIREZ, FRANCISCO O., and JOHN BOLI (1987) "The Political Construction of Mass Schooling: European Origins and Worldwide Institutionalization", *Sociology of Education* **60** (January): 2–17.

RAU, WILLIAM C. (1980) "The tacit conventions of the modernity school: An analysis of key assumptions", *American Sociological Review*, **45** (2): 244–260.

RESNICK, LAUREN B. (1987) "Learning in School and Out", *Educational Researcher*, **16** (9): 13-20.

REUTERBERG, SVEN-ERIC and ALLAN SVENSSON (1983) "The Importance of Financial Aid: The Case of Higher Education in Sweden", *Higher Education*. **12**: 89–100.

RICHMOND, MARK (1987) "Educational change in postrevolutionary Cuba: a critical assessment", *International Journal of Educational Development*, **7** (3): 191–204.

ROGERS, BARBARA (1980) *The Domestication of Women*, London: Tavistock Publications.

ROHRER, WAYNE C. (1986) "Developing Third World Farming: Conflict Between Modern Imperatives and Traditional Ways", *Economic Development and Cultural Change*, **34** (2): 299–314.

ROSENHOLTZ, S.J. (1985) "Effective Schools – Interpreting the Evidence", *American Journal of Education*, **30** (3): 352–388.

ROSTOW, W. W. (1960) *The Stages of Economic Growth: A Non-Communist Manifesto*, Cambridge: The University Press.

ROSTOW, W. W. (1971a) *The Stages of Economic Growth* (2nd edition), Cambridge: The University Press.

ROSTOW, W. W. (1971b) *Politics and the Stages of Growth*, Cambridge: The University Press.

ROSTOW, W. W. (1978) *The World Economy*, London: Mac Millan

ROXBOROUGH, IAN (1976) "Dependency theory in the Sociology of development: Some theoretical problems", *West African Journal of Sociology and Political Science*, **1** (2): 116–133.

RUBINSON, RICHARD and DEBORAH HOLTZMAN (1981) "Comparative Dependence and Economic Development", *International Journal of Comparative Sociology*, **32**: 86–101.

RUTTER, MICHAEL, BARBARA MAUGHAN, PETER MORTIMORE and JANET OUSTON (1979) *Fifteen Thousand Hours: Secondary Schools and Their Effects on Children*, London: Open Books:

RYAN, JOHN (1974) *Educational Resources and Scholastic Outcomes: A Study of*

Rural Primary Schooling in Iran, Stanford University, unpublished Ph. D. thesis.

SAHA, LAWRENCE J. (1978) "Literature review", in TORSTEN HUSÉN, LAWRENCE J. SAHA and RICHARD NOONAN, *Teacher Training and Student Achievement in Less Developed Countries,* Washington, D.C.: The World Bank.

SAHA, LAWRENCE J. (1982) "National development and the revolution of rising expectations: Determinants of career orientations among school students in comparative perspective", in MARGARET ARCHER (ed.) *The Sociology of Educational Expansion,* London: Sage Publications.

SAHA, LAWRENCE J. (1983) "Social structure and teacher effects on academic achievement: A comparative analysis", *Comparative Education Review,* 27: 69–81.

SAHA, LAWRENCE J. (1988) "The Effects of Socio-Economic Development on Academic Performance and Life Plans: a Cross-National Analysis". *Paper Presented to the Meeting of the American Sociological Association,* August, Atlanta.

SAKYA, T.M. (1987) "Asia-Pacific Programme of Education for All (APPEAL): A Regional Programme. Paper presented to the Regional Seminar of the Sociology of Education Research Committee, International Sociological Association, Canberra, November.

SAMUELSON, PAUL A (1976) *Economics,* 10th ed., New York: Mc.Graw-Hill Book Company.

SANDIN, BENGT (1986) *Hemmet, gatan, fabriken eller skolan* ("The Home, the Street, the Factory or the School"), Lund. Arkiv.

SCHIEFELBEIN, ERNESTO and JOSEPH P. FARRELL (1982) *Eight Years of Their Lives.* Ottawa: International Development Research Centre.

SCHNAIBERG, ALLAN (1970) "Measuring modernism: Theoretical and empirical explorations", *American Journal of Sociology,* 76 (3) (November): 399–425.

SCHULLER, TOM and JARL BENGSTSSON (1977) "The strategy for equity: Recurrent education and industrial democracy", in JEROME KARABEL and A. H. HALSEY (eds.) *Power and Ideology in Education,* New York: Oxford University Press.

SCHULTZ, THEODORE W. (1961) "Investment in human capital; *American Economic Review,* 51 (March): 1–17.

SCHULTZ, THEODORE W. (1980) "Nobel Lecture: The economics of being poor", *Journal of Political Economy,* 88 (4) (August): 639–652.

SCHUMACHER, E. F. (1974) *Small is Beautiful,* London: Sphere Books.

SEGERSTEDT, TORGNY (1974) *Hotet mot den högre utbildningen,* Stockholm: Askild och Kärnekull.

SEIDMAN, ROBERT H. (1982) "The logic and behavioral principles of educational systems: Social independence or dependence?" in MARGARET ARCHER (ed.), *The Sociology of Educational Expansion,* London: Sage Publications.

SELOWSKY, M. (1982) "The Economic Effects of Investment in Children: A Survey of the Quantitative Evidence", in T.E. JOHNSON (ed.), *Child Development Information and the Formation of Public Policy: An International Perspective,* Springfield, III.: Charles C. Thomas.

SEWELL, WILLIAM H. and ROBERT M. HAUSER (1975) *Education, Occupation and Earnings: Achievement in the Early Career,* New York: Academic Press.

SEWELL, WILLIAM H. and ROBERT M. HAUSER (1980) "The Wisconsin Longitudinal Study of Social and Psychological Factors in Aspirations and Achievements", *Research in Sociology of Education and Socialization,* Vol. I, Greenwich: JAI Press.

SHAPIRO, H. SVI (1980) "Education and the state in capitalist society: Aspects of the sociology of Nicos Poulantzas", *Harvard Education Review,* 50 (3) (August): 321–331.

SHARP, DONALD W. and MICHAEL COLE (1974) *The Influence of Educational Experience on the Development of Cognitive Skills as Measured in Formal Tests* and Experiments: A Case Study from the Mexican States of Yucatan and Quintana Roo: A Final Report, New York: Department of Health, Education and Welfare.

SHIPMAN, M.D. (1971) *Education and Modernisation*, London: Faber & Faber.

SIANN, GERDA, and RUHI KHALID (1984) "Muslim traditions and attitudes to female education", *Journal of Adolescence*, **7** (1984):191–200.

SIMMONS, JOHN (1980) "An Overview of the Policy Issues in the 1980s", in JOHN

SINGHAL, SUSHILA (1984) "The Development of Educated Women in India: Reflections of a Social Phychologist", *Comparative Education*, **20** (3): 355.

SIMMONS (ed.), *The Educational Dilemma*, New York: Pergamon Press.

SIMMONS, JOHN and LEIGH ALEXANDER (1980) "Factors which promote school achievement in developing countries: A review of the research", in JOHN SIMMONS (ed.) *The Education Dilemma*, New York: Pergamon Press.

SJÖSTRAND, WILHELM (1958) *Pedagogikens historia*, Malmö: Gleerup.

SJÖSTRÖM, MARGARETA and ROLF SJÖSTRÖM (1982) *Literacy and Development*, Umeå: Umeå University, Pedagogiska Institutionen.

SMELSER, NEIL J. (ed.) (1973) *Karl Marx. On Society and Social Change*, Chicago: The University of Chicago Press.

SMITH, ADAM (1970 (1776)) *An Inquiry into the Nature and Cause of the Wealth of Nations*, London: Dent & Sons, Everyman's Libary.

SMITH, ADAM (1961) "Of wages and profit in the different employments of labour and stock", in TALCOTT PARSONS, EDWARD SHILS, KASPAR D. NAEGELE and JESSE R. PITTS (eds.) *Theories of Society*, New York: The Free Press.

SMITH, MARY LEE and GENE V. GLASS (1980) "Meta-analysis of research on class size and its relationship to attitudes and instruction", *American Educational Research Journal*, **17** (4) (Winter): 419–433.

SMITH, PETER and MARK BRAY (1988) "Educating an Elite: Papua New Guinean Enrolment in International Schools", in MARK BRAY and PETER SMITH (eds) *Education and Social Stratification in Papua New Guinea*, Melbourne: Longman Cheshire.

SOU (1948) *1946 ars skilkom missions betankande med forslag till riktlinjer for den svenska skolvasendets utveckling*, Stockholm: Ecklesiastikdepartmente (2&7).

STATISTICS/SWEDEN (1986) *Yearbook of Educational Statistics. 1986*, Stockholm: Statistics Sweden.

STROMQVIST, Nelly P. (1987) "The State and the Education of Women: Toward a Theoretical Understanding". Paper presented to the CIES annual meeting, Washington, D.C..

STONE, L. (1970) "Japan and England: A comparative study", in P. W. MUSGRAVE (ed.) *Society, History and Education*, London: Methuen.

STOUFFER, SAMUEL A. (1966) *Communism, Conformity and Civil Liberties*, New York: John Wiley & Sons.

SUTCLIFFE, CLAUD R. (1978) "The predictive power of measures of individual modernity: A critique of the paradigm of modernization", *Comparative Political Studies*, **11** (1) (April): 128–136.

SVENSSON, LENNART G. (1987) *Higher Education and the State in Swedish History*, Stockholm: Almqvist & Wiksel.

SVENSSON, NILS-ERIC (1962) *Ability Grouping and Scholastic Achievement*, Stockholm: Almqvist & Wiksell.

SZCZEPANSKI, JAN (1980) "Integration of theory and practice", in TORSTEN HUSÉN (ed.) *The Future of Formal Education*, Stockholm: Almqvist & Wiksell International.

SZEKELY, BEATRICE BEACH (1986) "The new Soviet educational reform", *Comparative Education Review*, **30** (3): 321–343.

SZEKELY, BEATRICE BEACH (1987) "Critical Commentary on the New Soviet Secondary School Mathematics and Science Curricula: Editor's Introduction", *Soviet Education*, **XXIX** (8): 3–9.

THIAS, HANS HEINRICH and MARTIN CARNOY (1972) *Cost-Benefit Analysis in*

Education: A Case Study of Kenya, Washington, D.C. International Bank for Reconstruction and Development (World Bank).

THOMAS, R. MURRAY (1970) "Who shall be educated? – The Indonesian case", in JOSEPH FISCHER (ed.) *The Social Sciences and the Comparative Study of Educational Systems*, Scranton, Pa.: International Textbook Co.

THORNDIKE, ROBERT L. (1973) *Reading Comprehension Education in Fifteen Countries*, Stockholm: Almqvist & Wiksell.

TILLY, CHARLES (1972) "The modernization of political conflict in France", in EDWARD B. HARVEY (ed.) *Perspectives on Modernization*, Toronto: University of Toronto Press.

TIMASHEFF, NICHOLAS S. (1964) *Sociological Theory: Its Nature and Growth*, New York: Random House, Revised edition.

TINBERGEN, J. *et. al.* (1976) *Reshaping the International Order*, A Report to the Club of Rome. New York: E. P. Dutton & Co.

TINKER, IRENE (1987) "Street Foods: Testing Assumptions About Informal Sector Activity by Women and Men", *Current Sociology*, **35**, (3) (Winter): 1–110.

TIPPS, DEAN (1976) "Modernization theory and the comparative study of societies: A critical perspective", in CYRIL E. BLACK (ed.) *Comparative Modernization: A Reader*, New York: The Free Press.

TODARO, MICHAEL P. (1977) *Economic Development in the Third World*, New York: Longman Publishing Co.

TOMIAK, J. J. (1972) *The Soviet Union*, Devon: David & Charles Publishers.

TORNEY, JUDITH V., A. N. OPPENHEIM and RUSSELL F. FARNEN (1975) *Civic Education in Ten Countries*, Stockholm: Almqvist & Wiksell.

TORNEY-PURTA, JUDITH and JOHN SCHWILLE (1986) "Civic values learned in school: policy and practice in industrialized nations" *Comparative Education Review*, **30** (1): 30–49.

TOURAINE, ALAIN (1973) *Production de la Société*, Paris: Editions du Seuil.

TROW, MARTIN (1961) "The second transfomation of American secondary education", *International Journal of Comparative Sociology*, **2**: 144–166.

TUIJNMAN, ALBERT, VINAYAGUM CHINAPAH and INGEMAR FÄGERLIND (1988) "Adult Education and Earnings: A 45-Year Longitudinal Study of 834 Swedish Men", *Economics of Education Review*, **7** (4): 423–437.

UNESCO (1967) *Qualitative Aspects of Educational Planning*, Paris: UNESCO, International Institute for Educational Planning (IIEP).

UNESCO (1970) *Educational Planning: A World Survey of Problems and Prospects*, Paris: UNESCO.

UNESCO (1978) *Study in Depth on the Concept of Basic Needs in Relation to Various Ways of Life and Its Possible Implications for the Action of the Organization*, Summary – UNESCO – Executive Board 105th Session, Paris, September.

UNESCO (1983) *Bibliographic Guide to Studies on the Status of Women: Development and Reputation Trends*, Paris: Unesco.

UNESCO (1983a) *Development of Education in the Least Developed Countries since 1970: a Statistical Study*, Paris: Unesco.

UNESCO (1983b) *Trends and Projections of Enrolment by Level of Education and by Age*, Paris: Unesco.

UNESCO (1985) *The Current Literacy Situation in the World*, Paris: UNESCO

UNESCO (1986) *Education of Girls in Asia and the Pacific*, Bangkok: Unesco Regional Office.

UNESCO (APEID) (1987) *Universal Primary Education for Girls-India*, Bangkok: Unesco, Principal Regional Office for Asia and the Pacific.

VAIZEY, JOHN (1972) *The Political Economy of Education*, London: Duckworth Publishing Co.

WAGAW, TESHOME G. (1979) *Education in Ethiopia: Prospects and Retrospect*, Ann Arbor: University of Michigan Press.

WAGNER, DANIEL, A. (1985) "Islamic Education: Traditional Pedagogy and Contemporary

Aspects", in TORSTEN HUSÉN and T. NEVILLE POSTLETHWAITE (eds.), *International Encyclopedia of Education*, Oxford: Pergamon Press.

WAGNER, DANIEL A. (ed) (1987) *The Future of Literacy in a Changing World*, Oxford: Pergamon Press.

WAGNER, DANIEL, A. LOTFI (1980) "Traditional Islamic Education in Morocco: Socio-historical and Psychological Perspectives", *Comparative Education Review*, 24: 238–251.

WAGNER, DANIEL A. and JENNIFER E. SPRATT (1987) "Cognitive Consequences of Contrasting Pedagogies: The Effects of Quranic Preschooling in Morocco", *Child Development*, 58 (5): 1207–1219.

WALKER, DAVID A. (1976) *The IEA Six Subject Survey: An Empirical Study of Education in Twenty-One Countries*, Stockholm: Almqvist & Wiksell.

WALLERSTEIN, I. (1979) *The Capitalist World Economy*, Cambridge: The University Press.

WALTERS, PAMELA BARNHOUSE (1981) "Educational Change and National Economic Development", *Harvard Educational Review*, 51 (1): 94–106.

WARD, F. CHAMPION (ed.) (1974) *Education and Development Reconsidered*, London: Praeger.

WARNER, W. LLOYD et. al. (1963) *The American Federal Executive*, New Haven, Conn.: Yale University Press.

WARREN, BILL (1980) *Imperialism: Pioneer of Capitalism*, London: Verso Publications.

WATSON-FRANKE, MARIA-BARBARA (1974) "Traditional educational concepts in the modern world: The case of the Guajiro Indians of Venezuela", *Sociologus*, 24 (2): 97–116.

WEBSTER, ANDREW (1984) *Introduction to the Sociology of Development*. London: Macmillan.

WEEKS-VAGLIANI, WINIFRED (1980) *Women in Development*, Paris: OECD.

WEIGEL, VAN B. (1986) "The Basic Needs Approach: Overcoming the Poverty of Homo Oeconomicus", *World Development*, 14 (12): 1423–1434.

WEILER, HANS N. (1978) "Education and development: from the age of innocence to the age of scepticism", *Comparative Education*, 14 (3) October: 179–198.

WEINBERG, IAN (1972) "The concept of modernization", in EDWARD B. HARVEY (ed.) *Perspectives on Modernization*, Toronto: University of Toronto Press.

WEIS, CAROL H. (1977) *Using Social Research in Public Policy-Making*, Lexington, Mass: Lexington Books.

WELLESLEY EDITORIAL COMMITTEE (1977) *Women and National Development: the Competition of Change*, Chicago: The University of Chicago Press.

WELLS, ALAN (1987) "Adult literacy: its impact on young adults in the United Kingdom" *Prospects*, XVII (2): 259–265.

WELCH, F. (1970) "Education in Production", *Journal of Political Economy*, 18 (Jan/Feb): 35–39.

WIDGREN, JONAS (1980) *Svensk invandrarpolitik*, Lund: Liber:

WILLIAMS, RAYMOND (1961) *The Long Revolution*, Harmondsworth: Penguin Books.

WILLIAMS, TREVOR, JEFF CLANCY, MARGARET BATTEN and SUE GIRLING–BUTCHER (1980) *School, Work, and Career: 17-year-olds in Australia*, Hawthorne, Victoria: Australian Council for Educational Research.

WILLIAMS, TREVOR, MARGARET BATTEN, SUE GIRLING–BUTCHER and JEFF CLANCY (1981) *School and Work in Prospect: 14-year-olds in Australia*, Hawthorne, Victoria: Australian Council for Educational Research.

WILLIAMS, TREVOR (1987) *Participation in Education*, ACER Research Monograph No. 30, Melbourne: Australian Council of Educational Research.

WILSON, DAVID N. (1984) "A Comparative Re-examination of the Notion of Institutional Transfer as Applied to Technical-Vocational Educational and Training in Developing Nations, *ILO/–CINTERFOR BULLETIN*, 1: 5–30.

WINBERG, CHRISTER (1975) *Folkökning och proletarisering*, Göteborg: Meddelanden fran historiska institutionen i Göteborg Nr. 10.

WINDHAM, DOUGLAS M. (1988) *Indicators of Educational Effectiveness and Efficiency*, Tallahassee: IIES, Florida State University.

WOBER, MALLORY (1975) *Psychology in Africa*, London: International African Institute.

WOLF, RICHARD M. (1987) "The Nature of Educational Evaluation", *International Journal of Educational Research*, **11** (1): 7–19.

WOLFE, BARBARA and JERE R. BEHRMAN (1986) "Child Quantity and Quality in a Developing Country: Family Backgrounds, Endogenous Tasks, and Biological Supply Factors", *Economic Development and Cultural Change*, **34** (4): 703–720.

WORLD BANK (1988) *World Development Report 1988*, Washington, D.C.: The World Bank.

WOOD, RICHARD H., Jr. (1988) "Literacy and Basic Needs Satisfaction in Mexico", *World Development*, **16** (3): 405–417.

WOODHALL, MAUREEN (1985) "Human Capital", in TORSTEN HUSÉN and T. NEVILLE POSTLETHWAITE (eds.), *International Encyclopedia of Education*, Oxford: Pergamon Press.

WORLD BANK (1974) *Education Sector Policy Paper*, Washington, D.C.: The World Bank.

WORLD BANK (1980a) *Education Sector Policy Paper*, Washington, D.C.: The World Bank.

WORLD BANK (1980b) *World Development Report, 1980*, Washington, D.C.: The World Bank.

WORLD BANK (1981) *World Development Report 1981*, Washington, D.C.: The World Bank.

WORLD BANK (1983)*World Tables: The Third Edition, Volume II: Social Data.* Baltimore: The Johns Hopkins University Press.

WORLD BANK (1986) *Financing Education in Developing Countries*, Washington: The World Bank.

WORLD BANK (1987) *World Development Report 1987*, Washington, D.C.: The World Bank.

WORLD BANK (1988) *World Development Repart 1988*, Washington, D.C.: The World Bank.

YOUNG, MICHAEL F. D. (ed.) (1971) *Knowledge and Control*, London: Collier–Macmillan.

ZEIGLER. HARMON and WAYNE PEAK (1971) "The political functions of the educational system", in EARL HOPPER (ed.) *Readings in the Theory of Educational Systems*, London: Hutchinson & Co.

ZHEN, LU (1988) "A Brief Introduction to the System of Higher School Enrolment Examinations in China", in STEPHEN P. HEYNEMAN and INGEMAR FÄGERLIND (eds), *University Examinations and Standardized Testing*, Washington, D.C.: The World Bank.

Name Index

Subject Index